Stewart Goetz is Ross Frederick Wicks Distinguished Professor in Philosophy and Religion at Ursinus College. He has written extensively on the philosophy of mind and action theory and his books include *Freedom, Teleology, and Evil* (2008), *Naturalism* (with Charles Taliaferro, 2008), and *The Soul Hypothesis* (edited with Mark Baker, 2011).

Charles Taliaferro is Professor of Philosophy at St. Olaf College. He is on the editorial board of the *American Philosophical Quarterly, Religious Studies, Sophia,* and *Philosophy Compass*. His books include *Consciousness and the Mind of God* (1994, 2004), *Naturalism* (with Stewart Goetz, 2008), *A Companion to Philosophy of Religion,* 2nd edition (edited with Paul Draper, Wiley-Blackwell, 2010), and *The Image in Mind* (with Jil Evans, 2010).

T0313617

Brief Histories of Philosophy

Brief Histories of Philosophy provide both academic and general readers with short, engaging narratives for those concepts that have had a profound effect on philosophical development and human understanding. The word "history" is thus meant in its broadest cultural and social sense. Moreover, although the books are meant to provide a rich sense of historical context, they are also grounded in contemporary issues, as contemporary concern with the subject at hand is what will draw most readers. These books are not merely a tour through the history of ideas, but essays of real intellectual range by scholars of vision and distinction.

Already Published

A Brief History of Happiness by Nicholas P. White
A Brief History of Liberty by David Schmidtz and Jason Brennan
A Brief History of the Soul by Stewart Goetz and Charles Taliaferro

Forthcoming

A Brief History of Justice by David Johnston

A Brief History of the Soul

Stewart Goetz and Charles Taliaferro

A John Wiley & Sons, Ltd., Publication

This edition first published 2011
© 2011 Stewart Goetz and Charles Taliaferro

Blackwell Publishing was acquired by John Wiley & Sons in February 2007.
Blackwell's publishing program has been merged with Wiley's global Scientific,
Technical, and Medical business to form Wiley-Blackwell.

Registered Office
John Wiley & Sons Ltd, The Atrium, Southern Gate, Chichester, West Sussex,
PO19 8SQ, United Kingdom

Editorial Offices
350 Main Street, Malden, MA 02148-5020, USA
9600 Garsington Road, Oxford, OX4 2DQ, UK
The Atrium, Southern Gate, Chichester, West Sussex, PO19 8SQ, UK

For details of our global editorial offices, for customer services, and for information
about how to apply for permission to reuse the copyright material in this book please
see our website at www.wiley.com/wiley-blackwell.

The right of Stewart Goetz and Charles Taliaferro to be identified as the authors of
this work has been asserted in accordance with the UK Copyright, Designs and
Patents Act 1988.

Wiley also publishes its books in a variety of electronic formats. Some content that
appears in print may not be available in electronic books.

Designations used by companies to distinguish their products are often claimed as
trademarks. All brand names and product names used in this book are trade names,
service marks, trademarks or registered trademarks of their respective owners. The
publisher is not associated with any product or vendor mentioned in this book. This
publication is designed to provide accurate and authoritative information in regard
to the subject matter covered. It is sold on the understanding that the publisher is
not engaged in rendering professional services. If professional advice or other expert
assistance is required, the services of a competent professional should be sought.

Library of Congress Cataloging-in-Publication Data
Goetz, Stewart.
 A brief history of the soul / Stewart Goetz and Charles Taliaferro.
   p. cm.—(Brief histories of philosophy)
 Includes bibliographical references and index.
 ISBN 978-1-4051-9633-8 (hardcover : alk. paper)—ISBN 978-1-4051-9632-1
(pbk. : alk. paper) 1. Soul. I. Taliaferro, Charles. II. Title.
 BD421.G64 2011
 128′.109—dc22

                                                      2010043497

A catalogue record for this book is available from the British Library.

This book is published in the following electronic formats: ePDFs 9781444395914;
Wiley Online Library 9781444395938; ePub 9781444395921

Set in 10.5/14pt Minion by Graphicraft Limited, Hong Kong

5 2015

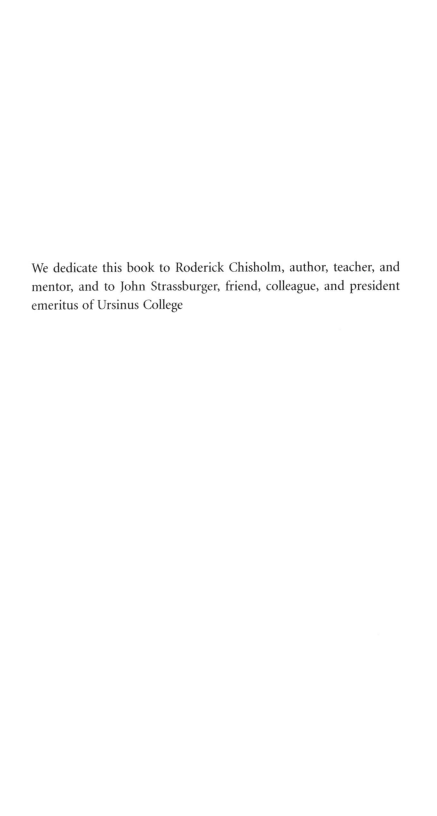

We dedicate this book to Roderick Chisholm, author, teacher, and mentor, and to John Strassburger, friend, colleague, and president emeritus of Ursinus College

Contents

Acknowledgments

We thank Nick Bellorini for inviting us to undertake this project, and Jeff Dean, Tiffany Mok, and Ben Thatcher of Wiley-Blackwell for their kind and generous support. We owe a special debt of gratitude to Manuela Tecusan for absolutely first-rate copy-editing advice. We are also deeply grateful to the John Templeton Foundation for providing financial assistance that supported our work on the book. Finally, we thank Tess Cotter for assistance in preparing the manuscript and Michael DelloBuono for compiling the bibliography.

Introduction

The current intellectual climate is quite hostile to the idea that we are embodied souls. The idea that there might be more to us than our physical bodies is out of step with contemporary secular philosophy. There is a prevailing assumption that we human beings and other animals are thoroughly physical–chemical realities. To be sure, physio-chemical organisms like us have extraordinary powers and capacities (powers to think and choose, and capacities to feel pleasure and pain), but most philosophers today think this does not make us in any way non-physical or entail that there is more to us than physio-chemical processes. Daniel Dennett offers this summary of the current materialist view of the natural world and the mind:

> The prevailing wisdom, variously expressed and argued for, is *materialism*: there is only one sort of stuff, namely *matter*—the physical stuff of physics, chemistry, and physiology—and the mind is somehow nothing but a physical phenomenon. In short, the mind is the brain. According to materialists, we can (in principle!) account for every mental phenomenon using the same physical principles, laws and raw materials that suffice to explain radioactivity, continental drift, photosynthesis, reproduction, nutrition, and growth. (Dennett 1991, 33)

From the standpoint of a comprehensive form of materialism, talk about "souls" only makes sense as a metaphor for referring to one's

A Brief History of the Soul, First Edition.

values or identity, as for instance in "Jones sold his soul to become a celebrity." The existence of the soul retains some life in fictional worlds such as J. K. Rowling's hugely popular Harry Potter books (a soul can be sucked out of a character by the kiss of a dementor) but not in the real world. In *Philosophy of Mind*, Jaegwon Kim says the following about the soul:

> The general idea [. . .] is that because each of us has a soul, we are the kind of conscious, intelligent, and rational creature we are. Strictly speaking, we do not really "have" souls, since we are in an important sense *identical with* our souls-that is, each of us *is* a soul. My soul is the thing that I am. Each of us "has a mind," therefore, because each of us *is* a mind. All that is probably a bit too speculative, if not totally fantastical, for most of us to swallow. (Kim 2006, 29)

The traditional account of the soul is still mentioned in the average philosophy of mind textbook, but rarely taken seriously. For example, in *The Problem of the Soul* Owen Flanagan contends that, if we recognize the soul at all, we need to see that it is the very same thing as the brain:

> The mind or the soul is the brain. Or better: Consciousness, cognition, and volition are perfectly natural capacities of fully embodied creatures engaged in complex commerce with the natural and social environments. Humans possess no special capacities, no extra ingredients, that could conceivably do the work of the mind, the soul, or free will as traditionally conceived. (Flanagan 2002, xii)

Is the prevalent materialist outlook beyond challenge? Could there still be a sound case for holding that there is more to being a human (and perhaps an animal, too) than physio-chemical processes?

In this book we explore the history of the idea that we are embodied souls. Many contemporary philosophers who reject the view that we are, or contain, souls yet acknowledge that such a view seems natural, and even a matter of common sense. William Lyons writes that the view "that humans are bodies inhabited and governed in some intimate if mysterious way by minds (or souls) seemed and still seems to be nothing more than good common sense" (Lyons 2001, 9). One way to bring out the apparent common sense of such a stance is to appreciate how we think about death. We often think that, when a person dies, the person either perishes or (if we subscribe to religious traditions) is with God or in some kind of afterlife, heaven or reincarnation. In any case, we often treat a person's dead body as a corpse (or remains), and not as the same thing as the man himself or the woman herself. Even to allow for the possibility of one's surviving the death of the body is to court the possibility that one is more than a body. Moreover, it is puzzling to think how it can be that all our sensations, conscious experiences, and so on are the very same thing as brain states. To be sure, there is an evident, clear sense in which our sensations are affected by the brain, and it appears that our bodily processes are affected by our beliefs and desires. But establishing a correlation between the mental and the physical is not the same thing as establishing their identity. Colin McGinn rightly points out the apparent distinction between the mental and the physical:

> The property of consciousness itself (or specific conscious states) is not an observable or perceptible property of the brain. You can stare into a living conscious brain, your own or someone else's, and see there a wide variety of instantiated properties—its shape, colour, texture, etc—but you will not thereby see what the subject is experiencing, the conscious state itself. (McGinn 1991, 10–11)

So, while many contemporary philosophers (including McGinn) deny the traditional belief that we are embodied souls and deny that consciousness is more than brain states, the belief that there is more to us than physical–chemical processes has some initial, common-sense credibility.

As it happens, we actually accept the truth of this apparent commonsense distinction of soul and body. In the philosophy of mind literature, the position we hold would customarily be called *substance dualism*, though the term "dualism" is so fraught with misunder-standing and meets with such derision that we will only use it spar-ingly. "Dualism" as a philosophical term is a late invention (so-called dualists, from Plato to Descartes, did not use any equivalent expres-sion in their languages, or any of its cognates). Indeed, ancient Greek does not even have a word for "dualism." We will, however, pay close attention to all the classical and contemporary objections to "dualism."

Our aim is to set before you a brief history of the idea that we are embodied souls. We are deeply committed to making this a fair and balanced history, but it will also contain a sustained investigation into what we may gain from this history for our thinking constructively about the soul today. One of our goals in this book is to explain, at least in part, why a history of the soul terminates with an age in which those who are learned deny the very existence of that which is the subject of this book. The arguments of those who deny the soul's existence are powerful and complex but, we hope to show, uncon-vincing. Even if we are unsuccessful, we believe that reading a history of the soul written by advocates of the soul will make for a more dramatic and interesting engagement than if the authors were to think that the notion of soul is only of antiquarian interest.

We are convinced that the time is right for a brief history of the soul. While a form of materialism that rejects the soul is the domi-nant position of the day, not all the materialists are content with the current state of play in their field. A life-long materialist, William Lycan finds himself not persuaded by the philosophical case for dualism; but he is not convinced by the case against it either—nor does he embrace the philosophical case for materialism:

> Being a philosopher, of course I would like to think that my stance is rational, held not just instinctively and scientistically and in the main-stream but because the arguments do indeed favor materialism over dualism. But I do not think that, though I used to. My position may be rational, broadly speaking, but not because the arguments favor it:

> Though the arguments for dualism do (indeed) fail, so do the arguments for materialism. And the standard objections to dualism are not very convincing; if one really manages to be a dualist in the first place, one should not be much impressed by them. (Lycan 2009, 551)

Although Lycan is not persuaded by arguments for dualism, there has been a renaissance of philosophical work on the soul over the past twenty years, which indicates that the case in favor of its existence is better than Lycan estimates. In light of this development, it is timely to consider the arguments for and against different conceptions of the soul (and thus for and against materialism) not just in contemporary philosophy, but also from a comprehensive, historical perspective.

Two final points before we get started: First, we make liberal use of quotations in our brief history, so that the many figures we cover can speak for themselves. We believe that all the main figures we cover have important things to say to us today, and we hope that this history will prompt you to read these fascinating philosophers directly. In a longer history, more of each philosopher would be represented and more philosophers would be part of the story. But here we are aiming to engage both newcomers and seasoned scholars in thinking or re-thinking the history of the soul and its bearing on our own thinking about human nature today.

Second, all subsequent references to the Platonic dialogues and works in the Aristotelian corpus can be consulted in the editions listed in the bibliography. When we wish to specify one translation rather than another for a quoted passage, we add the translator's name in a bracket.

Chapter 1

The Soul in Greek Thought

In this chapter our focus is on the two best known figures of ancient Greek philosophy: Plato (428/7–348/7 BCE) and Aristotle (384–322 BCE). There are other major philosophers in Greek thought, both before Plato and after Aristotle, and some of them hold a place of honor in the development of great future ideas, such as the hypothesis that the material world is made up of atoms, or the thesis that life evolved; but Plato and Aristotle are the most important ones in shaping the history of the soul.

Plato

Before diving into Plato's view of the soul, three important points need to be observed. First, because the central figure in Plato's dialogues is the philosopher Socrates, the question about which views are Socrates' and which are Plato's is not easy to answer, if it is answerable at all. For the sake of brevity and clarity of presentation, we will not enter the debate about this matter and we will not distinguish between Socrates' and Plato's thought. We will simply assume that Socrates' philosophical views about the soul are Plato's.

Second, we stress that Plato's treatment of the soul is *philosophical* in nature. It is necessary to emphasize this point because it is not uncommon in certain circles (e.g. theological; see Chapter 2) to find

A Brief History of the Soul, First Edition.
© 2011 Stewart Goetz and Charles Taliaferro. Published 2011 by Blackwell Publishing Ltd.

assertions to the effect that Plato invented the idea of the soul and, therefore, that the concept of the soul is a Greek idea. Nothing could be further removed from the truth. Belief in the existence of the soul is, as we pointed out in the Introduction, commonsensical in its nature, in the sense that it is espoused by the ordinary person. What Plato did was to philosophize about the nature of the soul in which ordinary people believe.

Third, the Greek term used in ancient philosophical texts and commonly translated as *soul* is *psyche*, a noun derived from the verb *psychein*, which meant *to breathe*. For philosophers, *psyche* came to stand, not for breath, but for the life of a being or for that which generates and constitutes the essential life of a being. The great philosopher and classicist A. E. Taylor offers this overview, in which he points out that *psyche* can involve (though this meaning is secondary) consciousness—a term that was probably coined in the seventeenth century by Ralph Cudworth, to stand for "awareness":

> Consciousness is a relatively late and highly developed manifestation of the principle which the Greeks call "soul." That principle shows itself not merely in consciousness but in the whole process of nutrition and growth and the adaptation of motor response to an external stimulation. Thus consciousness is a more secondary feature of the "soul" in Greek philosophy than in most modern thought, which has never ceased to be affected by Descartes' selection of "thought" as the special characteristic of psychical life. In common language the word *psyche* is constantly used where we should say "life" rather than "soul," and in Greek philosophy a work "on the *Psyche*" means what we should call one on "the principle of life." (Taylor 1955, 75)

As we shall see in different chapters, the definition of the soul is dynamic, though Plato's view on the soul or *psyche* has great historical significance, coming as it does as from the first major contributor to the philosophy of the soul. As an aside, we note that the term "soul" in English today is derived from *sawel/sawol* in Old English, as found in the Vespasian Psalter and in *Beowulf*. What, then, did Plato have to say about the soul? His thoughts are many and wide-ranging in scope, and they seem to develop over time in ways that sometimes present problems of consistency. We will focus on those thoughts that comprise the core of his view and, when appropriate, we will point out the tensions among them.

We begin with the end of Socrates' life. While Socrates is in prison and not long before he drinks the hemlock that will bring about his death, his friend Crito asks him about how he would like to be buried. "Any way you like, replied Socrates, that is, if you can catch me and I don't slip through your fingers. [. . .] I shall remain with you [Crito and other friends] no longer, but depart to a state of heavenly happiness [. . .] You [the other friends] must give an assurance to Crito for me [. . .] that when I am dead I shall not stay, but depart and be gone" (Plato 1961: *Phaedo*, 115C–D). From this response of Socrates to Crito's question it seems reasonable to infer that Plato believes the "person" Socrates is his soul (as opposed to his soul plus his body, or just his body).

Like most philosophers after him up until Descartes in the seventeenth century, Plato claims that the soul is that which imparts life to its body (*Phaedo*, 105C–D). Moreover, because the soul is that which gives life to its body and cannot acquire a property that is contrary to its essentially life-giving nature, the soul itself can never perish (*Phaedo*, 105D–E). Plato's rationale behind this view of properties is tenuous; but, for a start, we simply note that he thought of the soul as essentially and fundamentally alive, whereas he did not think this was the case with the body. The soul is indestructible or imperishable, and thereby the soul is unlike its body and other material things, which by nature are always changing and never keep to the self-same condition (*Phaedo*, 79C). When a person dies, the body may perish but the soul endures. Plato argues that, because change is always from contraries (e.g., that which becomes bigger does so from that which is smaller, and that which is darker comes from that which is lighter), the soul must have come from the realm of the dead and return there after completing its life in this world, only to return once again to the realm of the living (*Phaedo*, 70C–72E). While belief in reincarnation may strike western secular readers as preposterous, it is interesting to take note not only of the presence of a belief in reincarnation in the ancient west (one of the best known Presocratic philosophers, Pythagoras, taught reincarnation, and reincarnation is in evidence in one of the greatest Roman epic poems, Virgil's *Aeneid*, Book VI), but also of its widespread adherents today, among Hindus and Buddhists. In any case, given the way Plato describes reincarnation, the soul has to be thought of as something that is distinct from the body.

The soul's recurring journey from death to life and back again entails that it is embodied more than once. This view also seems to involve a concept of the soul as a substantial individual being, as opposed to a mode of the body. In the *Phaedo* the idea that the soul may be just a mode of the body is considered as an objection to the Socratic–Platonic position. An interlocutor in the dialogue raises this point. Could it be that what Socrates and Plato refer to as the soul is not a substantial individual entity, but more like a harmony? One may play a stringed instrument (a lyre, for example) and produce what appears to be more than the instrument (melodious sound); yet this is not a separate substance, but a mode of the lyre. Melodious sound is *the way a lyre sounds when played*, and if (so the interlocutor argues) the lyre is broken, the melodious sound will end:

> The body is held together at a certain tension between the extremes of hot and cold, and wet and dry, and so on, and our soul is a temperament or adjustment of these same extremes, when they are combined in just the right proportion. Well, if the soul is really an adjustment, obviously as soon as the tension of our body is lowered or increased beyond the proper point, the soul must be destroyed, divine though it is—just like any other adjustment, either in music or in any product of the arts and crafts, although in each case the physical remains last considerably longer until they are burned up or rot away. (*Phaedo*, 86C; Tredennick's translation)

In the dialogue, Socrates argues that the soul cannot be like the lyre and the music it makes, because the soul actually pre-exists the body; and, if the soul pre-exists the body, it is not identical with it. Socrates thereby seeks to break the analogy proposed, because *the way a lyre sounds* cannot exist before the lyre exists. The case for a pre-natal existence of the soul, developed in detail by Plato elsewhere in the same dialogue (and in others, too), deserves a brief comment here. For example, in the *Meno* he argues that knowledge is recollection of what the soul was aware of before birth:

> [A man] would not seek what he knows, for since he knows it there is no need of the inquiry, nor what he does not know, for in that case he does not even know what he is looking for. [. . .] Thus the soul, since it is immortal and has been born many times, and has seen all things both here and in the other world, has learned everything that is. So we need not be surprised if it can recall the knowledge of virtue or anything else which [. . .] it once possessed [. . .] for seeking and learning are in fact nothing but recollection. (*Meno*, 80E, 81D)

The most famous illustration of the "anything else" that is recalled by the soul involves the interrogation of a slave boy who, when prodded with the right questions, "rediscovers" a proof of the Pythagorean theorem (*Meno*, 85E–86A).

The Platonic case for pre-natal existence would be hard to defend today, but if it is even conceivable that the soul can pre-exist its body, then there is at least an appearance that the soul is not the body, and thus not a mere mode of the body. Another way to make Plato's case against the soul being a mere mode is to appeal to our understanding of ourselves as substantial beings existing over time. Arguably, when you love a person, you love a concrete individual. But if the person, or soul, is a mode of something else (say, a living animal body), then it appears that your beloved is a phase or a shape of his/her body. Is it plausible to believe that the object of your love is a certain aspect of that body? Isn't it more reasonable to believe that you love a substantial being and that, when your beloved dies, she is no more (at least not in this life), while her body remains? Socrates took something akin to this position and, in the *Crito*, he comforted his disciples, who were weeping over his immanent death, by claiming that they might bury his body, but he, Socrates, would be elsewhere. (We will return to this question when considering the work of Aristotle.)

Reincarnation means re-embodiment; and in Plato's account of the soul the material body is not only something that is ever changing, but also it is that which effectively serves as a prison for the soul, and as such is evil (*Phaedrus*, 250C). As we examine further Plato's view of the soul–body relationship, it is important to recognize that early philosophers were interested in the soul for more than purely theoretical reasons. They also sought to evaluate the moral and spiritual condition of the soul. According to Plato, the embodied soul is attracted by the pleasures of the body, such as those of food and drink and love-making (*Phaedo*, 64D). These pleasures distract the soul from its true purpose of being (what we might think of as the soul's meaning of life), which is to reason about and know (or recollect) what is true. However, Socrates says:

> I suppose the soul reasons most beautifully [without the need for recollection] when none of these things gives her pain—neither hearing nor sight, nor grief nor any pleasure—when instead, bidding farewell to the body, she comes to be herself all by herself as much as possible and when, doing everything she can to avoid communing with or even being in touch with the body, she strives for what *is*. (*Phaedo*, 65C; Brann's translation)

What *is* are the immaterial Platonic Forms or Ideas, which are abstract objects like the concepts of justice, circularity, rationality, humanness, and so on. The soul possesses knowledge when it is focusing on these Forms and philosophizing about them and their relationships with each other. The soul is happy when it beholds the Forms directly, because what it ultimately desires more than anything else is the truth (*Phaedo*, 66b).

Plato seems to regard reason/intellect as that which alone constitutes the essence of soul, and tells his readers that the soul is nourished
by reason and knowledge (*Phaedrus*, 247D). The less a soul is nourished by these, the greater its forgetfulness and resulting wrongdoing
and the lower its level of re-embodiment. Thus Plato claims that

> the soul that hath seen the most of being shall enter into the human
> babe that shall grow into a seeker after wisdom or beauty, a follower
> of the Muses and a lover; the next, having seen less, shall dwell in
> a king [. . .] or a warrior and ruler; the third in a statesman, a man
> of business, or a trader; the fourth in an athlete, or physical trainer,
> or physician. (*Phaedrus* 1961, 248D–E)

Elsewhere Plato states: "Of the men who came into the world, those
who were cowards or led unrighteous lives may with reason be supposed to have changed into the nature of women in the second generation" (*Timaeus*, 90E–91A). (While such a view would be labeled
sexist today, we should note that Plato held a higher view of women
than his contemporaries when he affirmed in the *Republic* that women
can make ideal rulers). Furthermore, "those who've made gorging and
abusing and boozings their care [. . .] slip into the classes of donkeys
and other such beasts" (*Phaedo*, 81E). In the *Timaeus* again, Plato
expresses the view that the "race of wild pedestrian animals [. . .] came
from those who had no philosophy in any of their thoughts [. . .] In
consequence of these habits of theirs they had their front legs and
their heads resting upon the earth to which they were drawn by
natural affinity" (*Timaeus* 1961, 91E).

Plato's position on pleasure and the body may seem to us today
as too derisive, and we will not defend it; but it is worth appreciating
that Plato's teacher Socrates, and probably Plato himself, were veter-
ans of a massive war, the Peloponnesian War (431–404 BCE) in which
their side (Athens and her allies) was decisively defeated. Perhaps Plato's
warnings about bodily pleasure and being prey to other sensory
desires stemmed from his (and other Athenians) belief that Athens'

entry into war was largely the result of a desire for worldly goods. His account on the soul definitely situates the soul as oriented toward more enduring goods than imperial wealth.

Let us consider further Plato's understanding of the soul–body relationship. We have already touched upon his view of how bodily pleasures seduce the soul away from its proper activity of contemplating the Forms. When the soul is seduced in this way, events in the body causally affect it. For example, the eating of foods, the drinking of liquids, and sexual intercourse cause the soul to experience pleasure. Plato was also aware that the soul moves its physical body when it pursues, among other things, bodily pleasures, some of which it should forego. How does the soul move the body? When discussing the concept of motion, Plato claims that that which can move itself is the most powerful and superlative kind of mover (*Laws*, 894D). At one point, Plato suggests defining the word "soul" as "the motion which can set itself moving" (*Laws*, 896A), and he thinks of the soul as "the universal cause of all change and motion" (896B) because motion in a series that has a beginning must begin with the motion of a self-mover (894E; 895B). Motion that is produced in a thing by that thing itself is most like or akin to the motion of thought (*Timaeus*, 89A) and, as a result, when the soul moves the body that is its vehicle (*Timaeus*, 69C), it is the soul that governs and the body that is governed (*Laws*, 896C). In short, it is our souls that move us wherever we go (*Laws*, 898E) and Plato seems to believe that the soul moves the body by first setting itself in motion.

The soul, then, is a self-mover that moves the body. Is there anything more that might be said about the soul's movement of the body? Plato believes that there is. In a passage in the *Phaedo*, at 97B–99D, Socrates informs his interlocutor that he once heard someone reading from a book by an earlier philosopher, Anaxagoras, in which the author claimed that mind is responsible for all things, and it orders the world and the objects in it in the best possible way. Socrates recollects how he thought he had discovered, to his great pleasure, a teacher after his own mind. However, upon reading Anaxagoras further, he discovered a man who did not acknowledge any kind of explanatory role for the mind. Socrates' words deserve quotation in full:

> And to me his [Anaxagoras'] condition seemed most similar to that of somebody who—after saying that Socrates does everything he does by mind and then venturing to assign the causes of each of the things I do—should first say that I'm now sitting here [in prison] because my body's composed of bones and sinews, and because bones are solid and have joints keeping them separate from one another, while sinews are such as to tense and relax and also wrap the bones all around along with the flesh and skin that holds them together. Then since the bones swing in their sockets, the sinews, by relaxing and tensing, make me able, I suppose, to bend my limbs right now—and it's through this cause that I'm sitting here with my legs bent. And again, as regards my conversing with you, he might assign other causes of this sort, holding voices and air and sounds and a thousand other such things responsible, and not taking care to assign the true causes—that since Athenians judged it better to condemn me, so I for my part have judged it better to sit here and more just to stay put and endure whatever penalty they order. Since—by the Dog—these sinews and bones of mine would, I think, long ago have been in Megara or Boeotia, swept off by an opinion about what's best, if I didn't think it more just and more beautiful, rather than fleeing and playing the runaway, to endure whatever penalty the city [Athens] should order. But to call such things causes is too absurd. (*Phaedo*, 98C–99A; Brann's translation)

More generally, Socrates is suggesting something like the following. When we go to explain our bodily actions, it is misguided to think that we can ultimately explain them in terms of physical causes alone, without any reference to purposes (ends or goals). In other words, there are at least two kinds of explanations, one that is causal and the other that is teleological (*telos* is the Greek word for purpose, end, or goal). While it is no doubt true that, if Socrates (contrary to fact) had fled to Megara, his bones and sinews would have been caused to move in certain ways, it is also true in such a case that the movements of his bones, sinews, and body to Megara would ultimately have been explained by the purpose for which Socrates was fleeing his cell in Athens. From the first-person perspective of Socrates (the perspective of self-awareness or introspection), this purpose would have been something like "so that I save my life." Moreover, as Socrates goes on to point out (*Phaedo*, 99B), there is a distinction between those things (in this case, bones, sinews, and the like) without which this purpose could not become active so as to do any explanatory work (what philosophers call "necessary conditions") and the purpose itself. To maintain that the necessary conditions are the explanation itself is, Socrates claims, a most serious mistake.

So far, we have primarily surveyed Plato's thoughts about the soul's *extrinsic* nature, as it relates to the body and to reincarnation. Plato has equally interesting and important views about the soul's *intrinsic* nature (its nature independently of its relationship to a physical body). What is not clear, however, is whether his views about the soul's intrinsic nature are consistent.

For example, on the one hand, as we have already seen, Plato maintains that the soul is indestructible and imperishable. He explains this fact about the soul in terms of its indissolubility (*Phaedo*, 80A–B). Unlike bodies, which are composite and whose components are constantly changing (*Timaeus*, 43A), a soul keeps to the self-same condition (*Phaedo*, 80B) and is thereby likely to be non-composite, or without parts (*Phaedo*, 78C). Plato also stresses that the soul is akin to the invisible Forms, which are grasped by thought and not by the senses (*Phaedo*, 79A–D).

On the other hand, Plato claims that the soul has "parts," whose existence is clearly manifested in everyday life. More specifically, the soul has three parts. On the one hand, there is the appetitive and lowest part of the soul, which does not comprehend reason (it is non-rational) but experiences pleasure and pain and has low desires (*Timaeus*, 71A, 77B). At the other extreme, there is the rational part of the soul (*Republic*, 440E), which is the part that beholds the Forms and ought to rule over the other two parts. In between these two parts of the soul is a third one, which is spirited in nature. This part's function is that of rising to the occasion, in support of the rational part, when that one is at odds with the appetitive part. As Plato views the life of the soul, excessive pains and pleasures are its greatest enemies insofar as they tempt the soul to engage in inappropriate behavior. Pleasure is the greatest incitement to evil action, while pain is a deterrent to action that is good (*Timaeus*, 69D). Excessive pleasures provoke abuse of food, drink, and sex, while excessive pains elicit cowardly behavior. Reason must govern the unreasonable eagerness to attain the former and avoid the latter, and in order to do so it harnesses the emotion (e.g. anger) of the high-spirited part of the soul to support reason in its battle with the appetites. Plato goes so far as to locate the three different parts of the soul in different areas of the body. The rational part is located in the head; the appetitive in the midriff; and the high-spirited in between the other two, midway between the midriff and the neck, "in order that being obedient to the rule of reason it might join with it in controlling and restraining the desires when they are no longer willing of their own accord to obey the word of command issuing from the citadel" (*Timaeus*, 70A).

Plato's assertion that the soul has parts is puzzling in light of his other claim, that the soul keeps to the self-same condition because it is likely without parts. Perhaps these three parts are not so much separable things that make up a soul (the way three people might make up a singing trio), but they are three capacities or powers possessed by a single soul. On this view, the appetitive part is the soul's capacity to be subject to appetitive urges, the rational part is the soul's power to reason, and so on. But, no matter how Plato's two positions may be reconciled (if they can be reconciled at all), they serve to highlight an important issue, which will be with us throughout the remainder of this book. This issue is the question of whether the soul has or lacks parts, whether it is complex or simple in nature. Plato raised this matter but did not clearly resolve it. The contemporary philosopher David Armstrong has used Plato in an effort to support the view that the self does have parts (Armstrong 1999, 23). He points out that in the *Republic* Plato argues for the existence of parts of soul from the fact that we are the subjects of, and can consider acting for the purpose of, fulfilling either one, but not both, of two competing desires:

> But, I [Socrates] said, I once heard a story which I believe, that Leontius the son of Aglaion, on his way up from the Piraeus under the outer side of the northern wall, becoming aware of dead bodies that lay at the place of public execution at the same time felt a desire to see them and a repugnance and aversion [. . .] (*Republic*, 439E)

Contrary to what Armstrong (and, perhaps, Plato) would have us believe, if these desires are parts of the self, they are not substantive parts in the sense of being substantial entities in their own right, whose loss would entail a corresponding substantial diminishment in the size of the self. To see that this is the case, we can suppose that Socrates loses one or both of the desires—to see the dead bodies and not to see them (the loss of a desire is not an uncommon experience that each of us has). Does Socrates experience a substantial loss of himself? Not in the least. *All* of him will remain after the loss of either or both of these desires. Socrates will have changed, but not in the sense that there will be less of him in a substantive sense. He will survive this kind of psychological change in his entirety. Therefore, we will need an argument other than the one brought forth by Armstrong from Plato to support the idea that the self has substantive parts.

Regardless of whether Plato ever espoused a clear position on the matter of the soul's substantive simplicity, he was aware of the soul's nature as a unit in perception and cognition and of the problem that this poses for the idea that the soul has parts. In a discussion about knowledge and perception in the *Theaetetus*, Socrates asks: "Is it more correct to say that we see and hear *with* our eyes and ears or *through* them?" Theaetetus responds, "I should say we always perceive through them, rather than with them," and Socrates retorts as follows:

Yes, it would surely be strange that there should be a number of senses ensconced inside us, like the warriors in the Trojan horse, and all these things should not converge and meet in some single nature—a mind, or whatever it is to be called—*with* which we perceive all the objects of perception *through* the senses as instruments. (*Theaetetus*, 184C–D)

In other words, Plato recognizes that it will not do to liken an individual mind to a group of individuals who are parts of a whole, where one person sees the lightning, another hears the thunder, yet another smells the rain, and yet one more feels the rain's impact on his skin, but there is no single individual that is aware of all of these things at once. No; one and the same individual simultaneously sees the lightning, hears the thunder, and smells the rain whose impact he feels on his skin. Hence Plato reasons that the senses through which we are aware of the thunderstorm must be instruments of the soul that somehow converge at the single point that is the soul itself, which is the subject of awareness. Were this convergence not to obtain, there would be no single soul or mind that is aware of all that is going on, but only a multiplicity of perceivers. A fact that deserves noting is that this *unity of consciousness* of which Plato was aware is still something that puzzles contemporary brain scientists. Thus, in commenting about contemporary speculations about consciousness, John Searle says:

I need to say something about what neurobiologists call "the binding problem." We know that the visual system has cells and indeed regions that are specially responsive to particular features of objects such as color, shape, movement, lines, angles, etc. But when we see an object we have a unified experience of a single object. How does the brain bind all of these different stimuli into a single, unified experience of an object? The problem extends across the different modes of perception. All of my experiences at present are part of one big unified conscious experience [. . .]. (Searle 1997, 33)

We will have more to say about the unity of consciousness in our discussions of subsequent philosophers' views of the soul.

Aristotle

Without question, the other major Greek philosopher of the soul was Aristotle. Though he was a student of Plato at the Academy in Athens, he was not one who blindly accepted his teacher's views. Some passed his scrutiny, others did not.

Like Plato, Aristotle believes that the soul gives life to its body. Because the soul is the first principle of living things (Aristotle 1986: *De anima*, 402ª), Aristotle maintains "that the ensouled is distinguished from the unsouled by its being alive" (*De anima*, 413ª). In short, *everything* that is alive has a soul, including organisms like plants and trees. One should not conclude, however, that Aristotle believes that plants and trees see, hear, and think. To avoid saying anything like this, he distinguishes between kinds of soul, which are hierarchically arranged. The lowest kind of soul, which is the kind that plants and trees have, is what Aristotle terms a "nutritive" soul. Whatever has it is alive (*De anima*, 415ª). It is best to think of a nutritive soul as the principle that is responsible for the nourishment, growth, and decay of an organism. "Now of natural bodies some have life and some do not, life being what we call self-nourishment, growth and decay" (*De anima*, 412ª).

According to Aristotle, one step up from the nutritive soul is the sensitive soul, which is the soul that accounts for perception in the form of touch, sight, smell, taste, and hearing. It is the existence of the sensitive soul that distinguishes animals from plants and trees. Nothing that is alive is an animal, unless it is able to perceive (*De anima*, 413ᵇ). Because animals both live and perceive, the question arises as to whether they have two souls, a nutritive one and a sensitive one. Aristotle makes it clear (at 414ᵇ) that they have only one soul, because the lower member of the hierarchical series (in this case, the nutritive) is present in the form of its powers (nourishment, growth, and decay) in the higher soul. In other words, the higher soul incorporates the powers of the lower into itself and thereby eliminates the need for the lower-level soul itself.

Human beings are animals, but different ones from beasts (non-human animals), so the question arises as to what distinguishes humans from the beasts. According to Aristotle, a human being possesses a kind of soul that is one step further up the ladder from the kind that is possessed by beasts. The kind of soul in question is one that enables a human being to think, suppose, and know (*De anima*, 413^b, 429^a). Its possession renders a human being a rational animal. In keeping with the point made in the previous paragraph, a human being does not have three souls but only one, where the rational soul incorporates the nutritive and perceptive powers that define the lower-level souls.

While Aristotle agrees with Plato about the existence of the soul and its life-giving power, he takes issue with several of his teacher's beliefs about the soul. For example, consider the issue of how the soul is related to the body. According to Plato, the soul's relationship to a body is *contingent*. The body you have now is not your body in virtue of some essential necessity; you could have had a different body. (And, if Plato is right about reincarnation, you will come to have a different body.) Formally, Plato's position can be put this way: while a rational soul A gives life to, and has, a human body B, A could have given life to, and could have had, human body D. Moreover, rational soul C, which gives life to, and has, D could have enlivened and had B. Indeed, on Plato's view, rational soul A could have had the body of a dog. Aristotle believes that this kind of radical contingency between a soul and its body is wrong:

> But there is one absurdity that this [Platonic view] has in common with most theories about the soul. The soul is connected with the body, and inserted into it, but no further account is given of the reason for

this nor of the condition that the body is in. Yet this would seem to be required. For it is by their partnership that the body acts and the soul is affected, that the body comes to be moved and the soul produces motion. And none of these is possible for things whose mutual connection is contingent. [. . .] The point is, however, that each body has its own form and shape. (*De anima*, 407ᵇ; Lawson-Tancred's translation)

Aristotle believes that an adequate account of the soul must be able to explain why it is that a *particular* soul has a *particular* body. Moreover, he claims somewhat cryptically that each body has its own form and shape, which might mean that, while all human bodies are just that—human—each nevertheless has its distinctive height and weight, skeletal structure and skin features, and so on, in virtue of its soul; and the Platonic kind of soul cannot account for these particularities of its body.

Before we explain Aristotle's account of the soul–body relationship, we believe it is important to point out that Aristotle concedes in the passage just cited that "most theories about the soul" acknowledge the contingency between a soul and its body that is included in the Platonic account. What explains this acknowledgment? It is not in the least implausible to think that part of the explanation is this: every one of us can easily conceive or imagine him- or herself having a different body than the one that he or she has. A male can easily conceive of himself having either a different male's body or the body of a female, and a female can easily imagine herself having either a different female body or that of a male. In a recent article in the *New York Times* entitled "Standing in Someone's Else's Shoes, Almost for Real," the author, Benedict Carey, reports that neuroscientists can create "body swapping" experiences, in which a subject can be "tricked" into adopting

any other human form, no matter how different, as [his or her] own. "You can see the possibilities, putting a male in a female body, young in old, white in black and vice versa," said Dr. Henrik Ehrsson of the

Karolinska Institute in Stockholm. [. . .] [T]he Karolinska researchers have found that men and women say they not only feel they have taken on the new body, but also unconsciously cringe when it is poked or threatened. (Carey 2008)

We cite Carey's article in the present context not because we believe that neuroscientists have discovered some new datum about something that people would be able to conceive for the first time in history, but because their work confirms the reality of something that human beings have always been able to do: to imagine themselves in bodies other than their own. In this instance, neuroscience teaches us nothing new. While Plato failed to provide the *complete* account of embodiment for which Aristotle was looking (as we pointed out in our discussion of Plato's view of the soul, he did have something to say about why one soul has the body of a human being and another has that of a beast), had Plato been able to respond to Aristotle, he might have countercharged that Aristotle failed to provide any plausible explanation for why or how it is that each of us can so easily imagine standing in the body of someone else and calling it his or her own.

What, then, is Aristotle's account of the soul–body relationship? At its core is the idea that the soul is the *form* or "first actuality of a body which potentially has life" (*De anima*, 412^a). To say that the soul is the form of the body means something like the following: the soul is an active or vital principle, which *informs* its body and gives to it its life and configuration (most generally, Aristotle is a "hylomorphist," which is to say that he believes an entity's matter or stuff is distinct from its form, where the latter, when combined with the former, makes that entity the kind of thing it is; the soul is a kind of form). By saying that the soul is a vital principle or a "first actuality" that informs its body, Aristotle intends to make clear that the soul is not, as Plato claimed, a primary substance that either does exist or could have existed on its own before it entered a body, or does or could survive the dissolution of the body and (once again) exist independently. The soul does not and could not do either of these things because it is not a *thing* or an *entity* that exists on its own and is distinct from its body:

> Now that it is impossible for [any of the three souls—nutritive, sensitive, rational] to preexist is clear from this consideration. Plainly those principles whose activity is bodily cannot exist without a body, e.g. walking cannot exist without feet. For the same reason also they cannot enter from outside. For neither is it possible for them to enter by themselves, being inseparable from a body, nor yet in a body, for the semen is only a residue of the nutriment in process of change. (Aristotle 1984b: *Generation of Animals*, 736^b)

If the soul is not a primary substance, then what is it in the case of a human being? Aristotle maintains that that which exists on its own is the individual soul–body composite—for example the individual man, Socrates. Thus, it is ultimately not the soul, as opposed to the body, that thinks, experiences pain and pleasure, desires, deliberates, and so on, but the individual man, Socrates, who is active with respect to some and passive with respect to others of these things. "Perhaps indeed it would be better not to say that the soul pities or learns or thinks but that the man does in virtue of the soul" (*De anima*, 408^b).

Though Aristotle denies, in opposition to Plato, that it is the soul as such that is the subject of what may be called psychological events, he is aware of the unity of consciousness that we discussed at the end of the previous section on Plato and of the problem it poses for a view that holds that distinct parts of the material body are subjects of distinct psychological capacities and of their actualizations:

> Therefore discrimination between white and sweet cannot be effected by two agencies which remain separate; both the qualities discriminated must be present to something that is one and single. [. . .] What says that two things are different must be one; for sweet is different from white. Therefore what asserts this difference must be self-identical, and as what asserts, so also what thinks or perceives. That it is not possible by means of two agencies which remain separate to discriminate

two objects which are separate is therefore obvious. (*De anima*, 426ᵇ; Smith's translation)

Aristotle's point seems to be that, if one subject apprehends whiteness and another apprehends sweetness, then it would not be obvious to either that what it apprehends is different from what the other apprehends. But it is obvious that whiteness is different from sweetness, which requires the existence of a single subject that is aware both of whiteness and sweetness and of their difference from each other.

In addition to highlighting the unity of consciousness, Aristotle also calls attention to the fact that, when we see and hear, we are aware that we are seeing and hearing (*De anima*, 425ᵇ). He makes the same point about walking and thinking:

> Moreover, when a person sees, he perceives that he sees; when he hears, he perceives that he hears; when he walks, he perceives that he walks; and similarly in all other activities there is something which perceives that we are active. This means that, in perception, we perceive that we perceive, and in thinking we perceive that we think. (Aristotle 1962: *Nicomachean Ethics*, 1170ᵃ; Oswald's translation).

In other words, our perceiving is transparent to us. But can we be aware of our seeing or hearing (and tasting, smelling, and touching) by seeing or hearing, and so on? Because each mode of sensation has its appropriate object (e.g. color of seeing, sound of hearing) and the respective act of sensing does not itself exemplify that object (e.g., seeing color is not itself colored), one is tempted to answer this question negatively. Aristotle seems to take the position that one should resist this temptation and affirm that each act of perception is not a simple act of perception but *involves* both the respective act of perception (e.g. seeing) and the sensing of that act of perception in that act itself. The alternative, he says, would be an infinite regress of modes of sensation (e.g., the distinct mode of sensation by which one perceives that one is seeing must now itself be the object of a yet further act of perceiving by a yet further distinct mode of sensation). But is an infinite regress of modes of sensation the only alternative? Might not one have an additional form of awareness (e.g., introspective awareness of oneself seeing when one sees, where not a faculty of oneself but one's self/soul is the subject endowed with that awareness), which is not itself the object of any further distinct act of awareness? In other words, one need not have an additional, distinct act of awareness whereby one is aware of oneself being aware of oneself seeing. We are not aware of any consideration that would reasonably disqualify this possibility.

Beyond noting that we are aware of our own selves sensing, Aristotle also alerts us to an important feature of our sense. In order to make his point, Aristotle distinguishes the special sensibles (color, sound, taste, smell, and touch), each of which is the object of only one sense (sight, and only sight, has color as its object; hearing, and only hearing, has sound as its object, and so on), from the common sensibles (movement, rest, number, shape, and size (*De anima*, 418ª)), each of which can be the object of more than one sense (e.g., both touch and sight can have movement as an object). An interesting feature of a sense object that is special, says Aristotle, is that it is an object about which it is impossible in one way, but not in another, to be deceived: "Each sense then judges about the special objects [sight of color, hearing of sound] and is not deceived as to their being a colour or sound, but only as to what the coloured or sounded thing is or where it is" (*De anima*, 418ª). As we will see in subsequent chapters, both Augustine and Descartes will make a similar point in their refutations of skepticism. Each one maintains that, while the soul might be deceived about the color of an object or about where a sound is coming from, it cannot be deceived about the fact that it seems to it as if that color belongs to an object and that that sound is coming from a certain direction. Aristotle goes on to state that, with respect to the common sensibles, "there is the greatest possibility of perceptual illusion" (*De anima*, 428ᵇ). It seems to us, however, that there is no greater possibility of error with regard to the common sensibles than there is with respect to the special sensibles. If we stay with Aristotle's way of conceptualizing the issue, then it seems correct to hold that we are not deceived by our sight and touch about there being a moving object, but only as to what the moving thing is or where it is, or even if there is a moving thing. Similarly, if we take the perspective of Augustine and Descartes, it seems correct to say that, while a soul might be mistaken about the actual movement of an object, it cannot be deceived about the fact that it seems as if an object is so moving.

As we have already stated, Aristotle claims that rational souls make it possible for human beings not only to sense but also to think. Moreover, he believes that, because everything is a potential object of thought, it is not possible for the faculty of thought to be anything material. "That part of the soul then that is called intellect (by which I mean that whereby the soul thinks and supposes) is before it thinks in actuality none of the things that exist. This makes it unreasonable that it be mixed with the body" (*De anima*, 429^a; Lawson-Tancred's translation). The idea here seems to be that, if the power of thought were of a material nature, then we could not know things as they really are, but would distort them—much as a colored lens distorts the color of a perceived object.

Aristotle reinforces the belief that the soul as intellect is non-bodily in nature by arguing that, because the soul is, or has, an intellect, it cannot be a quantity. He points out that, while the thought in which a soul engages has a unity, this unity is different from the one possessed by a quantity. Thought is unified by its logical connections (e.g. by the connection between "If A then B; A; hence B"), but a quantity is unified by a juxtaposition or arrangement of parts, which is a spatial issue. Some, says Aristotle, liken the soul to a circle. Will the soul, then, he responds, always be thinking without beginning or end? This is absurd, because

> all practical thought processes have termini—they are all for some purpose—and all contemplative thought processes are similarly limited by their arguments. Now every argument is either a definition or a

demonstration, and of these a demonstration is both from a starting-point and in a way has an end [...] and all definitions are obviously limited. (*De anima*, 407ª; Lawson-Tancred's translation)

Thus the fact that all reasoning has a beginning and an end should deter us from thinking that we can learn about the nature of the soul by considering the nature of a circle.

While Aristotle is not a soul–body dualist in the sense that he maintains that the soul is a substance in its own right, which is separable from its body, he believes that the distinctive nature of thought or intellect provides him with grounds for making some suggestive remarks about the possibility of separating the intellect from its material housing:

But nothing is yet clear on the subject of the intellect and the contemplative faculty. However, it seems to be another kind of soul, and this alone admits of being separated, as that which is eternal from that which is perishable, while it is clear from these remarks that the other parts of the soul [nutritive, sensitive] are not separable, as some assert them to be, though it is obvious that they are conceptually distinct. (*De anima*, 413ᵇ; Lawson-Tancred's translation)

According to Aristotle, the intellect is both theoretical and practical in its operations. That is, it can have as its subject matter both philosophical concerns (e.g., does every event have a cause?) and concerns about daily life (e.g., how do I get to the market from here?). The concerns of the practical intellect require motions of our bodies, and Aristotle is much interested in how it is that the soul–body complex (the individual human being) moves. He devotes a significant space (*De anima*, Book I) to cataloging how earlier theorists of the soul tried to account for the movements of those things that are alive, most especially human beings. For example, he notes that many philosophers believed that what is ensouled differs from that which is not, in virtue of the fact that the soul is that which produces movement (*De anima*, 403ᵇ). Moreover, because these philosophers thought that what is not itself moved is not capable of moving anything else, they held that the soul, because it produces motion, is itself in motion. Aristotle notes that Democritus asserted that the soul is a kind of fire made up of spherical atoms—because, when they are in motion, they are especially able to penetrate everything and to move it. He also makes mention of some of the Pythagoreans who held that the soul is like motes in the air, because they seem to be in constant motion even when there is complete calm. (*De anima*, 404ᵃ).

Aristotle's response to such views is that they are deeply mistaken: "All this has made it clear that the soul cannot be in motion, and if in general it is not in motion, obviously it is not moved by itself" (408ᵇ). According to him, the plain fact is that the soul is not a kind of body, but rather belongs to a body and is present in it (414ᵃ). Moreover, the soul need not be made up of things that are spatially in motion in order for it to be able to move its body, which is something it does. As far as Aristotle is concerned, Democritus, the Pythagoreans, and others who shared views like theirs were deeply mistaken about how the soul moves its body. In the case of human beings, Aristotle asserts that the soul produces motion "through some kind of choice and thought process" (*De anima*, 406ᵇ), where that choice and the thought process cannot be understood in terms of microscopic bodies in motion. Later on, Aristotle elaborates on his insight about how the soul moves the body, and he claims that movement is started by the object of desire, which attracts because it either is good or seems good.

> The object of desire is the point of departure for action. [. . .] In form, then, that which produces movement is a single thing, the faculty of desire as such. But first of all is the object of desire, which, by being thought or imagined, produces movement while not itself in motion. (*De anima*, 433ᵃ⁻ᵇ; Lawson-Tancred's translation)

Elsewhere Aristotle says that "the origin of action—its efficient, not its final cause—is choice, and that of choice is desire and reasoning with a view to an end" (*Nicomachean Ethics*, 1139ª; Ross' translation). Finally, there must be a causal connection between what is mental and what is bodily, "so that the organ whereby desire produces movement [. . .] is something bodily, whose investigation belongs with that of the common functions of body and soul" (*De anima*, 433ᵇ; Lawson-Tancred's translation).

Aristotle's view of how the soul moves the body seems to be as follows. The soul has the *faculty* or *capacity* of desire (*De anima*, 433ᵇ), whose *operations* (actualizations) are directed at what is good or believed to be good. This object of desire is an *end* or goal (what Aristotle calls a "final cause"), and the subject of the desire, the individual human being, reasons about how to achieve this goal; and this goal of the reasoning process is a *purpose* because "all practical thought processes have termini—they are all for some purpose" (*De anima*, 407ª). This desire and reasoning process produce, or bring about (in Aristotle's language, they "efficiently cause") the individual's choice to act, where that choice in turn produces the relevant bodily motions, which serve as the means to the achievement of the purpose, if all goes according to plan.

We conclude our discussion of Aristotle's account of the soul by noting that he affirms a causal connection between what is mental and what is bodily in nature. Though he denies that the subject of what is mental is a substantial soul that is ontologically distinct from its physical body, he nevertheless affirms the broadly Socratic teleological view that the ultimately purposeful actualization or activity of an individual's mental faculty is directly causally productive of an initial effect in a bodily organ of that individual whereby motion is produced in that individual's limbs. In short, Aristotle affirms a form of mental-to-physical causation that will later (with Descartes) become a major point of debate.

Chapter 2

The Soul in Medieval
Christian Thought

We continue the history of the soul with an exploration of the
philosophy of two outstanding medieval thinkers who have exercised
a massive impact on subsequent philosophy and theology: Aurelius
Augustinus or Saint Augustine (354–430 CE), who was especially
influenced by Plato; and Saint Thomas Aquinas (1225–1274), who
was especially influenced by Aristotle. While we shall be investigating
their *philosophy* of the soul, it is worth noting that their views about
the soul were also rooted in their religious faith. Hence we begin with
some brief general observations about this religious background
before diving back into the philosophy of the soul. It is necessary to
do so; for, in the last 50 years, it has been fashionable to think that
Christian teachings about the soul are too heavily influenced by Greek
thought, and not in keeping with the biblical portrait of human persons
as material beings. Might it be the case the Augustine's and Aquinas's
philosophy of the soul is at complete odds with the roots of their
religious tradition? Over the past twenty years, there has been a movement, often called Christian materialism, which seeks to repudiate
Augustine, Aquinas, and others in the name of biblical faith.

The Hebrew Bible (or Christian Old Testament) and the New
Testament affirm what might be called a holistic or integrated view
of human beings. We are not souls trapped inside our bodies. Still,
Hebrew and Christian sources also testify to a belief in the reality of

A Brief History of the Soul, First Edition.
© 2011 Stewart Goetz and Charles Taliaferro. Published 2011 by Blackwell Publishing Ltd.

an afterlife for individual persons. This is often described in terms of bodily resurrection (Ezekiel 37), but there is also an affirmation that, at death and prior to the resurrection, the soul (or the person) is with God. In Hebrew theology, one can see over time the gradual affirmation of the reality of an afterlife (Genesis 37: 35; Job 3: 13; Wisdom of Solomon 3: 1–4), and this seems to require some distinction between the soul (or person) and the body—as we find in Ecclesiastes 12: 6,7, where death is described in terms of "the dust [body] will return to the earth as it was, and the sprit will return to God who gave it." Moreover, the belief of ordinary people in the soul's existence is reflected in historical vignettes involving Jesus. For example, when Jesus asked his disciples what people thought about his identity, it appeared that some thought he was John the Baptist, others that he was Elijah, and others still that he was Jeremiah, or one of the prophets (Matthew 16: 13–14). Even Herod, who had John the Baptist executed, wondered if Jesus was John (Matthew 14: 2). Given that it is reasonable to assume that John the Baptist's body could easily be located, it only makes sense to conclude that people thought that Jesus might be John's soul, re-embodied. Belief in the soul's existence is also manifested in St. Paul's conviction that he might become disembodied before death. Thus, when Paul boasted to the Corinthians that he was caught up in paradise though he could not remember whether he was in his body or out of it (2 Corinthians 12: 2–4), he was simply presupposing that he was a soul that could exist outside his body. In sum, it is hard to square Christian teachings about the person being with God upon their death (Luke 23: 43) with materialism; for, if the person is the very same thing as the body, then if the body is destroyed, the person is destroyed, and it makes little sense to affirm that the person is somehow with God. So we suggest that, by affirming (as we shall see) that the soul is more than the body (and thus does not share the same fate as the body at death), Augustine and Aquinas did not abandon biblical faith upon having been seduced by Greek, pagan thought. Readers with theological interests will find John Cooper's *Body, Soul and Life Everlasting; Biblical Anthropology and the Monism–Dualism Debate* and N. T. Wright's *The*

New Testament and the People of God and *The Resurrection of the Son of God* excellent resources for further reflection.

Augustine

Aurelius Augustinus was trained as a rhetorician and taught rhetoric until he converted to Christianity at 33 years of age. As Gareth Matthews, one of today's foremost Augustinian scholars, notes, although Augustine was not by training a philosopher, he was one by character and temperament (Matthews 1992, x). Augustine says of human beings that "they go out and gaze in astonishment at high mountains, the huge waves of the sea, the broad reaches of rivers, the ocean that encircles the world, or the stars in their courses. But they pay no attention to themselves" (Augustine 1961: *Confessions*, X.8). Those who do pay attention to themselves will sooner or later turn to the matter of the soul, and Augustine tells us that "The question of the soul troubles many people, and I confess that I am among them" (Augustine 2004: *Letters*, 166, 2.3). Augustine devoted much time and thought to the soul, and some of the most significant points he makes on the subject will reappear, over a thousand years later, in the work of René Descartes.

We begin with the most general points that Augustine makes about the soul. Like his Greek predecessors, he maintains that the soul is the principle of life, so that everything that is ensouled is alive: "[E]ach substance either lives or does not live. But all that does not live is without soul" (Augustine 1947: *Immortality of the Soul*, 3.3). The following powers of the soul are the common possession of plants and human beings:

[T]he soul by its presence gives life to this earth- and death-bound body. It makes of it a unified organism and maintains it as such, keeping it from disintegrating and wasting away. It provides for a proper, balanced distribution of nourishment to the body's members. It preserves the body's harmony and proportion, not only in beauty, but also in growth and reproduction. Obviously, however, these are faculties which man has in common with the plant world; for we say of plants too, that they live, [and] we see and acknowledge that each of them is preserved to its own generic being, is nourished, grows, and reproduces itself. (Augustine 1950b: *Greatness of the Soul*, 33.70)

In addition to plants and human beings, beasts also have souls. God is the one "who made every soul, whatever be the nature of its life, whether it have life without sensation and reason, or life with sensation, or life with both sensation and reason" (Augustine 1993: *City of God*, VII.29). As ensouled, beasts are not only alive but they also possess one or more of the five senses of touch, taste, sight, smell, and hearing. What the beasts lack is the power of intellect: "[E]ven the souls of animals live, though they are not intelligent" (Augustine 1991: *On the Trinity*, X.2.6).

With the addition of the power of reason, we reach the kind of soul that is found in human beings. Of this soul, Augustine says that "[i]t seems [. . .] to be a special substance, endowed with reason, adapted to rule the body" (*Greatness of the Soul*, 13.22; cf. 33.72). With this claim, that the soul is a substance in its own right, we have an affirmation of Plato's and a renunciation of Aristotle's position on the soul. Given Augustine's affirmation of the soul's substantiality, it is no surprise to find him saying that "I myself am my soul" (ibid., 30.61). If we are our souls, however, then what is a human being? A human being, or man, is a soul endowed with reason, which is joined to its physical body: "We could also define man like this and say, 'Man is a rational substance consisting of soul and body'" (*On the Trinity*, XV.2.11; cf. VIII.8).

It is in Augustine's reflections about the substantial soul of a human being (which is the only kind of soul that will concern us in the next several chapters) that we discover some of the most important and original of his ideas. As Matthews points out, in Augustine's writings "we find, for the first time, an argument for dualism that is essentially internalist. This is the reasoning from what each mind can know about itself to the conclusion that minds are non-corporeal entities" (Matthews 2000, 134). The method of argument that Matthews describes as "internalist" in character is one that we will henceforth characterize as "first-person" in nature; by this we mean, as in Chapter 1, that it is rooted in self-awareness or introspection. We will contrast the first-person perspective with what we will call the "third-person" perspective, by which we mean one that it has its source in one of more of the five senses of touch, sight, hearing, taste, and smell.

Augustine believes that each of us knows what a soul is from the simple fact that each of us is one. He maintains that nothing is more intimately known and aware of its own existence than a soul, because nothing can be more present to the soul than itself (*Confessions*, VIII.4.9; X.2.5). Indeed, a soul "simply cannot not know itself, since by the very fact of knowing itself not knowing, it knows itself" (ibid., X.2.5). While Descartes' *cogito ergo sum* ("I think, therefore, I am") is roughly eleven hundred years distant in the future, Augustine is already well aware of what is known through self-awareness and of how it can be used to defeat skepticism. For example, in response to the skeptic, he says: "I will ask you first whether you yourself exist. Are you, perhaps, afraid that you are being deceived by my questioning? But if you did not exist, it would be impossible for you to be deceived" (Augustine 1964: *On Free Choice of the Will*, II.3). Elsewhere, and at greater length, we find the following:

> For we both are, and know that we are, and delight in our being, and our knowledge of it. Moreover, in these three things no true-seeming illusion disturbs us; for we do not come into contact with these by some bodily sense, as we perceive the things outside of us—colours, e.g., by seeing, sounds by hearing, smells by smelling, tastes by tasting, hard and soft objects by touching—of all which sensible objects it is the images resembling them, but not themselves which we perceive in the mind and hold in the memory, and which excite us to desire the objects. But, without any delusive representation of images or

phantasms, I am most certain that I am, and that I know and delight in this. In respect of these truths, I am not at all afraid of the arguments of the Academicians, who say, What if you are deceived? For if I am deceived, I am. For he who is not, cannot be deceived; and if I am deceived, by this same token I am. And since I am if I am deceived, how am I deceived in believing that I am? For it is certain that I am if I am deceived. Since, therefore, I, the person deceived, should be, even if I were deceived, certainly I am not deceived in this knowledge that I am. And, consequently, neither am I deceived in knowing that I know. For, as I know that I am, so I know this also, that I know. (Augustine, *City of God*, XI.26)

Not only can the soul not be deceived about its existence, but also it cannot be deceived about how things appear to it:

> But, says someone, I am deceived, if I give my assent. Do not assent more than that you know that it appears so to you. There is then no deception. I do not see how the Academic can refute him who says: I know that this presents itself to me as white; I know that this delights my ear; I know that this has a sweet smell for me; I know that this has a pleasant taste for me; I know that this feels cold to me. (Augustine 1950a: *Against the Academics*, 3.11.26)

Given that we cannot help but know that we exist and that the external world appears in a certain way to us, how do we know that other souls exist? According to Augustine, it is through knowledge of, and comparison with, the causal relationship between our souls and certain of our bodily movements that we believe that certain movements of other bodies that are similar to our own are produced by other rational souls (*On the Trinity*, VIII.4.9). Matthews states that, so far as he knows, Augustine is the first philosopher to put forth this argument from analogy for the existence of other minds (Matthews 2000, 136).

How does the soul know that it is not also a body? While at points Augustine argues for the non-bodily nature of the soul (e.g., he claims that the soul's ability to turn away from bodily things in thinking about such topics as God and itself makes it clear that it is not a body; Augustine 2002: *On Genesis*, VII.14.20), there are other places where he seems to believe that the soul is directly aware of its non-bodily nature. For example, in a difficult section of his work *On the Trinity*, in which he discusses the meaning of the Delphic injunction "Know thyself" (X.2.6), Augustine maintains it is clear from a first-person perspective that the whole soul knows whatever it knows. Given that this is the case, when the soul knows that *it* knows, it knows all of itself. Because the whole soul knows the whole of itself, there is nothing of or about itself that is hidden to itself. The famous medievalist scholar Etienne Gilson summarizes Augustine's view in the following way:

> [T]he mind [soul] knows its own existence with immediate evidence. When it discovers itself (even in doubt), it apprehends itself as an intelligence. It knows that it exists and lives, but the life it grasps is the life of a mind. Because it knows this, it is capable of knowing what it is and what it is not. Since it is intelligence, it certainly is what it knows itself to be, and it is certainly not what it does not know itself to be. (Gilson 1960, 46)

With his claim that the soul is directly aware of its non-bodily nature, Augustine seems to embrace what can rightly be considered a strong position on self-knowledge, one that entails that at any moment the soul is perfectly transparent to itself. This strong position can be contrasted with a weaker one. To explain this contrast, consider the idea that, from the first-person perspective, a soul could go looking for itself—which is a possibility that Augustine himself discusses (*On the Trinity*, X.2.6). Typically, when we go looking for something, we have an idea of that for which we are looking. For example, when we are working on a jigsaw puzzle, we have an idea of the shape and color of the piece for which we are looking, in light of our awareness of the shapes and colors of the adjacent pieces. In the case of the soul, we might ask if it is aware of the shape and color of some part of itself that makes intelligible the idea that it might go looking for, and find, some other part, which fits together with the part of which it is already aware. This suggestion seems laughable, but its laughableness conceals an important point about what the soul's awareness of itself does not include.

To clarify this important point about what the soul's awareness of itself fails to include, it is necessary to summarize briefly Augustine's account of what a body is. At one point in *On the Trinity*, he states: "There may of course be some bodies that are quite impossible to cut up or divide; but even so, if they did not consist of their parts they would not be bodies" (IX.1.7). Later in the same work he emphasizes that a body is that "whose part in a localized space is smaller than the whole" (X.3.9). Elsewhere, Augustine states that anything that is a body has length, width, and height (Augustine, *Greatness of the Soul*, 4.6; 6.10; 14.23). A necessary condition, then, of something's being a body, according to Augustine, is that it has substantive parts (parts that are such that, if an object has them, then that object is in principle divisible into those parts). Because a soul is not a body, it is "without extension and unable to be divided and partitioned at all" (*Greatness of the Soul*, 14.23). Therefore, says Augustine, a soul is something simple (ibid., 1.2; 13.22).

Given these things that Augustine tells us about the nature of a body and of a soul, the weaker position on a soul's self-knowledge is that this knowledge does not include the soul's awareness of itself having properties that would entail that it is a body. Stated slightly differently, the soul fails to be aware of itself exemplifying properties that entail that it is a body.

At this point, someone might retort that the soul often discovers that it loses and adds things to itself, and the fact that it makes these discoveries supports the position that it does have parts. For example, the soul knows that it comes to remember things that it did, or things it could not remember before; and it is aware that it loses and comes to have desires, fears, hopes, and so on. Surely this indicates that the soul is aware that it has parts and that it is a body.

This objection, however, is based on a confusion between complexity at the level of substance and complexity at the level of qualities or properties. One must be mindful of the fact that a soul–body dualist like Augustine maintains that, while a soul has multiple essential psychological powers and/or capacities (e.g., the power to think, the power to remember, the power to choose, the capacity to experience pleasure, the capacity to desire, the capacity to fear), these powers and capacities are not themselves substances (they are not substantive). Because they are properties and not substances, powers and capacities cannot be separated from or exist independently of the soul that has them, so as to become parts of other substances. They are not substantive, separable parts of a soul in the way in which a portion of a table (e.g. a top, or a leg) is a substantive, separable part of the table and can exist independently of the table and become a part of another substance (e.g. the leg of a table can become the leg of a chair). Thus a table, unlike a soul, is a complex entity or thing in virtue of the fact that it is made up of parts that are themselves substances (substantive parts). Contemporary physical scientists inform us that a table is actually a lattice structure of molecules bound together by attractive powers affecting appropriate capacities, and, when this lattice structure is broken by a sufficient force, the table breaks. A soul–body dualist like Augustine maintains that a soul, unlike a table or physical objects in general, is not a complex entity, because it has no substantive parts. Instead, it is substantively simple in nature. Thus complexity at the level of propertyhood is compatible with simplicity at the level of thinghood.

In light of the distinction between propertyhood and thinghood, it is helpful to consider what Matthews regards as Augustine's most persuasive argument for mind–body dualism (Matthews 2005, 51–52). The argument is as follows:

1   If the mind were made of some kind of physical stuff, then the mind, simply by being fully present to itself, would think (be aware) of the physical stuff it is made of.

2   The mind, simply by being fully present to itself, does not think (is not aware) of any physical stuff.

Therefore,

3   The mind is not made of any kind of physical stuff.

Matthews goes on to say that the greatest challenge both to the idea of full mind self-presence and to Augustine's argument comes not from materialist theories of the mind, but from the Freudian idea of the unconscious mind, in which beliefs and desires are not fully present to the mind. But Matthews believes the objection is answerable. After all, he points out, from the Freudian perspective even unconscious beliefs and desires must somehow be directly available to the thinking soul. Thus, while we might at first disavow having a certain desire, if we genuinely have it, it must be possible for us at some point to become aware of it and to admit that it is ours in light of the soul's full presence to itself. In short, the Freudian idea of a partially unconscious mind can be made compatible with Augustine's view that the mind is fully present to itself. Moreover, adds Matthews, it is important to realize that the materialist philosopher who tells us that our mind is composed of some material substance or other might get us to accept his materialist view of the self on the basis of some argument, but he will not be able to get us to realize this on the basis of the mind's full presence to itself. In the light of that presence, the mind is not aware of itself being physical.

As Matthews says, the argument above might be Augustine's strongest argument for dualism. And we can grant that it stands up well to the Freudian challenge. But it is highly questionable that the greatest challenge to Augustine's argument is the Freudian one. The materialist, whether Freudian or not, could invoke the distinction between properties and substances and concede, for the sake of argument, that, while mental properties like having a desire must at some point come under the light of the mind's full presence to itself, substantive parts of the mind (assuming that it has such parts) need not. For whatever reason, they could be hidden from the mind in such a way that the mind is unable to be aware of them. If this is the case, then premise (1) of Augustine's argument is false and the argument unsound.

The weaker position concerning the soul's self-knowledge, which is the position that, from the first-person perspective, the soul fails to be aware of itself as being bodily in nature, is defended by various contemporary philosophers in terms of the *self*'s awareness of itself. For example, Roderick Chisholm stresses that, with the perception of external objects, we know that

> whatever our perspective upon the perceived object may be, there will always be certain parts of the perceived object that we do perceive and certain other parts of the perceived object that we do not perceive. Moreover, and this is the important point about external perception, if we know that we are perceiving a certain physical thing, then we are also capable of knowing that we are perceiving something that is just a proper part of that thing. But the situation is different when we perceive ourselves to be thinking.
>
> I may perceive myself to be thinking and know that I am doing so and yet be unable to know whether I am perceiving any proper part of anything that I am perceiving. It may be, for all anyone knows, that whenever I perceive myself to be thinking, I *do* perceive some part of myself. This would be the case, for example, if I could not perceive myself to be thinking without perceiving some part of my body, and if, moreover, I were identical with my body or with that part of my body. But it is not true that, whenever I perceive myself to be thinking, I thereby perceive what I can *know* to be a part of myself. (Chisholm 1994, 100)

The materialists John Searle and Colin McGinn make points similar to Chisholm's about the nature of self-awareness in terms of consciousness:

> We are not aware in conscious experience of [. . .] the dimensions of our conscious experience [. . .] Although we experience objects and

events as both spatially extended and of temporal duration, our consciousness itself is not experienced as spatial, though it is experienced as temporally extended. (Searle 1992, 105, 127)

It is precisely [spatially defined properties] that seem inherently incapable of resolving the mind–brain problem: we cannot link consciousness to the brain in virtue of spatial properties of the brain. [...] [C]onsciousness defies explanation in such terms. Consciousness does not seem made up out of smaller spatial processes. [...] Our faculties bias us towards understanding matter in motion, but it is precisely this kind of understanding that is inapplicable to the mind–body problem. (McGinn 1991, 11–12, 18, footnote 21)

The fact that a soul is not aware, from the first-person perspective, of itself having substantial parts connects in an interesting way with the idea that the soul might, from the third-person perspective, go looking for (part of) itself in the spatial realm of bodies and of their substantial parts. How could a soul look for itself within the spatial nexus of wholes and their parts, when it fails to be aware of itself having parts that make its location in that domain intelligible? On what grounds could it justifiably identify itself with anything in that domain? Augustine's insight, that it is difficult to make sense of the idea that a soul does not know about, and yet might go looking for, itself resembles certain views in contemporary philosophical discussions about the mind. For example, in his now classic paper "What Is It Like to be a Bat?," Thomas Nagel expresses skepticism about the intelligibility of physicalism, which is the philosophical position that identifies mental events or states with physical events or states. As opposed to saying that physicalism is false, Nagel believes:

It would be truer to say that physicalism is a position we cannot understand because we do not at present have any conception of how it might be true. Perhaps it will be thought unreasonable to require such a conception as a condition of understanding. After all, it might be said, the meaning of physicalism is clear enough: mental states are states of the body; mental events are physical events. We do not know *which* physical states and events they are, but that should not prevent us from understanding the hypothesis. What could be clearer than the words "is" and "are"?

But I believe it is precisely this apparent clarity of the word "is" that is deceptive. Usually, when we are told that *X* is *Y* we know *how* it is supposed to be true, but that depends on a conceptual or theoretical background and is not conveyed by the "is" alone. We know how both "*X*" and "*Y*" refer, and the kinds of things to which they refer, and we have a rough idea how the two referential paths might converge on a single thing, be it an object, a person, a process, an event, or whatever. But when the two terms of the identification are very disparate it may not be so clear how it could be true. We may not have even a rough idea of how the two referential paths could converge, or what kind of things they might converge on, and a theoretical framework may have to be supplied to enable us to understand this. Without the framework, an air of mysticism surrounds the identification. (Nagel 1979, 176–177)

Is there, then, no way to demystify the identification of what is mental with what is physical? This question will periodically resurface in subsequent chapters. For now, we simply note that the issue is not as straightforward as many people assume, or perhaps would like to believe. Of course, one might simply stipulate that the self or mental states and events are identical with something physical (e.g. with the brain or brain states and events) and adopt ways of speech that reflect this stipulation. However, such a stipulation would not be philosophically significant. The philosophical question is whether there are any good reasons to think that such a stipulation and the corresponding conventions of speech are correct. Augustine is a philosopher whose reflections about the soul and its self-knowledge provide serious reasons for doubting that they are.

We will revisit the distinction between the strong and weak positions on the soul's self-knowledge when we examine Descartes' philosophy of the soul. Presently, we turn our attention to some of Augustine's thoughts about how the soul is related to the body and to the spatial realm that the latter occupies. Once again, his thoughts raise interesting and difficult issues. For a start, Augustine maintains that what is not corporeal (bodily) is not in space (*Immortality of the Soul*, 10.17). Given that the soul is not corporeal in nature, one would expect Augustine to maintain that the soul is not in space. Nevertheless, he affirms that the soul is in space, but not in the same way in which something corporeal is in space. How does a body occupy space? It does so by having each of its parts occupy parts of space. With a body that is spread out in space, smaller parts of it occupy smaller spaces and larger parts of it occupy larger spaces. The point is that a body as a whole is not present in each of the parts of space that are occupied by its parts. "Each mass that occupies space is not in its entirety in each of its single parts, but only in all taken together. Hence, one part is in one place; another in another" (ibid., 16.25). Augustine considers this way of occupying space to qualify as occupying space by diffusion. When it comes to the soul, Augustine says that, while the soul is in space, we must not think that the soul "is diffused throughout the whole body, as is the blood" (*Greatness of the Soul*, 30.61). In other words, in contrast to a body that occupies space by means of its parts occupying sub-regions of the space occupied by the whole, so that the whole body is not present in any of the spaces occupied by its parts, the soul is present in its entirety at one time, not only in the entire space that is occupied by its body, but also in each of the sub-regions of space that are occupied by that body's parts. Why maintain that the soul occupies space in this way?

> [Because] it is the entire soul that feels the pain of a part of the body, yet it does not feel it in the entire body. When, for instance, there is an ache in the foot, the eye looks at it, the mouth speaks of it, and the hand reaches for it. This, of course, would be impossible, if what of the soul is in these parts did not also experience a sensation in the foot; if the soul were not present, it would be unable to feel what has happened there. [. . .] Hence, the entire soul is present, at one and

the same time, in the single parts, and it experiences sensation as a whole, at one and the same time, in the single parts. (*Immortality of the Soul*, 16.25)

And again:

But if a body is only that which stands still or is moved through an area of space with some length, breadth and depth so that it occupies a larger place with a larger part of itself and a smaller place with a smaller part and is smaller in a part than in the whole, then the soul is not a body. It is, of course, stretched out through the whole body that it animates, not by a local diffusion but by a certain vital intention. For it is at the same time present as a whole through all the body's parts, not smaller in smaller parts and larger in larger parts, but more intensely in one place and less intensely in another, both whole in all parts and whole in the individual parts. (*Letters*, 166.2.4)

It is unclear to us what Augustine has in mind in this passage when he states that the soul is stretched out (present) in the entirety of its body "by a certain vital intention." What is clear is that he believes the soul is present in its entirety at each point in the space it occupies, for the following reason: When something touches (or damages) a soul's body at a particular location (e.g. a toe), the soul in its entirety experiences a sensation (e.g. pain) at that location. Moreover, if that body were simultaneously touched (or damaged) at a different spot (e.g. a finger) then the soul in its entirety would simultaneously experience pain at both locations. If the soul were spread out in space by local diffusion, one part of it occupying one area of space and another part occupying a different area, then one part of the soul would experience one pain and another part a different pain, but neither of the parts would experience the other's pain. However, this is not as things are. *One and the same* entity (the soul) is experiencing both pains, which leads Augustine to maintain that the soul in its entirety is simultaneously present at both locations.

Augustine nicely ties together, in the following quote, his point about how the soul occupies space and his belief that the soul is simple at the level of thinghood but complex at the level of propertyhood:

> When we come to a spiritual creature such as the soul, it is certainly found to be simple in comparison with the body; but apart from such a comparison it is multiple, not simple. The reason it is simpler than the body is that it has no mass spread out in space, but in any body it is whole in the whole and whole also in any part of the body. Thus when something happens even in some tiny little part that the soul is aware of, the whole soul is aware of it because it does not escape the whole soul even though it does not happen in the whole body. And yet even in the soul it is one thing to be ingenious, another to be unskillful, another to be sharp, another to have good memory; greed is one thing, fear another, joy another, sadness another; some of these things can be found in the soul without others, some more, some less; countless qualities can be found in the soul in countless ways. So it is clear that its nature is not simple but multiple. (*On the Trinity*, VI.2.8)

According to Augustine, then, the soul exists, is simple at the level of substancehood while complex at the level of propertyhood, and is embodied, though it and its body occupy the same space in different ways. From where, however, does a soul come? What of its origin? How does it come to be embodied? Throughout his life, Augustine struggled to answer these questions. In his work entitled *On Free Choice of the Will*, which was completed at the end of the fourth century, Augustine sets out four possibilities concerning the origin of a soul: (1) one soul (Adam's) was created and others come from it through sexual procreation; (2) every soul is created in each child who is born; (3) each soul exists elsewhere and is sent by God into a body of a human being at birth; (4) each soul exists elsewhere and of its own will slips into a body of a human being at birth (III.20–21). Augustine finds the question of Adam's original sin and of how human beings subsequent to Adam could inherit the guilt of that sin particularly vexing. For example, possibility (1) seems to Augustine to be the best answer to the problem of original sin, but at the expense of compromising the non-bodily nature of the soul. Possibility (2) maintains the integrity of the soul's noncorporeal nature but at the expense of a plausible explanation of how a soul could bear the guilt of Adam's original sin. In the end, it seems fair to say that Augustine never resolves to his own satisfaction the issue of original sin and its inheritance and the matter of the soul's origin.

Though Augustine is not able to resolve the problem of the soul's origin, he believes that others should not be forbidden from examining the matter:

> I do not intend [. . .] to cause anyone to think that we forbid that he who is able should examine [. . .] whether a soul is propagated by a soul, or whether each soul is created for an individual body, or whether, at divine will, they are sent from somewhere to rule and animate a body, or whether they enter bodies of their own will. (*On Free Choice of the Will*, III.21)

But, while he does not forbid others from seeking to answer the question of the soul's origin, he does have doubts about the importance of the issue:

> What does it matter to me if I do not know when I began to exist, since I know that I now exist and believe hopefully in my future existence? I do not trouble myself about my past, and, if my judgment about past events is mistaken, I do not take this error to be serious. Instead [. . .] I direct my course toward what I shall be. [. . .] [T]here is no harm for the man sailing to Rome to forget what shore he sailed from, as long as he knows where to direct his boat from the place where he is. It does him no good to remember the shore he set sail from, if he is wrecked upon a reef because he had a mistaken idea about the port of Rome. In the same way, it is not harmful to me if I do not retain the beginning of my span of life, as long as I know where I shall rest. (*On Free Choice of the Will*, III.21)

Where will a soul rest? Where does a soul go after its embodiment in this life? What of its destiny? While in his later years as a Christian Augustine focused on the resurrection of the body, he never ceased to believe that the soul is immortal. Thus the soul exists disembodied during the time between earthly death and resurrection. "But if after its human birth, which came about from Adam, it is reborn in Christ and belongs to his society, it will have rest after the death of the body and will receive back its body for glory" (*Letters*, 166, 2.5).

While Augustine looked for life after life as a great good, he also held that embodiment was a good, even a cluster of coordinated goods. In a telling, amusing passage in *The City of God* (XIX.12), Augustine notes that a healthy embodiment is essentially a state of peace. Rupturing that peace can bring about havoc:

> If anyone were to hang upside-down, the position of the body and arrangement of the limbs is undoubtedly perverted, because what should be on top, according to the dictates of nature, is underneath, and what nature intends to be underneath is on top. This perverted attitude disturbs the peace of the flesh, and causes distress for that reason. For all that, the breath is at peace with its body and is busily engaged for the latter's preservation; that is why there is something to endure the pain. And even if the breath is finally driven from the body by distresses, still, as long as the framework of the limbs hold together, what remains retains a kind of peace among the bodily parts; hence there is still something to hang there.

Augustine thereby breaks with Plato, who had a more ambivalent view of embodiment. In any case, Augustine holds that there is soul–body interaction. When we reach Descartes eleven hundred years later, the issue of how the soul interacts with its body will receive a good deal of attention. Augustine, by contrast, does not really discuss the issue. What he does say is that the soul–body union is something marvelous and beyond human comprehension (ibid., XXI.10).

Aquinas

Like Augustine, Thomas Aquinas was a prolific scholar, and to this day his work is accorded an authoritative position by the Roman Catholic Church. Pope Pius V pronounced him the "Angelic Doctor" in 1567. Aquinas regularly refers to Aristotle as "the Philosopher," and his high regard for and use of Aristotle's philosophy in explicating issues that are integrally related to his Christian belief makes apt either the description that he Aristotelianizes Christianity or the description that he Christianizes Aristotle. As we will see, Aquinas advocates a largely Aristotelian view of the soul, and this ultimately generates some particularly difficult questions for his Christian belief in the resurrection of the body and life in the world to come.

Aquinas embraces Aristotle's view that there are different kinds of souls. First and foremost, the soul is the root principle of life (Aquinas 1970: *Summa theologiae*, Ia. q.75.1). Plants are alive and thus have a nutritive soul, but beasts are not only alive, they can also sense things, and human beings are alive, sense things, and engage in reasoning. A beast, however, does not have two souls, and a human being does not have three. Rather, a beast has only one soul, endowed with both nutritive and sensitive powers, while a human being possesses a single soul, a rational or intellective soul, with nutritive, sensitive, and intellectual powers.

> [I]f the form of non-living body confers on matter "actual being" and "being a body," the form of plant will confer on it this too, and "life" besides; and the sentient soul will confer this too and besides it will confer "sentient being"; and the rational soul will also confer this and besides it will confer "rational being". [. . .] So also the intellectual soul virtually contains the sentient soul, because it has this and still more, yet not in such a way that there are two souls. (Aquinas 1949: *On Spiritual Creatures*, III).

"It is," says Aquinas, "by the same principle [a soul], therefore, that one is a man, an animal, and a living thing" (Aquinas 1975: *Summa contra Gentiles*, II.58.3). "Hence a rational soul gives to the human body whatever a nutritive soul gives to plants and whatever a sensitive soul gives to brute animals, and in addition something more. And therefore the soul in a human being is nutritive, sensitive and rational" (Aquinas 1984: *Questions on the Soul*, XI).

One rational soul, with its multiplicity of nutritive, sensitive, and intellectual powers, assures the unity of an individual human being as a primary substance or fundamental being. Were there three souls in a man, he would be several things and at best accidentally, but not unqualifiedly one. How is it that this one soul is united with its body? Aquinas asks whether this unity can be accounted for in terms of a relationship of mixture and answers "No." The answer must be "No" because an intellectual soul is immaterial in nature and, therefore, shares no matter in common with its body by means of which the two could be mixed (*Summa contra Gentiles*, II.56). Can a human soul be united to its body by way of bodily contact? Once again, Aquinas answers "No," because contact between bodies occurs at their extremities (points, lines, or surfaces), but an intellectual soul, because it is immaterial, has no bodily extremities (ibid.).

There is, however, a different kind of contact than that which occurs at bodily extremities. It is a contact of, or by, power that relates a mover to that which it moves. Although Aquinas affirms that a soul has and exercises its power to move its body, he rejects Plato's appeal to this kind of unifying contact to explain the unqualified unity of the soul–body composite. One problem with a mere unity of contact by power is that a soul and its body end up being separate substances. "On the Platonic theory that the soul [as a substance] is united to the body as its motor only [. . .] it inevitably follows that there is some other substantial formative principle constituting the body as something the soul can move" (*Summa theologiae*, Ia. q.76.4). Another problem for explaining the unqualified soul–body unity of a human being in terms of a mere unity between mover and moved is that it does not by itself exclude the possibility for a soul to have a different body than the one it actually has, which is something that is excluded by unqualified oneness. "Just as, accordingly, it is essential to the soul that it be the form of a body, so it is essential to 'this soul,' insofar as it is 'this soul,' that it have a relation to 'this body'" (*On Spiritual Creatures*, IX.ad 4). In support of this point, Aquinas favorably quotes Aristotle's criticism of earlier philosophers who discussed the soul, namely that they failed to say anything about its proper recipient,

> "as if it were possible, as in the Pythagorean fables, that any soul might put on any body." It is, then, impossible for the soul of a dog to enter the body of a wolf, or for a man's soul to enter any body other than a man's. But the proportion between man's soul and man's body is the same as between this man's soul and this man's body. Therefore, the soul of this man cannot possibly enter a body other than its own. (*Summa contra Gentiles*, II.73.4; cf. *On Spiritual Creatures*, IX.ad 4)

How, then, if not by mixture or by either form of contact, can the unqualified unity of the soul–body relationship be explained? To answer this question, Aquinas turns to categories taken from Aristotle and insists that the soul is the *form* of the body. What does this mean? The contemporary Thomist scholar Eleonore Stump (1995, 506) suggests that we think of a form as a configurational state that organizes matter. For example, the form of water is that which configures a relationship between hydrogen and oxygen atoms to form the higher-level substance that is the water molecule. When material components like hydrogen and oxygen atoms are combined by a form into something of a higher level in nature, a substance comes into existence. Now, in the case of a human being, a soul is the form that organizes material components into a living organism with it internal organs, limbs, and so on and makes that organism capable of human action, both bodily and mental. Thus the shape (a kind of organization) of a body (and of its organs) "results from the soul" (*On Spiritual Creatures*, IV.ad 9). Elsewhere Aquinas clarifies the idea that the soul is the form of the body by contrasting it with the view that the soul is like a sailor in a ship:

Therefore, a human soul is the form of its body. Again, if a soul were in its body as a sailor is in a ship, it would not give to its body nor to its parts their specific nature; whereas the contrary seem to be true from the fact that when the soul leaves its body, the individual parts of the body do not retain their original names except in an equivocal sense. For the eye of a corpse, like the eye in a portrait or the eye of a statue, is only equivocally called an eye, and the same would be true of any other part of the body. Furthermore, if a soul were in its body as a sailor is in a ship, it would follow that the union of soul and body is accidental. Consequently death, which signifies the separation of soul and body, would not be a substantial corruption [but rather a separation of two substances], and this is obviously false. (*Questions on the Soul*, I)

In Aquinas' view, then, a human being is neither a soul alone nor a body alone, but body and soul together (*Summa theologiae*, Ia. q.75.4). "[B]ody and soul are not two actually existing substances; rather the two of them together constitute one actually existing substance" (*Summa contra Gentiles*, II.69.2)—a human being. Thus the soul alone is not a member of a species, but is a part of the human species, which the body–soul composite is (*Questions on the Soul*, III). At times we might speak as if the soul is the man, as when St. Paul writes that "the inward man [the soul] is renewed day by day" (2 Corinthians 4: 16). But this is no more than a manner of speaking (*Summa theologiae*, Ia. q.75. 4. ad 1). Just as I can say that I was hit, even though it was my car that I was driving that was hit, so also St. Paul can say that it is the soul that is being renewed, even though it is the man as a whole that is the subject of renewal. Similarly, not only may we say that the soul understands "inasmuch as the soul, which is [the man's] formal part, has this proper activity, just as the activity of any proper part is attributed to the whole" (*On Spiritual Creatures*, II.ad 2), but also "it is much better to say that the man understands with his soul" (*Summa theologiae*, Ia. q.75.2. ad 2).

The soul is the form of the body. As such, it is spatially present in the body. What is the nature of this spatial presence? Aquinas points out that

> if the soul were joined to the body as a mere motor it could be said
> to be, not in every part of the body, but only in the one through which
> it moved the others. But because the soul is united to the body as its
> form it has to be whole in the whole and whole in every part.
> (*Summa theologiae*, Ia. q.76.8)

This wholeness of the soul in every part of its body is not quantita-
tive in nature, with one part of the soul in one part of its body and
another part of the soul in a different part of its body. According to
Aquinas, any corporeal substance is a body with dimension and
shape and "is altogether composite and divisible" (*On Spiritual
Creatures*, V.ad 2; cf. *Summa theologiae*, Ia. q.76.7.ad 2). Because the
soul is not corporeal, it is indivisible (*Summa contra Gentiles*, II.50;
65), with the result that, when it is present at a point in the body, all
of it is there at that point:

> The simplicity of a soul [. . .] is not to be conceived in the same way
> as that of a point, which has a determinate location in a continuum,
> and thus, because it is simple in this way, cannot at one and the same
> time be in diverse parts of a continuum. But [. . .] a soul [is] said to
> be simple because [it is] entirely without quantity; and consequently
> it cannot come into contact with a continuum except by applying [its]
> power to it. (*Questions on the Soul*, X.ad 18)

While the soul, as a subsistent entity, is simple and indivisible, "still
it has a multiplicity of powers" (ibid., IX.ad 14; cf. Aquinas 1975, II.72).
Examples of such powers are the power to see, the power to hear, the
power to smell, the power to think, and the power to will. Aquinas
maintains that, while the powers of sight, and sound, and smell require
the operation of their respective bodily organs—eyes, ears, nose
(*Summa contra Gentiles*, II.72), the powers of thought and will do
not make use of a bodily organ. "[I]t is clear [. . .] that some of the
soul's activities, namely understanding and willing, do not take place
in bodily organs" (*Summa theologiae*, Ia. q.77.5). Are all of the powers present in each and every part of the body? Aquinas answers "No."

While "the whole soul is in every section of the body in its whole perfection of nature, [. . .] all its powers are not in every section of the body; rather, its power of sight is in the eye, hearing in the ear, and so forth" (ibid., q.Ia.76.8). "Consequently the soul is in diverse parts through diverse powers, and it is not necessary that the soul be in each part through all of its powers" (*Questions on the Soul*, X.ad 13). Moreover, because "some of the soul's powers, namely the intellect and the will, are in it by virtue of its surpassing the entire scope of the body [they do not make use of bodily organs], [. . .] [they] are not said to be in any part of the body" (*Summa theologiae*, Ia. q.76.8.ad 4). In short, "if the soul's wholeness is taken in the sense of wholeness of power [as opposed to wholeness of subsistent form], not only is the soul not wholly in every part, but neither is it wholly in the whole body" (*On Spiritual Creatures*, IV).

Aquinas is well aware that, while a soul might be the form of its body and thereby bestow existence on the latter and on all of its organs, there are certain movements of a human being, namely its bodily actions, which require explanation beyond that which is provided by a soul's formal structuring, organizing, and life-giving powers. This explanation of bodily action is ultimately given in terms of the powers of will and intellect. According to Aquinas, "[t]here is in all things appetite for the good since as the philosophers teach, the good is what all desire. [. . .] In things possessed of understanding [this appetite] is called intellectual or rational appetite, and this is will" (*Summa contra Gentiles*, II.47.2). Moreover,

> desire takes place by way of a turning of the desirer toward the thing desired. Now if the good desired were present in the desirer of its very self, it would not be proper to it to do any moving toward the attainment of the desired good. And hence one should say that the desired good, which moves as an end, is something other than the desirer, which moves as an agent. (*On Spiritual Creatures*, VI.ad 10)

The following is a simple example of an explanation of a bodily action: a person desires to get something to eat (the good), ascertains through use of his intellect how to obtain the desired food, and intends an action to obtain that food. Aquinas, following Aristotle, believes that this mental sequence of events produces an effect on the person's heart, which ultimately leads to the willed bodily movement:

> [T]he soul moves the body through knowledge and appetite. However, the sentient and the appetitive power in an animal have a definite organ, and thus the movement of the animal originates in that organ which is the heart, according to Aristotle. Thus, then, one part of the animal is what does the moving and the other is the part that is moved, so that the moving part may be taken to be the primary organ of the appetitive soul, and the remainder of the body is what is moved. But because in man the moving is done by the will and the intellect, which are not acts of any organ, the thing that does the moving will be the soul itself, considered on its intellectual side, whereas the moved thing will be the body, considered as something which is perfected by that soul in corporeal being. (*On Spiritual Creatures*, III. ad 4; cf. *Summa contra Gentiles*, II.72)

Aquinas' ascription of a motor function to the heart should not be taken to suggest that he was completely ignorant of the brain and the role it plays in our mental life. He states that,

> if anyone wants to examine also the particular organs of the human body, he will discover that they are organized so that a human being might sense most effectively. Consequently, because a well ordered brain is necessary for the effective condition of the internal sense powers, for example, the imagination, the memory and the cogitative power, a human being was made in such a way that in proportion to his size he has a brain that is larger than that of any other animal. (*Questions on the Soul*, VIII)

Moreover, Aquinas points out that, "if certain corporal organs have been harmed, the soul cannot directly understand either itself or anything else, as when the brain is injured" (*On Spiritual Creatures*, II.ad 7).

With our survey of Aquinas' account of the existence and nature of the soul as a background, we turn now to his treatment of the afterlife, which in its own way helps illuminate his conception of the soul. As we have stated, Aquinas maintains that the fundamental or primary substance is the individual human being, which is a soul–body composite. This entails that the soul of a human being is not a substance in its own right. Given that it is not, and that the souls of plants and beasts perish with the death of their respective organisms (*Summa theologiae*, 1a. q.75.3; cf. *Questions on the Soul*, XIV.ad 1), it is only natural to wonder if the human soul can survive the death of the body it informs. Because Aquinas believes that "it is impossible that natural appetite should be in vain" and "man naturally desires to exist forever" (*Summa contra Gentiles*, II.79.6), and as a Christian theist he believes that the Bible attests to the existence of the afterlife ("there are myriad passages of sacred Scripture which proclaim the immortality of the soul": ibid., II.79.17), he affirms that the soul is immortal and survives death. Therefore Aquinas faces the problem of explaining how this survival is possible for something that is not a substance in its own right. His solution is to say that the soul can *subsist*, even though it is not a substance. While both a substance and a subsistent form can exist on their own, the latter (in the form of a soul) is not a complete member of its species (which is that of being a human being). At this point, Stump suggests, for illustrative purposes, that we liken a soul as a subsistent form to an unfinished house (e.g. one with no more than its foundation laid and its walls erected), which exists on its own but is not a complete member of its species (being a house) (Stump 1995, 517). One thing that follows from the fact that a soul is not a substance in its own right is that a soul is not a person. "[The soul] cannot be called 'this something,' if by this phrase is meant [. . .] [a] person, or an individual situated in a genus or in a species" (*On Spiritual Creatures*, II.ad 16). Similarly, "[n]ot every particular substance is [. . .] a person, but rather, that which has the full nature of the species. Thus a hand or foot cannot be called a [. . .] person. Nor, likewise, can the soul, as

it is a part of human nature" (*Summa theologiae*, Ia. q.75. 4.ad 2).
And, finally,

> The soul is a part of human nature; and hence, although it can exist
> apart from the body, it ever can be reunited, and therefore cannot be
> called an "individual substance," or a "hypostasis" or "first substance"
> any more than a hand or any other part. So we can neither define it
> nor speak of it as a "person." (Aquinas 1965: *Summa theologiae*, Ia.
> q.29.1.ad 5)

All of this leads Aquinas to deny that he is his soul: *Anima autem
cum sit pars coporis homini, not est totus homo, et anima mea non est
ego* ("However, the soul, since it is part of man's body, it is not the
whole man, and I am not my soul"; cf. Aquinas, n.d.: *Commentary
on the First Epistle to the Corinthians*, paragraph 924, and Van Dyke
2009, 196). Elsewhere (in his commentary on Peter Lombard's
Sentences), Aquinas says that "[t]he soul of Abraham is not Abraham
himself, properly speaking, but is part of him" (quoted in van Dyke
2007, 376).

Aquinas' views about the soul as it relates to the self or to the "I"
and personhood are, to say the least, somewhat puzzling. Surely one
of the reasons why the soul's existence is of interest to so many people
is the fact that they desire to survive death and be in a better world.
In their minds, if the soul, which is their "I," exists, there is a real
possibility that this desire will be satisfied. The following words of
the Roman Catholic priest Richard John Neuhaus express this point
of view quite clearly:

> More common in the history of thought [than views that minimize
> the significance of death] is the idea of the immortality of the soul.
> The essential person, it is said, is the soul. [. . .] Surely we should not
> deny that there is an "I"—call it the soul—that is distinct from, if not
> independent from, the body. I am, after all, reliably told that every
> part of the body, down to the smallest molecule, is replaced several
> times in my lifetime, and yet "I" persist. [. . .]

I want to insist upon, if you will forgive the awkward term, the "I-ness" of the soul. It is not as though I *have* a soul in the way I have a liver or a kidney. [. . .] The soul is one with the enduring "I" that embraces, that defines, that gives form to my essential identity—an identity that includes my body. And yet I believe, in a faith disposed toward the future that we call hope, that it endures through its temporary separation from the body. (Neuhaus 2002, 71–72)

The Oxford don and Christian apologist C. S. Lewis shares Neuhaus's belief about the "I-ness" of the soul. In response to an apparent query of a Mrs. Frank L. Jones about the nature of the soul, Lewis writes: "What is a soul? I am. (This is the only possible answer: or expanded, 'A soul is that which can say I am'" (Lewis 2007, 10).

Yet Aquinas maintains that the soul is not the referent of the "I," and is not a person. If he is right, will it be of any benefit to the individual person to have his or her soul survive death? Who or what will survive? Aquinas' view is even more puzzling given his belief that the soul will be able to think and exercise its will when disembodied (Aquinas 1968b: *Summa theologiae*, Ia. q.89). How can a soul that thinks and wills apart from its body not refer to, and think of, itself as "I"? Can it not think and know that it is "I" who now, as disembodied, thinks and knows? And if it can do that, does it not also think and know that it is a *person* who is now thinking and knowing? Moreover, Aquinas holds that a disembodied soul feels joy and sadness from intellectual, but not bodily, desire (*Summa theologiae*, Ia. q.77.ad 5). Once again, however, does the disembodied soul not know that it is its "I" that is experiencing joy and sadness? And is that which thinks, knows, wills, and experiences joy and sadness not a person?

Aquinas himself touches upon the present issues concerning the "I"-ness and personhood of the soul in terms of prayers to the saints. An objection to the view that the saints (who are persons) in heaven pray for us is that, on Aquinas' view, "the soul of Peter is not Peter. If therefore the souls of the saints pray for us, so long as they are separated from their bodies, we ought not to call upon Saint Peter, but on his soul, to pray for us: yet the Church does the contrary" (Aquinas 1981: *Summa theologiae*, IIa.–IIae. Q.83.11.obj 5). In response to the objection, Aquinas grants the point that the soul is not Peter, but says that we invoke a saint like Peter under the name by which he was known in this life and will be known when re-embodied in the resurrection, a name that refers to the whole of body plus soul (Aquinas 1948: *Summa theologica*, IIa.–IIae. Q.83.11ad 5).

With regard to these issues involving the soul, personhood, and the "I," Stump observes that "it is easy to become confused about Aquinas' position here" (2003, 52), and she maintains that his denial that a soul is a person needs to be read in the context of his other views. More specifically, she claims that proper weight must be given to the distinction between constitution and identity in Aquinas' thought. Stump clarifies her claim by pointing out that normally the integral parts that constitute a human being include two hands, but a human being can exist without being in this normal condition (e.g. an individual can have one or both of his hands amputated and continue to exist as a human being). "Analogously, the metaphysical constituents of a human being normally include matter and substantial form, but Aquinas thinks that a human being can exist without being in the normal condition in this way either" (ibid.). Thus a person (human being) can "exist when it is constituted only by one of its main metaphysical parts, namely the soul. And so although a person is not identical to his soul [the latter being a constituent of the former], the existence of the soul is sufficient for the existence of the person" (ibid., 53).

As we will see later in Chapter 4, some philosophers (for instance Joseph Butler and Thomas Reid) believe that an approach like that suggested by Stump in defense of Aquinas begs a central question, which is whether a human being who exists after the loss of one or both of her hands is strictly speaking the same human being as the one who existed with both hands intact. They claim that, while there is no reason to contest that we loosely and popularly talk as if the same human being existed with and without the hands, this is just a manner of speaking, which can be explained by nothing less than the existence of a soul that is a person and remains the same through any and all the changes in the physical body. The identity of the soul, which is *strict*, gets transferred to the human being (which is a composite of soul and body) whose sameness is no more than *loose* in nature.

Regardless of what one thinks about Aquinas' view of the relationship between soul and body, there is still the matter of how a soul that is not an individual substance in its own right can subsist apart from its body. As a way of teasing out what is at issue here, we turn to Aquinas' account of ontological individuation, which is a topic dealing with what makes an individual thing the individual entity that it is, and thereby distinct from other individual entities. According to Aquinas, "matter is the principle of numerical distinction within the same species" (*On Spiritual Creatures*, I.ad 19; cf. Aquinas 1968a: *On Being and Essence*, 2.4). This implies that, if more than one member of a species exists (e.g. if two human beings exist), one member is ontologically distinct from another because each possesses a distinct portion of matter. "Moreover, things specifically the same [the same in species], but numerically diverse, possess matter. For the difference that results from the form [in the case of a human being, the soul] introduces specific diversity [difference of species]; from the matter, numerical diversity" (*Summa contra Gentiles*, II.93.3). So, while a human being is alive, its soul is ontologically distinct from the soul of another human being, because the matter the one informs in order to make a human being is different from the matter informed by the other to make it a human being. As Aquinas states, this is a relational account of the soul's individuation. "A soul is not individuated by matter out of which it is composed [because it is not composed of any matter], but rather because of its relation to the matter in which it exists" (*Questions on the Soul*, VI.ad 13). And again:

> For just as it belongs to the human soul by its specific nature to be
> united to a particular species of body, so this particular soul differs
> only numerically from that one as the result of having a relationship
> to a numerically different body. In this way are human souls indi-
> viduated in relation to bodies [. . .]. (*Summa contra Gentiles*, II.75.6)

By hypothesis, however, after death a soul does not inform any matter,
and therefore has no body. How, then, can it be ontologically distinct
from other disembodied souls? Once again, we turn to Stump for an
answer on Aquinas' behalf. She insists that the present concern about
how disembodied souls are individuated is misplaced:

> It is possible for one separated soul to be distinguished from another
> on the basis of its *past* connection with matter, rather than on the
> basis of a present connection with matter. The disembodied soul of
> Socrates is the substantial human form which at some time in the past
> configured *this* matter, the matter that was part of Socrates in his em-
> bodied state. The disembodied soul of Plato is the substantial human
> form which at some time in the past configured the matter that was
> part of Plato in *his* embodied state. It remains the case, then, that
> matter individuates, even in the case of disembodied souls. Matter
> individuates a disembodied form in virtue of its past connection
> to matter. (Stump 2003, 54)

Despite the ingenuity of such an answer, what remains puzzling is
how the existence of a soul in the present can be explained by a
relationship to something in the past, which no longer exists. The idea,
which Aquinas endorses (see the next paragraph), that God creates
an entity such as a soul and continuously keeps it in existence makes
sense, because God exists at the same time as that which He causes
to exist. Moreover, to maintain that it is God who creates a soul and
keeps it in existence right now, disembodied, but that it is a relationship
of that soul to a no longer existing body that explains the ontological individuation of that soul right now, only confuses matters more.
This is because it is reasonable to think that God's creation of, and

continuously sustaining in existence of, an entity like a soul entails that that entity is already individuated prior to any additional relationship into which it might enter.

We leave here issues concerning a soul's disembodiment and return briefly to the nature of a soul's embodiment in this life. How does a soul come to be united with its body in the first place? Not surprisingly, Aquinas answers that God creates a soul and infuses it into matter, to produce a soul–body composite or human being: "the soul is created immediately by God alone" (*Summa contra Gentiles*, II.87.3; cf. Aquinas 1964: *Summa theologiae*, Ia. q.90.2). But God's creation of a soul is the end of a process that includes the arising and passing away of vegetative (nutritive) and sensitive souls:

[I]n the generation of an animal and a man, wherein the most perfect type of form exists, there are many intermediate forms and generations—and, hence, corruptions, because the generation of one thing is the corruption of another. Thus, the vegetative [nutritive] soul, which is present first (when the embryo lives the life of a plant), perishes, and is succeeded by a more perfect soul, both nutritive and sensitive in character, and then the embryo lives an animal life; and when this passes away it is succeeded by the rational soul introduced from without [by God], while the preceding souls existed in virtue of the semen. (*Summa contra Gentiles*, II.89.11).

And consequently it is said the nutritive soul exists first, but [. . .] is superseded in the process of generation, and that another soul takes its place, a soul that is not only nutritive but also sensitive; and this soul is superseded by yet another soul which at one and the same time is nutritive, sensitive and rational. (*Questions on the Soul*, XI.ad 1)

Thus, according to Aquinas, growth and organization of an embryo occur first because of the presence of a nutritive soul and then because of the presence of a sensitive soul, where the appearance of the latter supplants the existence of the former. Each of these souls is transmitted biologically. A rational soul arrives on the scene from the outside (non-biologically), through the direct creative action of God; and this soul, in good Aristotelian fashion, includes both nutritive and sensient powers.

Why does God create souls? To explain Aquinas' answer to this question, we begin with a comment of his that is critical of the Platonic perspective on embodiment, which is highly intellectualist in nature. Aquinas maintains that, if the Platonists were right that a human being is a soul using a body, then,

> if the impediment of a body were removed, the soul would return to its true nature and understand intelligible objects simply [. . .] as other subsistent immaterial substances [e.g. angels] do. However, in this case the soul would not be joined to the body for the good of the soul, that is, if its understanding were worse when joined to the body than when separated, but only for the good of the body. Now this is unreasonable [. . .]. (*Summa theologiae*, 1a. q.89.1)

And:

> It also seems to be a consequence of this [Platonic] position that the union of a soul to its body is not natural; for whatever is natural to some thing does not hinder its proper operation. Consequently, if union with a body hinders the soul's intellectual understanding, it will not be natural for a soul to be united to a body but contrary to nature; and so it follows that a human being who is constituted by the union of soul and body will not be a natural being, and this seems to be absurd. (*Questions on the Soul*, XV)

Aquinas' point is that, if the soul's purpose for existing were that it understand Forms (universals), and this were best accomplished when the soul was disembodied, then a soul's embodiment would not be in the best interest of a soul. The question, then, is: Why are souls embodied? And Aquinas believes that the Platonists never answered this questioned satisfactorily. Unlike the Platonists, he believes that embodiment is in the best interest of the soul. "For the union of soul and body does not take place for the sake of the body, namely, that the body may be ennobled, but for the sake of the soul, which needs the body for its own perfection" (*On Spiritual Creatures*, VI). In what way does the body serve a soul's perfection? In an intellectualist spirit not far from that of the Platonists', Aquinas holds that embodiment promotes the perfection of the soul by enabling it to understand.

> But a soul is united to its body in order that it might understand, which is a soul's essential and principal operation. And consequently it is necessary that the body which is united to a rational soul be the kind of body that is best fitted for being of service to the soul in whatever understanding demands. (*Questions on the Soul*, VIII.ad 15)

So, while the Platonists were wrong in holding that a soul best understands when it is disembodied, they were correct in holding that understanding perfects the soul and is its principal end or purpose for existing.

According to Aquinas, however, a soul can understand when it is disembodied. Indeed, what separates his view from the Platonists' is not the claim that a disembodied soul cannot know species (Forms), but that it only does so after its embodiment in this life, and not before: "But it [a soul] receives such species [Forms] only after it is separated from its body, and not from the first moment of its existence, as the Platonists held" (*Questions on the Soul*, XV. ad 9). But if a soul can know Forms in its disembodied state, why is it embodied at all? Aquinas' answer seems to be that the perfection of the universe requires not only the existence of every possible type of being, and thus the existence of both non-intellectual and intellectual beings (*Summa contra Gentiles*, II.46), but also the existence, within the genus of intellectual beings, of some that are non-embodied (ibid., II.91.6) and of some that are embodied. Humans, therefore, occupy a midpoint between purely immaterial rational beings like angels and beings like brutes, who have non-rational souls in material bodies.

As we noted earlier in this chapter, Aquinas criticizes Plato for holding the view that a soul is related to the body as a mover to that which is moved. This view entails that there is causal interaction between a soul and a body. Does Aquinas deny such causal interaction? If Stump is right, he does. She maintains that, although on Aquinas' account the soul is a subsistent part of a human being, his concept of "part" enables him to avoid difficult questions, which will arise for Descartes (see Chapter 3), about how it is that a soul causally interacts with the body. One type of part is an integral part, examples of which are the roof of a house and the head of a body. A soul as a part of a human being is not an instance of this type of part. Rather, it is an instance of a metaphysical type of part. As a metaphysical kind of a part, a soul does not causally interact with the matter it informs ("on Aquinas' account, there is no efficient causal interaction between the soul and the matter it informs," Stump 1995, 518), but rather has causal influence in the sense that a human being (a composite of which the soul is a metaphysical part) has causal influence on objects in the material world.

One cannot help but suspect that the supposed difference between an integral and a metaphysical part is a distinction without a difference. If a soul is a subsistent entity that is distinct from, and can survive, the body it informs, then one cannot help but believe that questions about causal interaction between it and the body are legitimate, just as questions about how a roof is causally related to the walls, foundation, and so on of a house of which they are all parts, or about how a head is causally related to the neck, arms, and so on of the body of which they are all parts are legitimate.

The issue of causal interaction has loomed large in the history of how the soul relates to the body. No advocate of the existence of the soul has had his view of this matter subjected to more scrutiny than Descartes. Indeed, his soul–body dualism has proved to be a lightning rod for those who believe that causal interaction between a soul and its body is deeply problematic. It is to Descartes' treatment of the soul that we turn in the next chapter.

Chapter 3

The Soul in Continental Thought

We now turn to philosophy of the soul in the early modern era, an era that is most often identified as the birth of modern science with Kepler, Copernicus, Galileo, and Newton. The sixteenth and seventeenth centuries saw the emergence of a powerful scientific worldview, in which mechanical explanations of matter in motion dominated. As Christian theists, modern scientists like Newton retained a comprehensive teleological account of the cosmos (the cosmos was created and is sustained by God's purposive will), but explanations of the material world privileged impersonal mathematical forces. How might the soul fit into, or be related to, such a world?

We have used the term "dualism" sparingly until now, partly (as we pointed out in the Introduction) because this term is fraught with misunderstanding. For example, many believe that dualism implies the Platonic thesis that embodiment is bad for the soul. However, not all who distinguish between soul (mind or person) and body share Plato's denigration of embodiment. It is not an essential element of dualism. Dualism can also be potentially misleading, as it suggests that its advocates are first and foremost those who posit two fundamental realities or kinds of things ("dualism" essentially means "two-ism"). Historically, however, what we now call "dualism" emerged from an affirmation of the soul (mind, experience, and so on) and the

A Brief History of the Soul, First Edition.
© 2011 Stewart Goetz and Charles Taliaferro. Published 2011 by Blackwell Publishing Ltd.

thesis that the soul is not identical with (or the very same thing as) the body. "Dualism" was therefore more of a project against *monism* (the idea that there is only one kind of thing) and for the affirmation that there is more to persons than their bodies. Rather than beg a movement of restriction (there are only two sorts of things), dualism was an affirmation of plurality (there is more than body). This is a point we will return to in our final chapter. Presently, we turn to the thought of Descartes, and then to that of Malebranche and Leibniz.

Descartes

Mention the word "soul" or "mind" today among academics and they almost immediately think of René Descartes (1596–1650). Such has been the influence of Descartes that one of us, as a graduate student, heard a professor tell his undergraduate introductory philosophy class that Descartes *invented* soul–body dualism. Though this professor should have known better, his statement reflects the profound impact Descartes has had on subsequent philosophizing about the soul. What explains the influence of Descartes is ultimately the power of his thought—and it is to this thought that we now turn.

In ruminations that are reminiscent of Augustine's philosophy about the soul, Descartes wrestles with skepticism and presents his Augustinian answer to it in terms of knowledge of his self or soul. For the purpose of discovering that about which he cannot be mistaken, Descartes assumes the existence of an evil deceiver and concludes with certainty that he (Descartes) exists:

> But there is some deceiver or other, very powerful and very cunning, who ever employs his ingenuity in deceiving me. Then without doubt I exist also if he deceives me, and let him deceive me as much as he will, he can never cause me to be nothing so long as I think that I am something. So that after having reflected well and carefully examined all things, we must come to the definite conclusion that this proposition: I am, I exist, is necessarily true each time that I pronounce it,

or that I mentally conceive it. (Descartes 1967, I: *Meditations on First Philosophy II*, 150)

As was the case with Augustine, Descartes maintains that that about which he is certain extends beyond his own existence and includes how things appear to him:

> Finally, I am the same who feels, that is to say, who perceives certain things, as by the organs of sense, since in truth I see light, I hear noise, I feel heat. But it will be said that these phenomena are false and that I am dreaming. Let it be so; still it is at least quite certain that it seems to me that I see light, that I hear noise and that I feel heat. That cannot be false [. . .] [A]lthough the things which I perceive and imagine are perhaps nothing at all apart from me and in themselves, I am nevertheless assured that these modes of thought that I call perceptions and imaginations, inasmuch only as they are modes of thought, certainly reside (and are met with) in me. (Descartes, *Meditations II*, 153, 157)

In summary, Descartes is certain that he exists and that things appear to him in various ways. Through the course of an argument that has been the subject of enough literature to comprise a sizeable library, Descartes concludes that the self about whose existence and appearances he cannot be mistaken is a thing that thinks: "But what then am I? A thing which thinks. What is a thing which thinks? It is a thing which doubts, understands, (conceives), affirms, denies, wills, refuses, which also imagines and feels" (ibid., 153). In short, a thing that thinks is a mind, and a mind is a soul. Descartes makes clear in his synopsis to his *Meditations* that he considers the terms "soul" and "mind" to be interchangeable ("the mind [or soul of man (I make no distinction between them)]": Descartes 1967, I: *Synopsis of the Meditations*, 141). And, contrary to Aquinas and in sympathy with Augustine, Descartes maintains that the "I" is the soul ("Accordingly this 'I'—that is, the soul by which I am what I am— is [. . .] indeed easier to know than the body, and would not fail to be whatever it is, even if the body did not exist", Descartes 1985: *Discourse on the Method*, 127) and a substance in its own right ("[W]e can see that our soul [. . .] is a substance which is distinct from the body [. . .]" (Descartes 1985: *Description of the Human Body*, 314), where "the notion of substance is just this—that which can exist by itself, without the aid of any other substance" (Descartes 1967, II: *Reply to Objections IV*, 101).

Though he believes in the existence of soul, Descartes decisively rejects certain characterizations of it that his philosophical predecessors had largely taken for granted. Most notably, Descartes dismisses the idea that the soul gives life to the body. As he sees things, the body is its own substance, which is rightly likened to a mechanism or machine whose movements can largely, but not entirely (in the case of willed movements), be explained without any reference to the soul:

> And as a clock composed of wheels and counter-weights no less exactly observes the laws of nature when it is badly made, and does not show the time properly, than when it entirely satisfies the wishes of its maker, [. . .] [so also] if I consider the body of a man as being a sort of machine so built up and composed of nerves, muscles, veins, blood and skin, that though there were no mind in it at all, it would not cease to have the same motions as at present, exception being made of those movements which are due to the direction of the will, and in consequence depend upon the mind [as opposed to those which operate by the disposition of its organs], [. . .] (Descartes, *Meditations VI*, 195)

Elsewhere, Descartes makes clear that viewing the human body as a mechanism renders the Aristotelian vegetative and sensitive functions of the soul superfluous:

> I should like you to consider, after this, all the functions I have attributed to this machine—such as the digestion of food, the beating of the heart and arteries, the nourishment and growth of the limbs, respiration, waking and sleeping, the reception by the external sense organs of light, sounds, smells, tastes, heat, and other such qualities,

the imprinting of the ideas of these qualities in the organ of the "common" sense and the imagination, the retention or stamping of these ideas in the memory, the internal movements of the appetites and passions, and finally the external movements of all the limbs (movements which are so appropriate not only to the actions of objects presented to the senses, but also the passions and the impressions found in the memory, that they imitate perfectly the movements of a real man). I should like you to consider that these functions follow from the mere arrangement of the machine's organs every bit as naturally as the movements of a clock or other automaton follow from the arrangement of its counter-weights and wheels. In order to explain these functions, then, it is not necessary to conceive of this machine as having any vegetative or sensitive soul or other principle of movement and life, apart from its blood and its spirits, which are agitated by the heat of the fire burning continuously in its heart—a fire which has the same nature as all the fires that occur in inanimate bodies. (Descartes 1985: *Treatise on Man*, 108)

Descartes believes that, because the body is a mechanism, death should not be defined as the demise of the body, which would take place as a result of the departure of the life-giving soul:

[L]et us consider that death never comes to pass by reason of the soul, but only because some one of the principal parts of the body decays; and we may judge that the body of a living man differs from that of a dead man just as does a watch or other automation (i.e. a machine that moves of itself), when it is wound up and contains in itself the corporeal principle of those movements for which it is designed along with all that is requisite for its action, from the same watch or other machine when it is broken and when the principle of its movement ceases to act. (Descartes 1967, I: *The Passions of the Soul I*, 333)

In Descartes' mind, death is the irreversible breakdown of the bodily machine, and the soul leaves the body because of this brokenness:

[F]rom observing that all dead bodies are devoid of heat and consequently of movement, it has been thought that it was the absence of the soul which caused these movements and this heat to cease; and thus, without any reason, it was thought that our natural heat and all the movements of our body depend on the soul: while in fact we ought on the contrary to believe that the soul quits us on death only because this heat ceases, and the organs which serve to move the body disintegrate. (Ibid.)

Why have others ascribed life-giving power to the soul? Descartes believes at least part of the explanation is as follows:

Since childhood [...] we have all found by experience that many bodily movements occur in obedience to the will, which is one of the faculties of the soul, and this has led us to believe that the soul is the principle responsible for all bodily movement. Our ignorance of anatomy and mechanics has also played a major role here. For in restricting our consideration to the outside of the human body, we have never imagined that it has within it enough organs or mechanisms to move of its own accord in all the different ways which we observe. Our error was reinforced by our belief that no movement occurs inside a corpse, though it possesses the same organs as a living body, and lacks only a soul. The other functions [than thinking, willing, etc.] which some people attribute to the soul, such as moving the heart and the arteries, digesting food in the stomach and so on, do not involve any thought, and are simply bodily movements; further, it is more common for a body to be moved by another body than for it to be moved by a soul. Hence, we have less reason to attribute such functions to the soul than to the body. (Descartes 1985: *Description of the Human Body*, 314–315)

Not only does Descartes break with the views of his predecessors when he maintains that soul does not give life to the body and that death is the irreparable brokenness of the mechanical body, but he also parts ways with those who came before him by holding that the soul is not located in the space occupied by its physical body. Indeed, from what Descartes says about the nature of body and mind, it follows that the soul is simply not located in space. Consider what he says about the nature of a body:

> By the body I understand all that which can be defined by a certain figure; something which can be confined in a certain place, and which can fill a given space in such a way that every other body will be excluded from it; which can be perceived either by touch, or by sight, or by hearing, or by taste, or by smell: which can be moved in many ways not, in truth, by itself, but by something which is foreign to it, by which it is touched [. . .]: for to have the power of self-movement, as also of feeling or thinking, I did not consider to appertain to the nature of body [. . .]. (Descartes, *Meditations II*, 151)

Later, in "Meditation VI," Descartes adds the following thoughts about the nature of a body: "I possess a distinct idea of body, inasmuch as it is only an extended and unthinking thing [. . .] Moreover, "body is by nature always divisible [. . .]" (*Meditations VI*, 190; 196). In short, according to Descartes, a body is that which is extended with a certain shape or figure in a given space, is divisible into parts that are themselves extended, shaped, and so on, is movable but not capable of self-movement, and is perceivable by one or more of the five senses.

What about a mind? Descartes maintains that it has a nature that is the exact opposite of that had by a body. A mind is a thinking thing, and a thinking thing is a thing that is not extended:

> I rightly conclude that my essence consists solely in the fact that I am a thinking thing [or a substance whose whole essence or nature is to think]. And [. . .] inasmuch as I am only a thinking and unextended thing [. . .] it is certain that this I (that is to say my soul by which I am what I am), is entirely and absolutely distinct from my body. (Ibid., 190)

In addition, he notes that "in the first place [. . .] there is a great difference between mind and body, inasmuch as body is by nature always divisible, and the mind is entirely indivisible" (ibid., 196). Again, mind and body [. . .] are really substances essentially distinct one from the other [. . .] This is further confirmed [. . .] by the fact that we cannot conceive of body excepting in so far as it is divisible, while the mind cannot be conceived of excepting as indivisible. For we are not able to conceive of the half of a mind as we can do of the smallest of all bodies; so that we see that not only are their natures different but even in some respects contrary to one another. (Descartes, *Synopsis of the Meditations*, 141)

Concerning the lack of movement of the soul, Descartes says the following:

I observe also in me some other faculties such as that of change of position [. . .] which cannot be conceived [. . .] apart from some substance to which they are attached, and consequently cannot exist without it; but it is very clear that these faculties [. . .] must be attached to some corporeal or extended substance, and not to an intelligent substance, since in the clear and distinct conception of these there is some sort of extension found to be present, but no intellection at all. (Descartes, *Meditations VI*, 190)

In summary, according to Descartes, a soul is that which is non-extended and, thereby, without any shape in a given space, is not divisible into parts and is not moveable in the sense that it cannot change spatial position. Therefore, Descartes believes that a soul is not located in space, period.

At this point, it is important to pause in order to make clear that Descartes never claims that it looks to him as if he is a non-spatial being. On the contrary, to those who have come before him and maintained that the soul is spatially located in its physical body he explicitly concedes that it initially seems to him, too, that he was located in the space occupied by his physical body. In some comments about his pre-*Meditations* thoughts concerning what he is, Descartes says: "I did not stop to consider what the soul was, or if I did stop, I imagined that it was something extremely rare and subtle like a wind, a flame, or an ether, which was spread throughout my grosser parts" (*Meditations II*, 151). In other words, Descartes tells us that initially it looked to him as if his soul filled the space inhabited by his body. It is the idea that the soul fills its body that Descartes seeks to capture when he says that he (his soul) is not merely lodged in his body, in the way a seaman (pilot) is present on or in his ship:

> Nature also teaches me by these sensations of pain, hunger, thirst, etc., that I am not only lodged in my body as a pilot in a vessel, but that I am very closely united to it, and so to speak so intermingled with it that I seem to compose with it one whole. For if that were not the case, when my body is hurt, I, who am merely a thinking thing, should not feel pain, for I should perceive this wound by the understanding only, just as the sailor perceives by sight when something is damaged in his vessel; and when my body has need of drink or food, I should clearly understand the fact without being warned of it by confused feelings of hunger and thirst. (Descartes, *Meditations VI*, 192)

Descartes insists that, while the soul is sometimes able to discover damage to the body by means of external sense perception, as when one sees the damage done to one's foot by an object that fell on it, the soul is also able to apprehend that damage by means of feeling pain in the foot. This internal sense observation (proprioception) suggests that the soul is literally in the foot. It is this kind of consideration that leads him to say, in terms reminiscent of Augustine and Aquinas, that "the soul is really joined to the whole body, and that we cannot, properly speaking, say that it exists in any one of its parts to the exclusion of the others" (Descartes, *The Passions of the Soul I*, 345), and "that I [. . .] understand mind to be coextensive with the body, the whole in the whole, and the whole in any of its parts" (Descartes, *Reply to Objections VI*, 255). However, given the nature of body and mind, the idea that the soul is literally present in the space occupied by the physical body cannot be substantiated. Some of Descartes' thoughts about the phenomenon of phantom limb help to explain further the relationship between a spatial body and a non-spatial soul. In commenting about how our external senses sometimes deceive us and undermine our confidence in them, Descartes points out that our internal, proprioceptive senses are no less likely to deceive us:

> I from time to time observed that those towers which from afar appeared to me to be round, more closely observed seemed square, and that colossal statues raised on the summit of these towers, appeared as quite tiny statues when viewed from the bottom; and so in an infinitude of other cases I found error in judgments founded on the external senses. And not only in those founded on the external senses, but even in those founded on the internal as well; for is there anything more intimate or more internal than pain? And yet I have learned from some persons whose arms or legs have been cut off, that they sometimes seemed to feel pain in the part which had been amputated, which made me think that I could not be quite certain that it was a certain member which pained me, even although I felt pain in it. (Descartes, *Meditations VI*, 189)

In other words, just as visual experiences might mislead us about the size and distance of physical objects, so also the experience of pain might mislead us as to the existence of a limb in which it seems to occur. But Descartes believes that the deception involving experiences of pain goes much further than this. Given what is revealed in the case of phantom limb, we have grounds to conclude that our pains (and we ourselves, because it is we who experience pains) are not literally located in the space where they seem to be. This is the case even with fully intact bodies. What occurs, both when our bodies are and when they are not intact, is that the soul *represents* our pains as having spatial locations, which strictly speaking they do not:

> [W]hen I feel pain in my foot, my knowledge of physics teaches me that this sensation is communicated by means of nerves dispersed through the foot, which, being extended like cords from there to the brain, when they are contracted in the foot, at the same time contract

the inmost portions of the brain which is their extremity and place of origin, and then excite a certain movement which nature has established in order to cause the mind to be affected by a sensation of pain represented as existing in the foot. But because these nerves must pass through the tibia, the thigh, the loins, the back and the neck, in order to reach from the leg to the brain, it may happen that although their extremities which are in the foot are not affected, but only certain ones of their intervening parts (which pass by the loins or the neck), this action will excite the same movement in the brain that might have been excited there by a hurt received in the foot, in consequence of which the mind will necessarily feel in the foot the same pain as if it had received a hurt. (Ibid., 196–7)

From this it is quite clear that, notwithstanding the supreme good-ness of God, the nature of man, inasmuch as it is composed of mind and body, cannot be otherwise than sometimes a source of deception. For if there is any cause which excites, not in the foot but in some part of the nerves which are extended between the foot and the brain, or even in the brain itself, the same movement which usually is pro-duced when the foot is detrimentally affected, pain will be experienced as though it were in the foot, and the sense will thus naturally be deceived. (Ibid., 198)

At this point, we must be careful not to ascribe to Descartes a view that he does not hold, namely the belief that the pains we feel are actually located in the space of the brain. While this view is popular among contemporary materialists, who deny the existence of the soul and affirm that we are our brains or parts thereof, it is not espoused by Descartes. Rather, he believes that our pains are located in our souls, which are not themselves located in space, although they are represented as being present in the different extremities of our phys-ical bodies. The same goes for the pain experienced after a good knock on the head. Even this pain is not located in the head, though it is represented as being there.

To sum up, because the soul feels pains as if it were in the body's feet, hands, or head, or experiences hunger as if it were in the mid-section of its body, Descartes insists that the soul is joined to the entire body, even though it is not located in space:

> [T]he soul is really joined to the whole body, and [. . .] we cannot, properly speaking, say that it exists in any one of its parts to the exclusion of the others, because it is one and in some manner indivisible, [. . .] and because it is of a nature which has no relation to extension, nor dimensions, nor other properties of the matter of which body is composed, but only to the whole conglomerate of its organs, as appears from the fact that we could not in any way conceive of the half or the third of a soul, nor of the space it occupies, and because it does not become smaller owing to the cutting off of some portion of the body, but separates itself from it entirely when the union of its assembled organs is dissolved. (Descartes, *The Passions of the Soul I*, 345)

Although the soul is joined to the entire body in the sense that it feels as if it is present in the entirety of it, Descartes believes that the soul is related to one part of it in a distinctive way, which makes possible the external perception of bodies (both our own and all others), the undergoing of passions (pains, pleasures, emotions of joy, love, sorrow, hate) and the performance of mental actions (willings). The one part of the body to which the soul is related in this distinctive way is the pineal gland, which is itself tied to the body's organs and limbs by means of an internal network of nerves and muscles. In Descartes' own words:

> It is likewise necessary to know that although the soul is joined to the whole body, there is yet in that a certain part in which it exercises its functions more particularly than in all the others; and it is usually believed that this part is the brain, or possibly the heart; the brain, because it is with it that the organs of sense are connected, and the heart because it is apparently in it that we experience the passions. But, in examining the matter with care, it seems as though I had clearly ascertained that the part of the body in which the soul exercises its

functions immediately is in nowise the heart, nor the whole of the brain, but merely the most inward of all its parts, to wit, a certain very small gland which is situated in the middle of its substance [. . .] whereby the animal spirits [corpuscular bodies that move very quickly] in [the brain's] anterior cavities have communication with those in the posterior, that the slightest movements which take place in it may alter very greatly the course of these spirits; and reciprocally that the smallest changes which occur in the course of the spirits do much to change the movements of this gland. [. . .] The machine of the body is so formed that from the simple fact that this gland is diversely moved by the soul [. . .] it thrusts the spirits which surround it towards the pores of the brain, which conduct them by the nerves into the muscles, by which means it causes them to move the limbs. (Ibid., 345–347)

To convey Descartes' thought at this juncture, consider an example where the pineal gland is moved by the soul. Right now, one of us is presently typing this part of the chapter on Descartes on his keyboard, and this is done by moving the fingers. Similarly, each of us will likely be going to his refrigerator at some point in the day to get some food. On Descartes' view, what happens on occasions like these is that the soul wills that its body move in certain ways (e.g. it wills movements of the legs) and, all other things being equal, the willing itself causes an initial movement in the pineal gland that in turn produces movements of animal spirits that ultimately lead, by means of the body's internal network of nerves and muscles, to the body moving as willed:

And the activity of the soul consists entirely in the fact that simply by willing something it brings about that the little gland to which it is closely joined moves in the manner required to produce the effect corresponding to this volition. [. . .] [W]hen we want to walk or move our body in some other way, this volition makes the gland drive the spirits to the muscles which serve to bring about this effect. (Descartes 1985: *The Passions of the Soul I*, 343–344)

According to Descartes, willing an action leads to a movement of the pineal gland, which produces additional movements in the animal spirits, and these in turn ultimately reach the relevant limbs to produce movements in them. In perception, the process of movement is basically reversed: movements of the animal spirits in bodily extremities ultimately produce movements of the pineal gland, which result in the soul's experiencing pain and pleasure, seeing, hearing, tasting, and the rest. Again, in Descartes' own words:

> [T]he sensation of pain is excited in us merely by the local motion of some parts of our body in contact with another body; so we may conclude that the nature of our mind is such that it can be subject to all the other sensations merely as a result of other local motions. [. . .] [W]e know that the nature of the soul is such that different local motions are quite sufficient to produce all the sensations in the soul. What is more, we actually experience the various sensations as they are produced in the soul, and we do not find that anything reaches the brain from the external sense organs except for motions of this kind. In view of all this we have every reason to conclude that the properties in external objects to which we apply the terms light, colour, smell, taste, sound, heat and cold [. . .] are, so far as we can see, simply various dispositions in those objects which make them able to set up various kinds of motions in our nerves which are required to produce all the various sensations in our soul. (Descartes 1985: *Principles of First Philosophy*, 284–285)

In other words, the color, smell, taste, or sound of external bodies are no more than dispositions or powers of those objects to produce movements in the perceiver's body that ultimately lead, via movements of the animal spirits and of the pineal gland, to the soul experiencing color, smell, taste, or sound. The color, smell, taste, or sound perceived is not in the external body but in the soul:

> It is clear, then, that when we say that we perceive colours in objects, this is really just the same as saying that we perceive something in the

objects whose nature we do not know, but which produces in us a certain very clear and vivid sensation which we call the sensation of colour. (Ibid., 218)

According to Descartes, just as the soul represents a pain as being in the foot, when it is really not there but is in the non-spatial soul, so the soul also represents a color as being in a body, when it is really not there but in the non-spatial soul:

[O]n seeing a colour, for example, we supposed we were seeing a thing located outside us which closely resembled the idea of colour that we experienced within us at the same time. [...] The same thing happens with regard to everything else of which we have sensory awareness, even to pleasure and pain. [...] [W]e generally regard them not as being in the mind alone [...] but as being in the hand or foot or in some other part of our body. But the fact that we feel a pain as it were in our foot does not make it certain that the pain exists outside our mind, in the foot, any more than the fact that we see light as it were in the sun, makes it certain the light exists outside us, in the sun. (Ibid., 216–217)

Overall, it seems fair to say, then, that, while Descartes is willing to deny the appearances in connection with the nature of the soul's embodiment—saying, for instance, that the appearance of the soul's being spatially located is illusory—and also in connection with the location of the sensory qualities it perceives—saying, for instance, that the appearance of there being redness in the flag is illusory, as is the appearance of pain being in the foot—he is not willing to deny what he believes to be the appearance of a causal interaction between a soul and its body: "That the mind, which is incorporeal, can set the body in motion—this is something which is shown to us not by any reasoning or comparison with other matters, but by the surest and plainest everyday experience" (Descartes 1970, 235). If he is right, what is the case with regard to the soul–body relationship is that a substance, which is essentially spatially extended, divisible into other bodily parts, and movable (but without color, taste, or smell), causally interacts with another substance, which is essentially not spatially extended, indivisible into parts, and unmovable (but experiences pleasure, pain, color, or taste). Movements in corpuscular entities (the animal spirits) produce results in the soul via the pineal gland ("We know for certain that it is the soul which has sensory perceptions, and not the body", Descartes 1985: *Optics*, 164) that involve neither spatial movements nor corpuscles, while non-spatial willings produce spatial movements of corpuscular entities and hence of bodily limbs. The following is Descartes' description of what is involved in seeing, hearing, and experiencing heat:

> [R]egarding light and colour [. . .], we must suppose our soul to be of such a nature that what makes it have the sensation of light is the force of movements taking place in the regions of the brain where the optic nerve-fibres originate, and what makes it have the sensation of colour is the manner of these movements. Likewise, the movements in the nerves of the tongue make it taste flavours; and, in general, movements in the nerves anywhere in the body make the soul have a tickling sensation if they are moderate, and a pain when they are too violent. But in all this there need be no resemblance between the ideas which the soul conceives and the movements which cause these ideas. (Ibid., 167)

> As regards heat [as corpuscular motion], the sensation we have of it may, I think, be taken for a kind of pain when the motion is violent, and sometimes for a kind of tickling when the motion is moderate. And since we have already said that there is nothing outside our thought which is similar to the ideas we conceive of tickling and pain, we may well believe also that there is nothing which is similar to the idea we conceive of heat; rather, this sensation may be produced in us by anything that can set up various motions in the minute parts of our hands or of any other place in our body. (Descartes 1985: *The World*, 84)

It did not take very long for puzzlements to arise about the idea of causal interaction between the soul and the body. One of the most noteworthy of Descartes' correspondents on the matter of his views was a certain Princess Elizabeth of Bohemia (1618–1680). In a letter dated June 16, 1643, she writes as follows:

> For it seems that all determination of movement takes place by the propulsion of the thing moved, by the manner in which it is propelled by that which moves it, and by the qualification and shape of the surface of this latter. Contact is required for the first two conditions, and extension for the third. You yourself entirely exclude extension from the notion you have of the mind, and a touching seems to me incompatible with an immaterial thing. (Descartes 1958: *Letters*, 250–251)

In response to the princess, Descartes states that he has said almost nothing in his *Meditations* on the matter of the soul's union with the body and that he really cannot say much about how it is that they causally affect each other: "for soul and body [operating] together we have no notion save that of their union" (ibid., 252). The causal connection is a primitive or basic relation upon which not much, if any, light can be shed. In a letter to another correspondent named Arnauld, Descartes says that,

> though we are not in a position to understand, either by reasoning or by any comparison drawn from other things, how the mind, which is incorporeal, can move the body, none the less we cannot doubt that it can, since experiences the most certain and the most evident make us at all times immediately aware of its doing so. This is one of those things which are known in and by themselves and which we obscure if we seek to explain them by way of other things. (Ibid., 262)

And to another questioner, Pierre Gassendi, Descartes answers

> that the whole problem [of how the soul can move the body if it is in no way material] arises from a supposition that is false and cannot in any way be proved, namely that if the soul and the body are

two substances whose nature is different, this prevents them from being able to act on each other. (Descartes 1984: *Appendix to the Fifth Set of Objections and Replies,* 275)

As just noted, Descartes tells Princess Elizabeth that he has said almost nothing about the union of soul and body in his *Meditations.* To this day, a debate continues about whether Descartes believes that this union just is the causal interaction between soul and body or instead believes that it is accounted for by a more basic metaphysical relationship, which makes such interaction possible (Hoffman 1986). However this debate is resolved, two points are worth making here.

First, in a letter to Regius Henricus, a professor of medicine who was an admirer of Descartes' views, Descartes insists that a human being is made up of a soul and a body and that this is not explained by a

mere presence or proximity of one to the other, but by a true substantial union. For this there is, indeed, required a natural disposition of the body and the appropriate configuration of its parts; but the union differs from position and shape and other purely corporeal modes, because it reaches the incorporeal soul as well as the body. (Descartes 1970, 130)

Earlier in the same letter, Descartes has told Regius that,

whenever the occasion arises, in public and in private, you should give out that you believe that a human being is a true *ens per se,* and not an *ens per accidens,* and that the mind and the body are united in a real and substantial manner. You must say that they are united not by position or disposition [. . .] but by a true mode of union, as everyone agrees, though nobody explains what this means and so you need not do so either. (Ibid., 127)

Second, regardless of whether Descartes believes that causal interaction just is a soul–body union or he holds that it is itself grounded in something metaphysically deeper, he insists that it does occur. And given its importance in the history of thought about the soul, we will have something of our own to say about this matter in Chapter 5.

For now, we turn to another criticism that has been raised against Descartes' view. This criticism is that, if we grant to Descartes that this soul–body causal interaction occurs, then it is incumbent upon him to specify where in the body it takes place. As we have seen, Descartes conjectures that the locus of interaction is at the pineal gland in the brain; but this answer has not withstood either the test of time or that of science. In light of this failure, philosophers like Armstrong have asserted the following:

> Where in the brain do these first physical effects on the way down [from an initial mental willing], and these last physical effects on the way up [e.g. from bodily damage], occur? Descartes, who added anatomy and dissection to all his other scientific interests, suggested the pineal gland because it lay at the centre of the brain. It was an ingenious suggestion, but it can be disproved empirically. The gland can even be excised without affecting mental functioning. The neurophysiologist Sir John Eccles, who is a Dualist, suggests other locations: points where the firing or inhibition of neurons might occur as a result of small changes in electrical charge. His idea is that these changes in charge could be the direct effects, and direct causes, of happenings in the mental substance. [. . .] The point here is that the Dualist is in rather urgent need of some such scientific theory, preferably one that can be experimentally tested. (Armstrong 1999, 19)

Is the dualist interactionist in urgent need of a scientific theory about the place of interaction between soul and body that can be scientifically tested? It is not readily apparent why this is the case. After all, as Descartes points out, our first-person awareness of our willing (or choosing) to move our limbs does not provide us with an awareness of the point of causal interaction:

> It is true that we are not aware of the way in which our mind discharges the animal spirits into this or that nerve; for this does not depend

on the mind alone, but on the mind's union with the body. Yet we
do have knowledge of all the action by which the mind moves the nerves,
in so far as such action is in the mind, since it is no other than the
inclination of the will to this or that movement of the limbs; and this
inclination of the will is followed by the flow of the animal spirits into
the nerves, and by all that is requisite for the movement—all this being
due to the appropriate disposition of the body, of which the mind can
be ignorant, and to the mind's union with the body, of which the mind
is certainly aware; otherwise the mind could never incline its will to
the moving of the limbs. (Descartes, *Letters*, 261–262)

It is not possible, then, to discover the point of causal interaction
between body and soul from our awareness of our willing (choosing) to move our limbs. Is there anything else, which we are aware
of from the first-person perspective, that would suggest the place of
causal interaction? Descartes believes that there is. Though this is not
mentioned by Armstrong, Descartes has a reason other than the
central location of the pineal gland for maintaining that that gland
is the locus of causal interaction. This additional reason arises out of
Descartes' belief that the soul is substantively simple (it has no
substantive parts) and is, therefore, an indivisible unit. This belief is
supported (or at least not contradicted) by what Descartes is aware
of introspectively (from the first-person perspective):

[I]n the first place [. . .] there is a great difference between mind and
body, inasmuch as body is by nature always divisible, and the mind
is entirely indivisible. For, as a matter of fact, when I consider the mind,
that is to say, myself inasmuch as I am only a thinking thing, I cannot distinguish in myself any parts, but apprehend myself to be
clearly one and entire; and although the whole mind seems to be united
to the whole body, yet if a foot, or an arm, or some other part, is
separated from my body, I am aware that nothing has been taken away
from my mind. And the faculties of willing, feeling, conceiving, etc.
cannot be properly speaking said to be its parts, for it is one and the
same mind which employs itself in willing and in feeling and understanding. (Descartes, *Meditations VI*, 196)

Armed with the idea that he is a simple soul that is aware of itself simultaneously being the subject of willing, feeling, understanding, and so on (in other words, aware of what philosophers today term "the unity of consciousness"), he concludes that the locus of causal interaction should equally be singular in nature:

> The reason which persuades me that the soul cannot have any other seat in all the body than this gland wherein to exercise its functions immediately, is that I reflect that the other parts of our brain are all of them double, just as we have two eyes, two hands, two ears, and finally all the organs of our outside senses are double; and inasmuch as we have but one solitary and simple thought of one particular thing at one and the same moment, it must necessarily be the case that there must somewhere be a place where the two images which come to us by the two eyes, where the two other impressions which proceed from a single object by means of the double organs of the other senses, can unite before arriving at the soul, in order that they may not represent to it two objects instead of one. And it is easy to apprehend how these images or other impressions might unite in this gland by the intermission of the [animal] spirits which fill the cavities of the brain; but there is no other place in the body where they can be thus united unless they are so in this gland. (Descartes, *The Passions of the Soul I*, 346)

> [S]ince our soul is not double, but single and indivisible, it seems to me that the part of the body to which it is most immediately joined should also be single and not divided into a pair of similar parts. I cannot find such a part in the whole brain except this gland. (Descartes 1970: *Letters*, 75)

As Armstrong points out in the quote above, the singular pineal gland failed to be the bodily organ for which Descartes was looking. Nevertheless, the reasoning from the unity of consciousness that took Descartes to the pineal gland continues to exert its force among contemporary neuroscientists. Citing Searle again (see Chapter 1):

I need to say something about what neurobiologists call "the binding problem." We know that the visual system has cells and indeed regions that are specially responsive to particular features of objects such as color, shape, movement, lines, angles, etc. But when we see an object we have a unified experience of a single object. How does the brain bind all of these different stimuli into a single, unified experience of a single object? The problem extends across the different modes of perception. All of my experiences at present are part of one big unified conscious experience. (Searle 1997, 33)

And the science writer Sandra Blakeslee asserts the following about neuroscientists:

For scientists who study the human brain, even its simplest act of perception is an event of astonishing intricacy.

Consider this: It is a beautiful spring day and you are walking down a country lane, absorbed in thought. Birds are chirping, roses are in bloom and the sun feels warm on your face. Suddenly, you hear a dog bark and you switch your attention to seeing if the animal means to bite.

Years of research have shown that the brain absorbs a scene like this by carving it into components and analyzing each chunk of information along separate pathways. As the eyes gaze at the rose, it is not the whole image of the rose that is transmitted to the brain. Instead, something very puzzling takes place. The nerve cells in the retina immediately break down the image into separate components, like its contours, textures and colors. As the ear hears birds chirping, separate cells respond to each frequency while others compute the direction and intensity of the sound. Cells in the skin that respond to warmth channel their input to yet another part of the brain.

Each population of sensory cells, from the eye, ear, nose and skin, sends its information to its home area on the outer surface of the brain, a thin, deeply furrowed sheet of cells known as the cerebral cortex.

The sensations in one instant of a spring morning have thus become represented by millions of activated cells in many different regions of the cortex. That much is known. A still baffling question for scientists is, how does the brain bind these fragmented pieces of information into a single coherent image? The nature of the reassembly process, known as the binding problem, is intimately related to the age-old question of consciousness, since an answer to the binding problem would go far to defining the physical basis of the conscious mind. (Blakeslee 1995)

A significant point here is that neuroscientists consider the binding problem to be a problem *because of what we are aware of from the first-person perspective*, which is that we are unified subjects of consciousness. Neuroscientists look for a single spot in the brain to which the information from the various modes of perception is sent and bound together, and they do so because they are well aware of themselves as unified subjects of consciousness. In short, the existence of the binding problem is itself evidence of the nature of our unified experience, as known from the first-person perspective. When Descartes tells us that he "cannot distinguish in myself any parts" (Descartes, *Meditations VI*, 196), he is not making something up.

But what about our main point of concern, which is that Descartes takes his first-person knowledge of the soul's apparent simplicity to imply that causal interaction between a soul and its body must occur at a single point in the latter? Is Descartes right about this? It is not clear that he is. Regardless of whether the soul is non-spatial in nature (Descartes) or is present in its entirety at each point in the space occupied by the body (Augustine and Aquinas), it seems to be the case that the soul might simultaneously interact with the body at multiple points in the latter. Moreover, rather than the body containing a single point that performs the binding function, it may well be that the soul itself performs that function. If it does, then we cannot learn anything about the locus of causal interaction from our first-person awareness of ourselves as unified subjects of experience.

Is it possible to discover the (or a) point of causal interaction from the third-person perspective, by means of observation that employs one or more of our five senses? The answer to this question is not as straightforward as one might expect. For example, from the third-person perspective, what would count as evidence that a place in the body is the point of causal interaction? Would the failure to find a sufficient physical cause of a particular brain event (e.g. an event in the motor cortex) on the occasion of an apparently willed, purposeful bodily movement provide evidence that the brain event in question must have been caused by a mental event? Not necessarily. It is true that, if a soul makes, say, an undetermined choice (act of will) to act that directly produces a physical event that ultimately leads to a leg movement toward the refrigerator (and we assume that the leg movement would not have occurred without that choice), then there must have occurred an initial physical event of a specific kind that had no physical cause (or no sufficient physical cause). But would the failure to find a (sufficient) physical cause of this physical event (one that leads to the leg movement) be evidence of that event's being the locus of causal interaction? The answer to this question depends upon certain assumptions that one brings to the data. For example, on the one hand, if one is a committed physicalist (one who denies the existence of the soul), then one would likely respond to this failure to find a (sufficient) physical cause either by maintaining that the physical event, though it had no (sufficient) physical cause, was identical with the stated choice (one might say this if one, even though a physicalist, believes in the occurrence of causally undetermined choices); or by maintaining that the physical event had a (sufficient) physical cause, which has not yet been discovered. On the other hand, if one is a committed dualist interactionist, then one believes in causal interaction, as Descartes suggests, on the basis of one's first-person experience, *before* one does any scientific investigative work. Thus the failure to find a (sufficient) physical cause of a physical event is not the basis for one's belief in causal interaction. One might, like Descartes, take this failure to find a (sufficient) physical cause as defeasible evidence for a locus of causal interaction. However, if subsequent scientific work overturns this initial failure, one will not conclude (as Descartes most certainly would not have concluded) either that dualist interactionism is false or that the soul does not exist. Rather, one will conclude that the locus of causal interaction has not yet been discovered.

In the end, then, it seems as if Armstrong is mistaken when he claims "that the Dualist is in rather urgent need of some such scientific theory, preferably one that can be experimentally tested" (Armstrong 1999, 19) in support of interactionist dualism. It seems that the truth or falsity of interactionist dualism does not hinge on what is or might be discovered in science. If a reader finds this conclusion problematic, we will argue further in support of it in Chapter 6, when we consider the argument from causal closure against dualism.

Before leaving the topic of causal interaction, it is relevant to point out in what way Descartes believes it to be relevant to the issue of why one considers one's body to be one's *own* body. Most of us probably never give a moment's thought to why we regard a certain body as ours. We simply think and talk about it as *my* body. However, we think of, and regard, many other things as *mine*. For example, most of us regard a car as *mine* because we have purchased it through an agreed form of business transaction. Or, we think of some other object as *mine* because we have inherited it. It is highly doubtful that either of these senses of "mine" is at all relevant when it comes to thinking of a particular physical body as *mine*. Why, then, does each of us regard a particular human body as *mine*? According to Descartes, we do so because each of us is causally attached to a particular body and, when events occur in it, we undergo various experiences:

Nor was it without reason that I believed that this body (which by a certain special right I call my own) belonged to me more properly and more strictly than any other; for in fact I could never be separated from it as from other bodies; I experienced in it and on account of it all my appetites and affections, and finally I was touched by the feeling of pain and the titillation of pleasure in its parts, and not in the parts of other bodies which were separated from it. (Descartes, *Meditations VI*, 188)

If Descartes is right about why one thinks of one's body as one's own, then an implication of his view is that one might come to think of a different body as one's own. For example, if one were regularly to experience pains and pleasures in an additional body when it was respectively struck and stroked, while all the time continuing to experience pain and pleasure in one's present body, then one would come to think of oneself having either two bodies or one body at two different points in space. As we shall see in Chapter 5, philosophers have attempted to use Descartes' causal interactionist explanation of why one regards one's body as *mine* to undermine the credibility of dualism.

Up to this point, we have examined Descartes' conception of the soul and of the issue of causal interaction. What we have not yet focused on is why Descartes believes that the soul exists and that dualism is true. This is a particularly difficult topic, and a source of much disagreement among Cartesian scholars. What we do in the following pages is summarize what we believe to be the arguments that Descartes gives in support of dualism and briefly assess their strengths and weaknesses.

One argument is as follows:

1   The body is essentially a divisible substance.
2   The soul is essentially an indivisible substance.

Therefore,

3   The soul and the body are distinct substances.

This argument is valid. What support does Descartes provide for the premises? Consider premise 2. As we quoted above, Descartes says that, when he considers his mind—that is to say, himself—he cannot distinguish any substantive parts but apprehends himself to be one and entire. Amputation of limbs of his body (which confirms the divisibility of his body) would not produce a substantive diminishment of his mind. (We note that Descartes does not say that amputation of a limb would not affect his mind in any way whatsoever. He would surely concede that amputation of a limb would cause pain, sadness, etc. Descartes is claiming that amputation would produce no *substantive* change in his mind.)

One response to Descartes' support for premise 2, a version of which we addressed in Chapter 1 when considering Armstrong's discussion of Plato, makes use of ordinary language. For example, André Gombay says the following:

> [W]e are bound to feel uneasy about [. . .] the [premise] about the mind or self having no parts. Isn't "part of me" a standard locution to report mental conflicts? Part of me trembles at the thought of scaling the North Face of the Eiger, yet I am dying to try. Ah, Descartes will reply, this is not a mental conflict. The phrase is a misnomer, there can be no such thing: for a conflict to arise there must be parties, and the mind has none. What is really happening here is a conflict between my mind on one side, and a bodily impulse on the other— so Descartes will argue at length in article 47 of the *Passions* [. . .] But this view is not very convincing. My predicament re the North Face does not feel at all like a typical conflict between mind and body— say, my wish to stifle a sneeze during a concert. It feels mental all round. (Gombay 2007, 107)

Gombay is surely correct: the conflict is ultimately mental all round. But the conflict does not support the position that the soul has substantive parts. As we argued in response to Armstrong in Chapter 1, all one need do is suppose (in this case) that both Gombay's fear of scaling the face of the mountain and his desire to try disappear. Is there any less of Gombay, in the sense that he has lost substantive parts of himself? Not in the least. He will survive this mental change in his entirety.

A more telling response to Descartes' support for premise 2 points out that his claim that "he cannot distinguish in myself any parts" (Descartes, *Meditations VI*, 196) admits of both a stronger and a weaker reading. On the stronger reading, Descartes is saying that he is aware that his soul has no substantive parts. In other words, he is aware that he is substantively simple. On the weaker reading, Descartes is saying that he is unaware, or fails to be aware, that his soul has any substantive parts. This might leave open the possibility that the soul has substantive parts, of which it is not aware. We say this reading *might* leave open this possibility, because failure-to-be-aware-of arguments are only as strong as the assumptions behind them. One critical assumption concerns whether or not it is reasonable to believe that one would be aware of the feature for which one is look-ing, if it is there. For example, if one concludes, while sitting at one's desk, that there is no tiger in one's office on the grounds that one fails to be aware of the presence of a tiger, then one seems justified in drawing this conclusion, because it is reasonable to assume that one would be aware of the presence of a tiger in the office if one were there. But things are different when it comes to something like a paper-clip. It is not reasonable to conclude, while sitting at one's desk, that there is no paper-clip on the office floor on the grounds that one fails to be aware of a paper-clip on the floor. It is not reasonable to draw this conclusion because the desk, the chair, the bookcases, and so on might obscure from view a paper-clip that is lying on the floor. In this case, the assumption that one would be aware of a paper-clip if a paper-clip were on the floor is not justified.

In the case of the soul, then, an all-important question for the weaker reading of Descartes' argument is whether it is reasonable to assume that one would be aware of a substantive part of the soul, if such a part were there. Stated slightly differently, what is at issue is the degree to which the mind is transparent to itself such that, if something is (i.e. exists) in one's mind, then one is aware of it. Descartes himself seems to believe that the mind is thoroughly transparent with respect to events occurring in it. For example, he states that "[t]he fact that nothing can exist in the mind, in so far as it is a thinking thing, of which it is not conscious, seems to me self-evident. [. . .] [T]here can exist in us no thought of which, at the very moment that it is pre-sent in us, we are not conscious" (Descartes, *Reply to Objections IV*,

115). He believes, however, that this transparency does not extend to the soul's faculties or powers, of which we are potentially, but not actually, always conscious:

> But it has to be noted that, while indeed we are always in actuality conscious of acts or operations of the mind, that is not the case with the faculties or powers of the mind, except potentially. So that when we dispose ourselves to the exercise of any faculty, if the faculty reside in us, we are immediately actually conscious of it; and hence we can deny that it exists in the mind, if we can form no consciousness of it. (Ibid., 115)

With regard to something like pain (which Descartes regards as an instance of thought), the transparency of the mind does not seem all that implausible. After all, what would it mean to say that one is experiencing pain, but is not aware of any pain? But, were there substantive parts of the soul, would they be similar to pain when it comes to the mind's transparency? Perhaps, in the end, the only way to answer this question is in terms of whether or not one already believes that one is or is not a soul. If one believes that it is plausible to hold that the mind is transparent because one is a substantively simple soul, then the weaker reading of Descartes' argument simply begs the question at issue. Indeed, one does not need the argument for the existence of the substantively simple soul, because one is already convinced of the existence of such a soul. If one is not convinced that the mind is transparent because one is not sure if one is a soul or a body, then the weaker reading of Descartes' argument does not amount to much of an argument.

A different argument that many claim to find in Descartes' writings is the so-called "modal argument" for dualism. This argument rests on two principles: the principle of the indiscernibility of identicals; and a modal epistemic principle. The first principle states that, for any A and B, if A is identical with B, then any property had by A is also had by B. According to this principle, if the soul is the body, whatever is true of the soul is true of the body (similarly, if water is H_2O, then whatever is true of water is true of H_2O). As for a modal epistemic principle, consider this Cartesian thesis:

> One has reason to believe a state of affairs is possible if one can conceive of (picture, image, consistently describe) the state of affairs obtaining, and if its obtaining is not incompatible with what one has independent reason for believing is necessary.

Note that this principle is not articulated in terms of certainty. One may have reason to believe a state of affairs to be possible and yet one may be mistaken. Taliaferro has defended this principle in different publications (Taliaferro 1994, 1997, 2001b).

The modal argument may be articulated succinctly. Following Descartes, we frame the argument in the first person.

1 Hypothesis: I am identical with my body.
2 If I am identical with my body, then whatever is true of me is true of my body.
3 There is reason to believe the following state of affairs is possible: I can exist without my body, and my body can exist without me. (Such a state of affairs seems conceivable, and it is not incompatible with what we have independent reason for believing is necessary.)
4 There is reason to believe I am not identical with my body.

A full-scale, deep evaluation of this argument would be too demanding; but consider its merits in light of two objections.

The argument begs the question   One could not reasonably claim that it is possible for a person to survive the demise of her body unless we already know the person is not identical with her body.

Two replies. First, a range of philosophers (D. M. Armstrong, David Lewis, and Lynne Baker) accept the first three premises but reject the conclusion; so it seems to be false that no one would accept premise 3 while also affirming premise 1. Lynne Baker, for example, thinks that materialism is true of human persons, but a human person can be recomposed as an immaterial being (Baker 2000). A Cartesian defense would then need to show that Baker's account of premise 3 is not as plausible as a dualist's account (see Taliaferro 2009).

Second, the charge of begging the question against the modal argument might lead to a rejection of what appears to be the legitimate use of thought experiments in virtually all domains of philosophy. In philosophy today it is standard practice to use what is called the example–counterexample method, which involves thought experiments. Imagine we are in a dispute about utilitarianism (which is the ethical theory that maintains that pleasure alone is intrinsically good and should be maximized for as many people as possible): we think that utilitarianism is an ethically valid position, whereas you think it is unjustified because it conflicts with what both of us grasp as the virtue of justice. In the example–counterexample method, we each use examples (real cases or imaginary ones, called "thought experiments") in order to test and clarify our respective positions. One can object to this whole project as question-begging because, for example, if we are utilitarians we might simply claim that, whatever examples you use to persuade us that we are undermining the virtue of justice, they obviously beg the question. We might reply to you: If our theory leads to the conclusion that it is just for us to torture the innocent, so be it. But, in practice, in ethics and other domains of philosophy, what is more common is that a good counterexample causes a philosopher to rethink his or her theory. In this case, most utilitarians today (and historically) have worked hard either to show that torturing the innocent would not lead to maximizing pleasure for as many people as possible or to show that some acts that seem wrong would actually turn out to be for the best (or for the least worst). In terms of the modal argument, then, the apparent conceivability of persons without bodies and vice versa does count as a reason for materialists to try to explain away the seemingly evident contingency of person and body. The modal argument thus provides one reason for materialists to seek to somehow overturn what appears to be possible.

The turning-the-argument-on-its-head objection   Perhaps we can reverse the argument: why not imagine that the person is identical with her body? If we can imagine that, wouldn't it be reasonable to believe it is impossible for a person to exist without her body, and vise versa?

This is an important objection (Zimmerman 1991), but imagining the identity of person and body cuts against what seems to be an evident contingency between person and body. This contingency seems not only apparent in dualist thought experiments of imagined disembodiment and re-embodiment (or body switching), but in two other sources: philosophical idealism and experimental reports. Concerning the first, there is a vital philosophical school of idealism, in the tradition of George Berkeley (1685–1753), according to which all ostensible material objects are mind-dependent, and even constituted by nonphysical sensations. This position has contemporary defenders (Foster 1993). Without an extensive treatment here it is difficult to assess it fairly, but we note that, even if idealism is false, if it is at least possibly true, then it offers a coherent portrait of persons without their corporeal bodies (as understood by most materialists). In terms of experiential testimony, while we do not wish to argue for dualism from paranormal data (or parapsychology), there are widespread reports of persons having out-of-body experiences (OBEs) in states of extreme trauma. Clearly there are various neurological explanations for such experiences; but, like idealism, it appears as though they present us with possible states of affairs (see Blanke 2009). They are not akin to reports of seeing a round triangle or observing water that is not composed of H_2O (both of which we know to be impossible, given the definition of "round" and "triangle" and the actual composition of water). A defender of the modal argument need not claim to *know* that the person–body relationship is contingent; the defender need only claim that there is reason to believe it is contingent (see Swinburne 1997, Part II).

Finally, we turn very briefly to Descartes' position on the soul's origin and its immortality and consider some of his thoughts on the body's identity through time. Like his Christian predecessors Augustine and Aquinas, Descartes affirms both that God creates the soul and that the soul is immortal. In a summary of an earlier treatise of his (of which his *World* and *Treatise on Man* are parts), he says the following:

> [T]he rational soul [. . .] cannot be derived in any way from the potentiality of matter, but must be specially created. [. . .] [O]ur soul is of a nature entirely independent of the body, and consequently [. . .] it is not bound to die with it. And since we cannot see any other causes which destroy the soul, we are naturally led to conclude that it is immortal. (Descartes 1985: *Discourse on the Method*, 141)

Though the soul is of a nature that entails that it is not bound to die with its body, it is nevertheless still not true, on Descartes' view, that the soul and the body fail to share any properties. For example, while one is and the other is not in space, both are temporal in nature and undergo changes during the time when they exist. Do both remain the same through time? Descartes believes that they do. His thoughts about the sameness of the human body, which we quote below, are particularly interesting in light of issues that will arise in the next chapter:

> I consider what exactly is the body of a man, and I find that this word "body" is very ambiguous. When we speak in general of a body, we mean a determinate part of matter, a part of the quantity of which the universe is composed. In this sense, if the smallest amount of that quantity were removed we would *eo ipso* judge that the body was smaller and no longer complete; and if any particle of the matter were changed we would at once think that the body was no longer quite the same, no longer *numerically the same*. But when we speak of the

body of a man, we do not mean a determinate part of matter with a determinate size; we mean simply that whole of the matter joined to the soul of that man. And so, even though that matter changes, and its quantity increases or decreases, we still believe that it is the same body, *numerically the same* body, provided that it remained joined in substantial union with the same soul; and we think that this body is whole and entire provided that it has in itself all the dispositions required to preserve that union. (Descartes, *Letters*, 156–157)

Descartes then uses the sameness of the soul to ground the identity of the body over time:

Nobody denies that we have the same bodies as we had in our infancy, although their quantity has much increased, and according to the common opinion of doctors, which is doubtless true, there is no longer in them any part of the matter which then belonged to them, and even though they do not have the same shape any longer; so that they are only *numerically the same* because they are informed by the same soul. [. . .] In that sense, [the human body] can even be called indivisible; because if an arm or a leg of a man is amputated, we think that it is only in the first sense of "body" that his body is divided—we do not think that a man who has lost an arm or a leg is less a man than any other. Altogether then, provided that a body is united with the same rational soul, we always take it as the body of the same man whatever matter it may be and whatever quantity or shape it may have [. . .] (Ibid., 157)

According to Descartes, each of us retains numerically the same body throughout life, even though this body loses and adds parts, because it remains joined to numerically the same soul. This claim will be challenged by the likes of Joseph Butler and Thomas Reid (in the next chapter) on the grounds that anything that changes parts cannot, strictly speaking, remain the same. According to them, it is because the soul does not change any parts (because it has none to change) that it alone (as opposed to the body) remains numerically the same entity through time.

Malebranche and Leibniz

A variety of soul–body dualisms emerged after Descartes' work, two of which proposed fascinating alternatives to the causal interaction between a soul and its body. For example, Nicholas Malebranche (1638–1715) assumes that a true causal agent knows both that he acts and how he acts, where the latter requires a knowledge of the necessary connection between cause and effect. Because no one knows how to cause, say, her arm to move (none of us knows what, if anything, she does to her brain to produce events that lead ultimately to the movement of her arm), she does not do so:

> [B]ut there is no man who knows what must be done to move one of his fingers by means of animal spirits. How, then, could men move their arms? These things seem obvious to me and, it seems to me, to all those willing to think, although they are perhaps incomprehensible to all those willing only to sense. (Malebranche 1980: *The Search after Truth*, 6.2.3)

How, then, do our limbs move, if we do not cause them to move? Malebranche defends the view that God causes a human body to move on the occasions when that body's soul wills that it move:

> Now it appears to me quite certain that the will of minds is incapable of moving the smallest body in the world; for it is clear that there is no necessary connection between our will to move our arms, for example, and the movement of our arms. It is true that they are moved when we will it, and that thus we are the natural cause of the movement of our arms. But *natural* causes are not true causes; they are only *occasional* causes that act only through the force and efficiency of the will of God [. . .]. (Ibid.)

Malebranche is a two-way occasionalist: he not only maintains that God causes the movement of a soul's body when the soul wills such movement, but he also maintains that God causes mental events on the occasions when the requisite physical events involving bodies occur. Indeed, Malebranche goes so far as to maintain that not even material bodies causally interact with each other: God is the ubiquitous causal agent in the entire created order.

The German Philosopher Gottfried Leibniz (1646–1716) is equally creative about the soul–body relationship and defends not only the view that there is no causal interaction between a soul and the physical body, but also the view that God is not the cause of events on those occasions when souls will bodily movements and the like, as Malebranche claims. Instead Leibniz maintains that God created the world in such a way that, whenever the soul wills its body to move, the body moves in harmony with the willing. Similarly, whenever the sufficient physical conditions obtain for the occurrence of mental events, the latter occur. This harmonious relationship between soul and body was pre-established by God at the time of creation (thus obviating the need for either interactionist or occasionalist causal relations); for this reason, Leibniz is known for advocating a pre-established harmony.

It is important to point out that neither Malebranche nor Leibniz substantively betters Descartes' position on the interaction issue. Each one merely kicks the question of causal interaction upstairs, relegating it to the relationship between God and a human body and/or between God and the physical world. After all, God is for all intents and purposes a soul (though one with great making properties such as being all-powerful, all-knowing, all-good, and the like); and, if there are any insuperable problems with a human soul interacting with a human body, then those same problems will simply reemerge in God's interaction with the physical world.

Leibniz's soul–body dualism is interesting for reasons other than the idea of a pre-established harmony. Of particular relevance for this brief history of the soul is the following argument from Section 17 of his *Monadology*:

It must be confessed, however, that Perception, and that which depends upon it, are inexplicable by mechanical causes, that is to say, by figures and motions. Supposing that there were a machine whose structure produced thought, sensation, and perception, we could conceive of it as increased in size with the same proportions until one was able to enter into its interior, as he would into a mill. Now, on going into it he would find only pieces working upon one another, but never would he find anything to explain Perception. It is accordingly in the simple substance, and not in the composite nor in a machine[,] that the Perception is to be sought. (Leibniz 1973, 254)

For Leibniz's mill, let us substitute the human brain. Then let us enlarge that brain and imagine ourselves walking through it and looking around. Leibniz maintains that we would never find any thoughts, hopes, fears, desires, pains, and so forth. We would only come across physical events that are in no way like the mental events for which we are looking. Hence, it is reasonable to suppose that a simple soul is the subject of these mental events.

One might respond that Leibniz's argument hinges on an outdated conception of mechanical interactions, involving pushes and pulls of material objects and, perhaps, the wheels, gears, rods, or levers that one might find in a mill. But this would be a mistake, because Leibniz would surely and rightly insist that a walk through an enlarged brain whose contents include electrochemical events involving neurons would fail to turn up any mental events. For present purposes, the important question is: Why is there no success in finding any mental events?

Peter van Inwagen has argued that the problem of not finding mental events in a brain is really just the problem of not being able to imagine how anything, including a simple soul, can think, feel, hope, desire, and so on:

For it is thinking itself that is the source of the mystery of a thinking physical thing. The notion of a non-physical thing that thinks is, I would argue, equally mysterious. How any sort of thing could think is a mystery. It is just that it is a bit easier to see that thinking is a mystery when we suppose that the thing that does the thinking is physical, for we can form mental images of the operations of a physical thing and we can see that the physical interactions represented in these images—the only interactions that can be represented in those images—have no connection with thought or sensation, or none we are able to imagine, conceive, or articulate. The only reason we do not readily find the notion of a non-physical thing that thinks equally mysterious is that we have no clear procedure for forming mental images of non-physical things. (Van Inwagen 2002, 176)

Van Inwagen seems to be arguing that, while we can imagine physical interactions and changes, we are unable to see how those imagined physical interactions and changes have anything to do with thought. This suggests that the problem for physicalism is that we cannot imagine how a physical thing thinks. However, says van Inwagen, what Leibniz overlooked is the fact that the same point can be made about simple substances: we cannot imagine how they can think. In general, we cannot imagine how anything can think. Therefore, physicalism is no worse off than dualism, contrary to what Leibniz's argument suggests.

Alvin Plantinga believes that van Inwagen has misstated the problem posed by Leibniz's argument. As Plantinga sees the issue,

[w]hat inclines us to reject the idea of a physical thing's thinking is not just the fact that we can't form a mental image of a physical thing's thinking. [. . .] It's rather that on reflection one can see that a physical object just can't do that sort of thing. [. . .] But (and here is the important point) the same clearly doesn't go for an immaterial thing's thinking; we certainly can't see that no immaterial thing can think. (Plantinga 2007, 114, 115, 116).

In considering Plantinga's response to van Inwagen, it is helpful to recall the distinction between the stronger and the weaker forms of awareness that were important for understanding Descartes' argument for the distinctness of the soul from its body. On the stronger reading of awareness, Descartes says that he is aware that his soul has no substantive parts. On the weaker reading of awareness, he says that he is unaware (or fails to be aware) of his soul having any substantive parts. As Plantinga understands Leibniz's argument, the problem for physicalism is not just that we weakly fail to be able to see or understand how a physical thing can think. Leibniz is rightly claiming that we strongly see or understand that a physical thing cannot think, whereas we do not strongly see that a simple soul cannot think.

Van Inwagen offers a different response to Leibniz's argument:

> In general, to attempt to explain how an underlying reality generates some phenomenon is to construct a representation of the working of that underlying reality, a representation that in some sense "shows how" the underlying reality generates the phenomenon. Essentially the same considerations as those that show that we are unable to form a mental image that displays the generation of thought and sensation by the workings of some underlying reality (whether the underlying reality involves one thing or many, and whether the things it involves are physical or non-physical) show that we are unable to form any sort of representation that displays the generation of thought and sensation by the workings of an underlying reality. (Van Inwagen 2002, 177–178)

Here, again, we can see the relevance of the distinction between the stronger and weaker forms of awareness, understanding, or representation. In this instance, van Inwagen is claiming that we are in the weaker sense unable to form a representation of how thought and sensation might be generated by underlying complex interactions of what is physical. However, the problem is that we are in the same position with respect to what is non-physical, in so far as we are unable to represent how underlying interactions of it might generate thought and sensation.

In response to van Inwagen, Plantinga points out that those who believe in the soul's existence hold that the soul is a substantively simple entity: "the dualist [. . .] typically thinks of an immaterial self, as soul, a thing that thinks, as *simple*" (Plantinga 2007, 116). Because it is simple, we can see, in the strong sense, that thoughts and sensations are not generated by any underlying interactions between parts, because a soul has no such parts. Hence the explanation of why we are unable to form a representation of the generation of thought by what is non-physical is completely different from the explanation of this inability with respect to what is physical.

Now, though an immaterial self is simple in the sense that it has no substantive parts, it does have properties. Moreover, according to Plantinga,

> a property P is *basic* to a thing x if x has P, but x's having P is not generated by the interaction of its parts. Thought is then a basic property of selves, or better a basic activity of selves. [Thus,] there isn't any *way* in which the self produces a thought; it does so immediately. To ask, "How does a self produce thought?" is to ask an improper question. There isn't any how about it. (Ibid., 116–117)

As we have seen in our brief history of the soul to this point, those who believe in the soul typically hold that the simple soul has a multiplicity of properties (the power to think, the power to will, and so on). In Plantinga's terminology, these are basic properties. Moreover, the exercisings of these powers are themselves simple in nature in the sense that they are events or occurrences with no event parts. Given that this is the case, what each of us sees, in the strong sense, is that acts of thought do not and cannot be generated by underlying realities, which would combine in some way to compose thoughts. This kind of generation of thought is impossible because thoughts have no event parts. They are simple events.

As we will see in the next chapter in our brief history of the soul, the issue of the soul's simplicity will continue to play a role in discussions about the nature of the self. In the mind of more than one philosopher, the soul's substantive simplicity will be of critical importance for developing adequate responses to different critics of the idea of the soul.

Chapter 4

The Soul in Locke, Butler, Reid, Hume, and Kant

In the Introduction to their book *Naturalization of the Soul: Self and Personal Identity in the Eighteenth Century*, Raymond Martin and John Barresi write as follows:

> At the beginning of the seventeenth century, European philosophers were still thinking about the self pretty much as philosophers had been thinking about it for the previous two thousand years. The self was the soul, an immaterial substance. But in Europe the seventeenth century was a time of momentous and soul-shattering intellectual transformation. [...] [B]y the end of the eighteenth century the self [had ceased to be the soul and] had become the mind, a dynamic natural system subject to general laws of growth and development. (Martin and Barresi, 2000, 1)

Part of the explanation for this replacement of the soul by the mind was the gradual acceptance of Descartes' idea that a soul does not give live to the body. The demise of this idea led to a more general cessation of talk about the soul altogether. But, while one could sensibly give up on the theoretical view that the self is a life-giving principle (and therefore that the self is a soul), one could not as easily abandon the non-theoretical truth that the self is a thing that thinks.

A Brief History of the Soul, First Edition.
© 2011 Stewart Goetz and Charles Taliaferro. Published 2011 by Blackwell Publishing Ltd.

After all, something must have *thoughtfully* theorized that the self is that which gives life to the body. Hence there was no reasonably denying that the self is a mind. Moreover, because the thing which thinks is commonly thought of as a person, the issue of the identity of persons became a topic of great interest. As Martin and Barresi point out, the replacement of the view of the self as a substantial and enduring immaterial soul with the idea of the self as a mind "involved movement away from [non-relational] accounts of personal identity, according to which the self is a simple persisting thing, toward relational accounts, according to which the self consists essentially of physical and/or psychological relations among different temporal stages of an organism or person" (Martin and Barresi, 2000, ix).

In this chapter we will examine some of the central figures who participated in this debate about the non-relational versus the relational conception of the self. Toward the end, we will critically interact with some comments of Martin and Barresi about the naturalization of the soul and will finish with a brief survey of some of Immanuel Kant's thought about the significance of our use of the first-person pronoun "I."

Locke

When asking oneself the question "What am I?," one might very well answer "I am a person." But what is a person? As we have seen in earlier chapters, philosophers like Plato, Augustine, and Descartes answered that a person is a rational, life-giving soul (though Descartes denied this function of the soul), where a rational, life-giving soul is a spiritual/immaterial substance. Philosophers such as Aristotle and Aquinas responded that a person is a human being, where a human being is a body that is infused and given life by a rational soul. All, however, agreed that the identity of a person over time depends upon the continued existence of the same soul. In *An Essay Concerning Human Understanding*, the first edition of which was published in

1689, John Locke (1632–1704) acknowledges the following view of the soul:

> But taking, as we ordinarily do [. . .] the Soul of a Man, for an immaterial Substance, independent from Matter, and indifferent alike to it all, there can from the Nature of things, be no Absurdity at all, to suppose, that the same Soul may, at different times be united to different Bodies, and with them make up, for that time, one Man. (Locke 1975: *An Essay Concerning Human Understanding*, II.XXVII.27)

This, as Locke says, is what we ordinarily believe about the soul. But what Locke goes on to write about the relationship between the soul and the person, or self, is far from ordinary.

The soul of a man, says Locke, is an immaterial substance (ibid.). What, then, is a man? "[T]he Identity of the same *Man* consists [. . .] in nothing but a participation of the same continued Life, by constantly fleeting Particles of Matter, in succession vitally united to the same organized Body" (ibid., II.XXVII.6). To support his understanding of what a man is, Locke states:

> I presume 'tis not the *Idea* of a thinking or rational Being alone, that makes the *Idea* of a *Man* in most Peoples Sense; but of a Body so and so shaped joined to it; and if that be the *Idea* of a *Man*, the same successive Body not shifted all at once, must as well as the same immaterial Spirit go to the making of the same *Man*" (*Essay*, II.XXVII.8).

From this statement about what a man is, one would naturally conclude that Locke believes a thinking or rational being is an immaterial spirit, that is to say, a soul. Things are not, however, as straightforward as they seem, because according to Locke a thinking or rational being is a person; and a person is not a soul (an immaterial substance), but that which, by means of its consciousness, can consider itself as itself across or over time (for Locke, considering oneself as oneself over time means remembering oneself). The persistence of a person through time, then, is to be understood in terms of the unifying role of consciousness and does not require the continued existence of the soul. The upshot is that different immaterial substances (souls) can be sequentially attached to the same person, as the following extended quotes make clear:

> [W]e must consider what *Person* stands for; which, I think, is a thinking intelligent Being, that has reason and reflection, and can consider itself as itself, the same thinking thing in different times and places; which it does only by that consciousness, which is inseparable from thinking, and as it seems to me essential to it: It being impossible for anyone to perceive, without perceiving, that he does perceive. When we see, hear, smell, taste, feel, meditate, or will anything, we know that we do so [consciousness is self-reflective]. Thus it is always to our present Sensations and Perceptions [. . .]. (*Essay*, II.XXVII.9)

> The Question being what makes the same *Person*, and not whether it be the same Identical Substance, which always thinks in the same *Person*, which in this case matters not at all. Different Substances, by the same consciousness (when they do partake in it) being united into one Person; as well as different Bodies, by the same Life are united into one Animal, whose *Identity* is preserved, in that change of Substances, by the unity of one continued Life. For it being the same consciousness that makes a Man be himself to himself, *personal Identity* depends on that only, whether it be annexed only to one individual Substance, or can be continued in a succession of several Substances. (*Essay*, II.XXVII.10)

> And therefore those, who place thinking in an immaterial Substance only [. . .] must show why personal Identity cannot be preserved in the change of immaterial Substances, or variety of particular immaterial Substances, as well as animal Identity is preserved in the change of material Substances, or variety of particular Bodies [. . .]. (*Essay*, II.XXVII.12)

In summary, Locke maintains that "*personal Identity* consists, not in the identity of Substance, but [. . .] in the Identity of *consciousness*" (ibid., II.XXVII.19), where "Consciousness is the perception of what passes in a Man's own mind" (II.I.19), it being "altogether as intelligible to say, that a body is extended without parts, as that any-thing *thinks without being conscious of it*, or perceiving, that it does so" (ibid.). In other words, Locke understands or defines personal iden-tity over time in terms of memory.

Now, says Locke,

> *Self* is that conscious thinking thing (whatever Substance [. . .] whether Spiritual, or Material, Simple, or Compounded, it matters not) which is sensible, or conscious of Pleasure and Pain, capable of Happiness or Misery, and so is concern'd for it *self*, as far as that consciousness extends. [S]*elf* is not determined by Identity or Diversity of Substance [. . .] but only by Identity of consciousness" (*Essay*, II.XXVII.17, 23).

Locke claims that consciousness extends beyond the present moment, and he maintains that remembering is itself an event that fixes or creates the moments at which the self or person existed in the past. Memory is the glue that brings and binds together earlier and later stages of a person:

> For since consciousness always accompanies thinking, and 'tis that that makes everyone to be, what he calls *self*; and thereby distinguishes himself from all other thinking things, in this alone consists *personal identity*, *i.e.*, the sameness of a rational Being: And as far as this consciousness can be extended backwards to any past Action or Thought, so far reaches the Identity of that *Person*; it is the same *self* now it was then; and 'tis by the same *self* with this present one that now reflects on it, that that Action was done" (*Essay*, II.XXVII.9).

> For as far as any intelligent Being can repeat the *Idea* of any past Action with the same consciousness it had of it at first, and with the same consciousness it has of any present Action; so far it is the same *personal self*. For it is by the consciousness it has of its present Thoughts and Actions, that it is *self* to it *self* now, and so will be the same *self* as far as the same consciousness can extend to Actions past or to come. [. . .] The same consciousness uniting those distant Actions into the same *Person*, whatever Substances contributed to their Production. (*Essay*, II.XXVII.10)

To avoid any confusion about what he is claiming, Locke emphasizes that it is consciousness, as opposed to any material substance, that fixes personal identity:

> That [it is consciousness that unites distinct actions into the same person], we have some kind of Evidence in our very Bodies, all whose Particles, whilst vitally united to this same thinking conscious self, so that we feel when they are touch'd, and are affected by, and conscious of good or harm that happens to them, are a part of our *selves*: *i.e.* of our thinking conscious *self*. Thus the Limbs of his Body is to every-one a part of *himself*: He sympathizes and is concerned for them. Cut off an hand, and thereby separate it from that consciousness, we had of its Heat, Cold, and other Affections; and it is then no longer a part of that which is *himself*, any more than the remotest part of Matter. Thus we see the *Substance*, whereof *personal self* consisted at one time, may be varied at another, without the change or personal *Identity*: there being no Question about the same Person, though the Limbs, which but now were a part of it, be cut off. (*Essay*, II.XVII.11)

And it is consciousness, as opposed to any immaterial substance, that determines personal identity:

> Let anyone reflect upon himself, and conclude, that he has in himself an immaterial Spirit, which is that which thinks in him, and in the constant change of his Body keeps him the same; and is that which he calls himself: Let him also suppose it to be the same Soul, that was in *Nestor* or *Thersites*, at the siege of *Troy* [. . .] which it may have been, as well as it is now, the Soul of any other Man: But he, now having no consciousness of any of the Actions either of *Nestor* or *Thersites*, does, or can he, conceive himself the same Person with either of them? Can he be concerned in either of their Actions? Attribute them to him-self, or think them his own more than the Actions of any other Man, that ever existed? So that this consciousness not reaching to any of the Actions of either of those Men, he is no more one *self* with either of them, [. . .] the same immaterial Substance without the same con-sciousness, no more making the same Person by being united to any

Body, than the same Particle of Matter without consciousness united to any Body, makes the same Person. But let him once find himself conscious of any of the Actions of *Nestor*, he then finds himself the same Person with *Nestor*. (*Essay*, II.XXVII.14)

Butler

Locke's views about the self (person) and the soul brought forth responses from others. For example, a critic named John Sergeant pointed out in 1697 that "Consciousness of any Action or any Accident we have now, or have had, is nothing but our Knowledge that it belong'd to us." Thus "a Man must be the same, [before] he can know or be Conscious that he is the same" (quoted in Martin and Barresi 2000, 40). However, without doubt the most notable critics of Locke were Joseph Butler and Thomas Reid. According to Butler (1692–1752), who was an Anglican clergyman, "consciousness is a single and indivisible power" and, because it is this sort of thing, "the subject in which it resides must be so too" (Butler 1897: *The Analogy of Religion* 24–25). Then Butler introduces an analogy involving the impossible division of the motion of an indivisible particle of matter into the motion of its parts; and he goes on to argue, by means of this analogy, that, if a self (what Butler refers to as a living being) by hypothesis could be divided into parts, then each separate part of it would have the power of consciousness in itself. However, this would imply the existence of multiple consciousnesses, which is contrary to the indivisible nature of the self. Moreover, given the indivisible nature of the self, not only is it "easy to conceive, that we may exist out of bodies, as in them," but also it is "[easy to conceive] that we might have animated bodies of any other organs and senses wholly different from these now given us" (ibid., 26). Butler concedes that the "simplicity and absolute oneness of a living agent cannot indeed, from the nature of the thing, be properly proved by experimental observations" (ibid.). Nevertheless, given that these are consistent with the self's unity, "they plainly lead us to *conclude* certainly, that our gross organized bodies [. . .] are no part of ourselves; and therefore show us, that we have no reason to believe their destruction to be ours: even without determining whether our living substances be material or immaterial" (ibid., 26–27). Thus, for Butler, it seems to be the self's simplicity, and not its immateriality, that guarantees its survival of death.

Given Butler's view of the self or living being, it comes as no surprise that he believes the idea of personal identity to be indefinable. Though it is indefinable, it is not at all difficult to understand what this idea is.

> For as, upon two triangles being compared or viewed together, there arises to the mind the idea of similitude, or upon twice two and four, the idea of equality: so likewise, upon comparing the consciousness of one's self or one's own existence in any two moments, there as immediately arises to the mind the idea of personal identity. And as the two former comparisons not only give the idea of similitude and equality; but also shows us, that two triangles are alike, and twice two and four are equal: so the latter comparison not only gives us the idea of personal identity, but also shows us the identity of ourselves in those two moments [. . .]. (Butler 1897: *Of Personal Identity*, 317–318)

Because of his conviction that comparing the consciousness of one's self in any two moments immediately convinces one of one's personal identity, Butler takes Locke to task for the latter's claim that consciousness *makes* personal identity. Consciousness, says Butler, cannot make personal identity, though it most certainly can *ascertain* it:

> But though consciousness of what is past does thus ascertain our personal identity to ourselves, yet to say, that it makes personal identity, or is necessary to our being the same persons, is to say, that a person has not existed a single moment, nor done one action, but what he can remember; indeed none but what he reflects upon. And one should really think it self-evident, that consciousness of personal identity

presupposes, and therefore cannot constitute, personal identity; any more than knowledge, in any other case, can constitute truth, which it presupposes. (Ibid., 318)

Butler goes on to point out that, while Locke's claim that we are necessarily conscious of what we are presently doing and feeling is most certainly correct, the latter is mistaken when he claims that present consciousness of past actions or feelings is a necessary condition of one's either having performed those actions or having had those feelings: "But though present consciousness of what we at present do and feel is necessary to our being the persons that we now are; yet present consciousness of past actions or feelings is not necessary to our being the same persons who performed those actions, or had those feelings" (ibid., 318–319). Moreover, Butler argues that Locke's assertion that a person is a thinking, intelligent being but not a substance is incoherent, because a being is nothing other than a substance: "The question then is, whether the same rational being is the same substance; which needs no answer, because Being and Substance, in this place, stand for the same idea" (ibid., 320). And it is because a person or self is a substance that all its "successive actions, enjoyments, and sufferings, are actions, enjoyments, and sufferings, of the same living being. And they are so, prior to all consideration of its remembering or forgetting: since remembering or forgetting can make no alteration in the truth of past matter of fact" (ibid., 324).

Butler's mention of the sameness of a living being provides the natural basis for summarizing his thoughts about one concept of sameness—namely, that which is strict and philosophical, as it applies to persons—and another concept of sameness—namely, that which is loose and popular, as it applies to vegetation. According to Butler,

[w]hen a man swears to the same tree, as having stood fifty years in the same place, he means only the same as to all the purposes of property and uses of common life, and not that the tree has been all that time the same in the strict and philosophical sense of the word. For

he does not know, whether any one particle of the present tree be the same with any one particle of the tree which stood in the same place fifty years ago. And if they have not one common particle of matter, they cannot be the same tree in the proper philosophical sense of the word *same*: it being evidently a contradiction in terms, to say they are, when no part of their substance, and no one of their properties, is the same: no part of their substance, but the supposition: no one of their properties, because it is allowed, that the same property cannot be transferred from one substance to another. (Ibid., 319–320)

Butler then draws the following conclusion:

And therefore, when we say the identity or sameness of a plant consists in a continuation of the same life, communicated under the same organization, to a number of particles of matter, whether the same or not; the word *same*, when applied to life and to organization, cannot possibly be understood to signify, what it signifies in this very sentence, when applied to matter. In a loose and popular sense then, the life and the organization and the plant are justly said to be the same, notwithstanding the perpetual change of the parts. But in a strict and philosophical manner of speech, no man, no being, no mode of being, no anything, can be the same with that, with which it hath indeed nothing the same. Now sameness is used in the latter sense, when applied to persons. The identity of these, therefore, cannot subsist with diversity of substance. (Ibid., 320)

In summary, it is Butler's view that, when we are concerned with the sameness (identity) of a person or self, we are concerned with the strict sameness that excludes any change of substance. Thus, were a person, contrary to fact in Butler's view, to consist of two or more substances joined together, the loss (or acquisition) of one or more of those substances would entail the going out of existence of that person and, perhaps, its replacement by another person. When it comes to vegetation like a tree, however, we make use of a concept of sameness that allows for the continued existence of the same tree, even though it undergoes a continuous replacement of substances over the course of time. Loosely speaking, the tree is the same over that period of time, even though strictly speaking it is not.

Reid

Thomas Reid (1710–1796), who, like Butler, was a man of the cloth, was also equally critical of Locke's views of personal identity. For starters, Reid asserts that none of us could even reason about something like the existence and nature of the soul without the conviction of his or her personal identity:

> We may observe, first of all, that [the conviction that every man has of his identity] is indispensably necessary to all exercise of reason. The operations of reason, whether in action or in speculation, are made up of successive parts. The antecedent are the foundation of the consequent, and, without the conviction that the antecedent have been seen or done by me, I could have no reason to proceed to the consequent, in any speculation, or in any active project whatever. (Reid 1872, I: *Essays on the Intellectual Powers of Man*, 344)

Having drawn our attention to the conviction that each of us has regarding his or her personal identity, Reid takes aim at Locke's claim that the same consciousness (and thus, on Locke's view, the same person or self) might be attached to more than one substance. Were this possible, two or more substances might remember the same past action or feeling, with the result that

> two or twenty intelligent beings may be the same person. And if the intelligent being may lose the consciousness of the actions done by him, which surely is possible, then he is not the person that did those actions; so that one intelligent being may be two or twenty different persons, if he shall often lose the consciousness of his former actions. (Ibid., 351)

In Reid's estimation, one—if not the—fundamental problem with Locke's treatment of personal identity is his understanding of "consciousness." At its heart, Locke's account confuses consciousness, which is a current awareness of what is present, with memory, which is about past events:

> Mr. Locke attributes to consciousness the conviction we have or our past actions, as if a man may now be conscious of what he did twenty years ago. It is impossible to understand the meaning of this, unless by consciousness be meant memory, the only faculty by which we have an immediate knowledge of our past actions. [. . .] If a man can be conscious of what he did twenty years or twenty minutes ago, there is no use for memory, nor ought we to allow that there is any such faculty. The faculties of consciousness and memory are chiefly distinguished by this, that the first is an immediate knowledge of the present, the second an immediate knowledge of the past. (Ibid., 351)

While Reid's central claim seems sound, we point out that it is neither the faculty of consciousness that provides immediate knowledge of what is present nor the faculty of memory that provides immediate knowledge of what is past, but the actualization or use of these faculties that provides what Reid describes. As Reid himself says about the faculty of smelling, "[t]he faculty of smelling is something very different from the actual sensation of smelling; for the faculty may remain when we have no sensation" (Reid 1872, I: *An Inquiry into the Human Mind*, 110). Reid goes on to argue that Locke confuses personal identity with the evidence we have for it:

> It is very true, that my remembrance that I did such a thing is the evidence I have that I am the identical person who did it. And this, I am apt to think, Mr. Locke meant. But to say that my remembrance that I did such a thing, or my consciousness, makes me the person who did it, is, in my apprehension, an absurdity too gross to be entertained by any man who attends to the meaning of it; for it is to attribute to memory or consciousness a strange magical power of producing

its object, though that object must have existed before the memory or consciousness which produced it. (Reid, *Essays*, 352)

According to Reid, the mistake Locke makes in confounding consciousness with memory provides the occasion for making clear that a memory about what one did or suffered *presupposes* a belief in one's personal identity, and therefore cannot be used to give an account of it. Put slightly differently, in terms of the first person: whenever I remember doing or suffering something I remember that the *I*, of which right now I cannot but be conscious, did or suffered something in the past. Hence, memory by nature presupposes the very personal identity that Locke invokes memory to explain. In Reid's own words: "There can be no memory of what is past without the conviction that we existed at the time remembered" (ibid., 341). That a memory of a self (person) about itself includes a reference to that self in the memory implies that the self is a permanent entity or substance, which has existed from the time referred to in the memory to the time at which the memory is occurring. Someone might ask, says Reid, how one knows, what evidence one has, that such a permanent self exists.

> To this I answer, that the proper evidence I have of all this is remembrance. I remember that twenty years ago I conversed with such a person; I remember several things that passed in that conversation; my memory testifies not only that this was done, but that it was done by me who now remembers it. If it was done by me, I must have existed at that time, and continued to exist from that time to the present. [. . .] Every man in his senses believes what he distinctly remembers, and everything he remembers convinces him that he existed at the time remembered. (Ibid., 345)

Consider the alternative: I remember someone having done action A or having suffered some event S, but my memory does not include me as its subject. Can I infer that I either did A or suffered S? Certainly not directly. After all, someone else could have done A or suffered S, which would make it difficult for me to ascertain who actually did

A or suffered S. My memories would be subjectless and leave open the issue of who was the agent or patient. But my memories are not subjectless and do not leave it to me to find out who was the subject. Rather, they inform me directly that I did A or suffered S.

There is one other significant mistake that, Reid believes, undermines Locke's treatment of personal identity. This mistake involves Locke's confusing events or occurrences, which an instance of consciousness is, with a substance, which is what a person is. The identity of a person does not consist in that which is constantly changing:

> Our consciousness, our memory, and every operation of the mind, are still flowing like the water of a river, or like time itself. The consciousness I have this moment can no more be the same consciousness I had last moment, than this moment can be the last moment. Identity can only be affirmed of things which have a continued existence. Consciousness, and every kind of thought, is transient and momentary, and has no continued existence; and, therefore, if personal identity consisted in consciousness, it would certainly follow, that no man is the same person any two moments of his life [. . .]. (Ibid., 352)

A moment ago we discussed how Reid argues that every memory includes a reference to the "I" that is doing the remembering. Reid also comments on what this "I" is like and affirms that it has many of the qualities already ascribed to it by others who, like him, believe in the existence of the soul. Most importantly, he insists that the person or self is without parts and, therefore, cannot be divided:

> [I]t is sufficient for our purposes to observe, that all mankind place their personality in something that cannot be divided, or consist of parts. A part of a person is a manifest absurdity.
>
> When a man loses his estate, his health, his strength, he is still the same person, and has lost nothing of his personality. If he has a leg or an arm cut off, he is the same person he was before. The amputated member is no part of his person, otherwise it would have a right to

a part of his estate, and be liable for a part of his engagements; it would be entitled to a share of his merit and demerit—which is manifestly absurd. A person is something indivisible, and is what Leibnitz calls a *monad*.

My personal identity, therefore, implies the continued existence of that indivisible thing which I call myself. Whatever this self may be, it is something which thinks, and deliberates, and resolves, and acts, and suffers. I am not thought, I am not action, I am not feeling; I am something that thinks, and acts, and suffers. My thoughts, and actions, and feelings, change every moment—they have no continued, but a successive, existence; but that *self*, or *I*, to which they belong, is permanent, and has the same relation to all the succeeding thoughts, actions and feelings which I call mine. [. . .]

The identity of a person is a perfect identity; wherever it is real, it admits of no degrees; and it is impossible that a person should be in part the same, and in part different; because a person is a *monad*, and is not divisible into parts. (Ibid., 345)

Reid's view is that our acquaintance with our own perfect identity is the source of our idea of identity. Our conviction about our own identity is natural and with us from the dawn of our own thinking (ibid.). In Butler's terms, the notion of identity that we acquire from ourselves is strict and philosophical in nature. Reid maintains that, when we come to objects of sense perception, however, we fail to find anything that fulfills this strict concept of identity. The identity of objects of sense is, says Reid, never perfect:

All bodies, as they consist of innumerable parts that may be disjoined from them by a great variety of causes, are subject to continual changes of their substance, increasing, diminishing, changing insensibly. When such alterations are gradual, because language could not afford a different name for every different state of such a changeable being, it retains the same name, and is considered as the same thing. Thus we say of an old regiment, that it did such a thing a century ago, though there now is not a man alive who then belonged to it. We say a tree is the same in the seed-bed and in the forest. A ship of war, which has successively changed her anchors, her tackle, her sails, her masts, her planks, and her timbers, while she keeps the same name, is the same.

The identity, therefore, which we ascribe to bodies, whether natural or artificial, is not perfect identity; it is rather something which, for the conveniency of speech, we call identity. [. . .] But identity, when applied to persons, has no ambiguity, and admits not of degrees, or of more and less. (Ibid., 346)

All in all, Reid's view of the self is very Cartesian in nature. We know our own identity is perfect because we have a far better knowledge of ourselves than we do of material objects. Reid approvingly says the following about Descartes' observations concerning the soul:

It was not in the way of analogy, but of attentive reflection, that he was led to observe, That thought, volition, remembrance, and the other attributes of the mind, are altogether unlike to extension, to figure, and to all the attributes of body; that we have no reason, therefore, to conceive thinking substances to have any resemblance to extended substances; and that, as the attributes of the thinking substances are things of which we are conscious, we may have a more certain and immediate knowledge of them by reflection, than we can have of external objects by our senses. (Reid, *Inquiry*, 205)

Hume

Reid believes that we are intimately acquainted with ourselves and know much about the self and its identity. In his view, each of us is acquainted with himself as a simple substance—or what was historically known as the soul. His fellow Scotsman, David Hume (1711–1776), begs to differ. According to Hume, none of us has evidence that he is a substance that remains self-identical for however long that he exists. Rather, the evidence that an individual has concerning what he is supports, at best, the belief that he is a serial bundle of perceptions:

> For my part, when I enter most intimately into what I call *myself*, I always stumble on some particular perception or other, of heat or cold, light or shade, love or hatred, pain or pleasure. I never can catch *myself* at any time without a perception, and never can observe any thing but the perception. [. . .] If any one, upon serious and unprejudic'd reflection, thinks he has a different notion of *himself*, I must confess I can reason no longer with him. All I can allow him is, that he may be in the right as well as I, and that we are essentially different in this particular. He may, perhaps, perceive something simple and continu'd, which he calls *himself*; tho' I am certain there is no such principle in me. [. . .] I may venture to affirm of the rest of mankind, that they are nothing but a bundle or collection of different perceptions, which succeed each other with an inconceivable rapidity, and are in a perpetual flux and movement. Our eyes cannot turn in their sockets without varying our perceptions. Our thought is still more variable than our sight; and all our other senses and faculties contribute to this change; nor is there any single power of the soul, which remains unalterably the same, perhaps for one moment. The mind is a kind of theatre, where several perceptions successively make their appearance; pass, re-pass, glide away, and mingle in an infinite variety of postures and situations. There is properly no *simplicity* in it at one time, nor *identity* in different; whatever natural propension we may have to imagine that simplicity and identity. (Hume 1978: *A Treatise of Human Nature*, 252–253)

> When I turn my reflexion on *myself*, I never can perceive this *self* without some one or more perceptions; nor can I ever perceive any thing but the perceptions. 'Tis the composition of these, therefore, which forms the self. (*Treatise*, 634)

The problem with Hume's position, however, as others such as Chisholm have pointed out, is that it certainly seems as if Hume repeatedly finds the self, which he says he cannot find, stumbling on different perceptions (Chisholm 1994, 97). How can Hume truly say that he cannot find himself, if he is right when he says that he is aware of himself stumbling on certain things such as heat or cold, light or shade, love or hatred, pain or pleasure? The problem for Hume is that what he cites as evidence for the position that there are only perceptions and no substantial self implies not only that there is heat or cold, light or shade, pain or pleasure, and so on, but also that there is a substantial self that finds these things, which implies that the self that finds the heat or cold is *the same self* as that which finds light or shade and the rest. Hence, not only does Hume find perceptions, but he also finds that *he* is the one who finds them (Chisholm 1994, 97). The conclusion that Hume should have reached is that every time he stumbles upon some particular perception he simultaneously stumbles upon the substantive self that is stumbling.

If Anthony Quinton is right, however, there is more to Hume's argument than meets the eye. He believes that Hume's search for his self provides an insight into a possible argument against the existence of the soul as a permanent, unchanging substance, which remains the same over time. Commenting on Hume, Quinton says: "Hume's search for a self over and above his particular perceptions was bound to fail" (Quinton 1975, 55). It was bound to fail, because,

> if it is held that the spiritual substance is [. . .] a permanent and unfaltering constituent of a person's conscious life, it follows that it must be unobservable and so useless for purposes of identification. Suppose that from its very first stirrings my consciousness has contained a continuous whistling sound of wholly unvarying character. I should clearly never notice it, for I can only notice what varies independently of my consciousness—the whistles that start and stop at times other than those at which I wake up and fall asleep. (Ibid.)

Quinton's point seems to be this: because a soul, if it exists, is a permanent and unchanging element of, or presence in, a person's conscious life (it is always present in consciousness), it does not vary independently of that conscious life and, therefore, it is unobservable. Hence, it comes as no surprise that Hume's search for it ended in failure.

In explaining why Hume never found the permanent self for which he was looking, Quinton seems to be making the following argument:

1   If one is (introspectively) aware of a permanent and unchanging soul, then one is aware of it as permanent and unchanging.
2   One cannot be aware of what is permanent and unchanging.

   Therefore,

3   One is not aware of a permanent and unchanging soul.

This argument is valid; but are all of its premises true? We believe there is good reason to doubt premise (2). Our doubt presupposes that a soul, if it exists, is a substance, and a substance is an entity that has essential powers and capacities, where powers are the basis for its actions and capacities are the basis for its passions, or for what happens to it (as opposed to what it does). For example, a soul has the power to think, the power to choose, the capacity to believe, the capacity to desire, the capacity to experience pain, the capacity to experience pleasure, and so on. Furthermore, there is an important distinction between a power and its exercising, and a capacity and its actualization. Reid is alluding to this distinction when he writes: "I am not thought, I am not action, I am not feeling; I am something that thinks, and acts, and suffers" (Reid, *Essays*, 345). Now, exercisings of powers and actualizations of capacities are changes, but they are changes in that which remains permanent. Thus, when Hume seeks to find his self, he is aware of changes (thinkings, choosings, experiences of pleasure and pain, and so forth), but he is also aware of these changes as changes in powers and capacities that are unchanging in the sense that they are permanent properties of the soul that has them. Therefore, when Hume is aware of the powers and capacities of his soul as involved in change (when he is aware of their exercisings and actualizations), he is simultaneously aware of them as unchanging bases for this change. And, because a soul just is the immaterial or spiritual substance that has these powers and capacities, he is aware of his soul (himself) as a permanent and unchanging immaterial substance whenever he is aware of the changes that are exercisings of its powers and actualizations of its capacities.

In Quintonian spirit, Martin and Barresi claim that,

> [a]s simple, immaterial substances, souls are not part of the natural world. Whatever exists or obtains, but not as part of the natural world, is inherently mysterious. Other peoples' souls cannot be observed either directly or indirectly. And since only the activities and not the substance of the soul is [*sic*] open to empirical investigation, there is no way to detect by observing an individual whether his soul remains the same. Hence, on the soul view, personal identity is inherently mysterious. (Martin and Barresi 2000, 16–17)

Marin and Barresi favor a Lockean account of the self, in which personal identity is explained in terms of what is observable. "Only by explaining personal identity in terms of things or relations that are observable can an account of it be developed on the basis of which one can determine empirically whether a person at one time and one at another are the same" (Martin and Barresi 2000, 17).

It seems to us that Martin and Barresi's comments do not withstand scrutiny. While it is no doubt true to hold that in some sense souls are not part of the natural order (for example, in Chapter 6 we point out that souls are non-natural in the sense that their actions are ultimately explained teleologically and not causally), this in no way makes personal identity inherently mysterious on the soul view. As we have just pointed out in our response to Quinton, souls are directly aware of the exercisings of their own powers and actualizations of their own capacities; and, because these powers and capacities are essential properties of the substantial souls that have or exhibit them, souls are directly aware of themselves as substances. This awareness is certainly not empirical in the sense that a soul sees, hears, or tastes the exercisings of its powers and the actualizations of its capacities. But its reality is in no way compromised because of this. So Martin and Barresi are simply mistaken when they say that the soul's activities, but not its substance, are open to empirical investigation. Neither is open to empirical investigation in the sense just defined, but both are nevertheless open to direct introspective awareness.

Moreover, while it is surely true, as Martin and Barresi state, that the souls of others cannot be directly observed, the claim that these souls cannot be indirectly observed seems groundless. As Augustine argued and we summarized in Chapter 2, we are able to observe the correlations between events involving our own souls and bodies, and our belief in the existence of other souls is indirectly supported by our observation of the bodily behavior of others, where it seems reasonable to believe that this behavior is accompanied by events occurring in the souls of others. Hence, when Martin and Barresi say that "[o]ther peoples' remembering, unlike their souls, can be observed indirectly," because "by listening to another talk one may be able to determine that they remember having experienced or done various things" (Martin and Barresi 2000, 17), we respond "Yes" and "No." It is true that when we hear another person talk we are able, because of the content of that talk, to ascertain that events of remembering are associated with it. But, because events of remembering are events in souls, we are also able to observe indirectly the existence of those souls.

Kant

Immanuel Kant (1724–1804) is without question one of the most important figures in the history of thought, and this is the case despite the fact that when one reads his work one is often not sure what he is claiming. In the words of Martin and Barresi, "While it is hard to read Kant and not believe that he was up to something important, often it is equally hard to be sure what that something was" (Martin and Barresi 2006, 172). This is certainly the case with a good bit of Kant's thought about the soul. In what follows, we focus on what seems clearest to us in Kant's treatment of the soul.

As we pointed out in the last section, Reid maintained that we cannot reason without a firm conviction that the "I" remains self-identical throughout the course of that reasoning. Like Reid, Kant is concerned with the role of the "I" in thought. He points out that the "I" is the logical subject in thought. What Kant seems to have in mind is something like the following: The having, apprehending, or contemplating of a thought logically requires the existence of a substantive "I" that has, apprehends, or contemplates the thought, where this "I" must be an irreducible unity. For example, consider the thought that grass is green (here we follow Strawson 2009, 379–380). This thought contains distinguishable elements, namely, "grass," "is," and "green." These parts of the thought must be present to the same, single, unified consciousness or "I." Otherwise there will be no comprehension of the thought "grass is green." Thus, if the part "grass" is had by one "I," the part "is" is had by another "I," and the part "green" is had by yet another distinct "I," no "I" will have the thought "grass is green." For an "I" to have that thought, each of the parts of the thought must be simultaneously present to, and apprehended by, the same "I." In other words, there must be a unified consciousness to which the parts of the thought are presented: "That [. . .] the I in every act of thought is *one*, and cannot be resolved into a plurality of subjects, [. . .] is something that lies already in the concept of thought, and is therefore an analytic proposition" (Kant 1965: *Critique of Pure Reason*, B407).

Lest one draw too strong a conclusion from this argument, Kant seems intent on maintaining that he is calling our attention to what is no more than a logical prerequisite of any thought. He is not arguing for the actual existence of a substantial, unified, conscious "I." Strawson summarizes Kant's point this way:

Certainly "the I who thinks or is conscious must *in such thought or consciousness* always be *considered* as a *subject,* and as something that does not merely attach to thought or consciousness like a predicate," but—this is Kant's central point—nothing follows from this about how things actually are, metaphysically speaking. (Strawson 2006, 190)

Perhaps one cannot draw a conclusion about the way the self is from the logical prerequisites of thought. However, it seems to us that Kant's point has a good bit more weight to it than he is willing to concede. As we saw in Chapter 1 with Plato and Aristotle and the dawn of philosophizing about the soul, the fact that our psychological life seems unified is hard to miss. It is a fact of everyday experience, which encompasses more than just thought. Thus, as one of us sits typing this section, he is aware of a pain on the sole of his left foot and, simultaneously, he hears the whirring of a fan in the air conditioning unit behind his desk, he tastes the salt in his mouth from a recently eaten cracker, and he sees the computer screen in front of him. All of these contents of sensory experience are present to him in one unified consciousness (there is not one self seeing, another tasting, another hearing, and another feeling; Hasker 1999, 122–146).

But is this unified consciousness a simple soul? We have already examined this issue at some length in previous chapters. We have nothing more to add at this point, except to say that philosophers like Strawson (see Strawson 2006, 2009) strike us as all too ready to dismiss as illusory various deep features of the self, like the unity of consciousness and its simplicity. Of course, arguments are given, in an effort to explain why it is that the soul does not exist and/or does not have the features that it seems to have. We have already canvassed some of these arguments in this and preceding chapters, and we will state and examine more of them in the following two chapters. For now, our point is simply this: if it really is plausible to maintain that we are in error about deep matters of the self such as its apparent simplicity, then one cannot help but wonder how it is that we supposedly manage to avoid error in our thought about anything else in the world, most particularly about those things that are supposedly physical in nature. We will return to this point in Chapter 8.

At present, we turn to one other issue that Kant raises about the soul. This is the matter of its persistence through time as the numerically same thing. Thus, when one of us thought about writing this section an hour ago, the thought of it was had by his "I." Subsequently, this *same* "I" thought about getting a bite to eat. And now, the thought of wrapping up this section is occurring to the very *same* "I." In Kant's own words, "In my own consciousness, therefore, identity of person is unfailingly met with" (*Critique of Pure Reason*, A362). But this identity of the "I" through time, like its unity at a moment of time, is no more than a logical condition of thought: "The identity of the consciousness of myself at different times is therefore only a formal condition of my thoughts and their coherence, and in no way proves the numerical identity of my subject" (ibid., A363).

To bolster his case that the identity of the "I" through time as a formal condition of thought does not entail the actual identity of the "I" through time, Kant presents the following possibility:

An elastic ball which impinges on another similar ball in a straight line communicates to the latter its whole motion, and therefore its whole state (that is, if we take account only of the positions in space). If, then, in analogy with such bodies, we postulate substances such that the one communicates to the other representations together with the consciousness of them, we can conceive a whole series of substances of which the first transmits its state together with its consciousness to the second, the second its own state with that of the preceding substance to the third, and this in turn the states of all preceding substances together with its own consciousness and with their consciousness to another. The last substance would then be conscious of all the states of the previously changed substances, as being its own states, because they would have been transferred to it together with the consciousness of them. And yet it would not have been one and the same person in all of these states. (Ibid., A364)

This seems to amount to an argument for thorough-going skepticism. After all, the same kind of argument might be formulated against the believed identity of a physical object through time. Thus, for all that the one of us who is working on this section right now knows, the computer that he presently sees in front of him might be different from the computer that he was working on moments ago, even though he believes it to be numerically the same computer. This is so because, unbeknownst to him, the present computer might have had, passed on to it, all the states of its predecessor computer, which itself replaced an even earlier computer upon absorbing all of its states, and so on. As we pointed out a moment ago, if it really is plausible to maintain that we are in error about deep matters of the self—in this case, about its persistence as numerically the same entity through time—then one cannot help but wonder how it is that we supposedly manage to avoid error in our thoughts about anything else in the world (in this case, about the persistence of physical objects as numerically the same things through time). Kant seems to regard as unproblematic the existence of billiard balls that remain self-identical through time. But why? Surely there is no more reason to be confident about the persistence of billiard balls than there is to be confident about the persistence of the self.

However, in the end, what seems to be of first importance is not whether our belief about our actual persistence through time is correct, but whether our belief, entertained in the present moment, that we are a substance that can persist being self-identical through time is correct. If we are genuinely aware that we are substances capable of enduring through time, then it seems that thought experiments like Kant's have far less bite to them. Given that we know that we are entities of this kind, our attention turns to reasons why we believe that we have persisted remaining self-identical through time. And the evidence provided by our memories (which, as we have already seen earlier in this chapter, was a subject much discussed by Locke and others) seems as good as any other that we have. Indeed, as we will point out in Chapter 7, it seems that any claim about the persistence of objects through time will ultimately require trust in our memories.

With our brief survey of Kant's thought about the soul completed, we turn in the next chapter to a topic that has remained at the forefront of discussions of the soul ever since Descartes. This is the topic of the causal interaction between the soul and the physical body. Our discussion in Chapter 5 will essentially take us from the seventeenth into the twentieth century, as the two philosophers whose arguments we discuss in it are two of the twentieth century's foremost critics of the soul's existence. They are Ernest Sosa and Jaegwon Kim. To their arguments we now turn.

Chapter 5

The Problem of Soul–Body Causal Interaction

As we discussed in Chapter 3, Descartes' development and defense of soul–body dualism brought front and center the issue of causal interaction between a soul and its body. As we also pointed out in Chapter 3, Descartes said very little about the issue of causal interaction, because he believed it was primitive in nature and, therefore, inexplicable in terms of any other relationship. In words to Gassendi that we have already cited, Descartes believed "that the whole problem [of how the soul can move the body if it is in no way material] arises from a supposition that is false and cannot in any way be proved, namely that, if the soul and the body are two substances whose nature is different, this prevents them from being able to act on each other" (Descartes 1984: *Appendix to the Fifth Set of Objections and Replies*, 275). In this chapter we examine some criticisms of the view that the soul causally interacts with the physical body.

Causation and Dualism

According to Descartes, each of us regards his or her physical body as "my body" because of the causal relationship he or she has with that body. In terms of the first person, "my body" is that body which

A Brief History of the Soul, First Edition.
© 2011 Stewart Goetz and Charles Taliaferro. Published 2011 by Blackwell Publishing Ltd.

directly moves when I will (intend or choose) that it move and which, when it is causally affected by other physical objects, directly causes me to experience pleasure and pain and a miriad of other sensations. Ernest Sosa has acknowledged that this is a promising analysis of ownership, until we consider what it is in virtue of which a causal relation obtains (Sosa 1984). According to Sosa, a causal relation obtains only if the appropriate noncausal conditions obtain. Consider the following two examples:

> Someone takes a picture of you, a photograph. Your image is imprinted on a piece of film. The film is imprinted with an image of a face that looks a certain way *because* you have a certain physiognomy. But your physiognomy causes the image on the film only in virtue of the fact that certain conditions hold at a given time with respect to you and the piece of film. The film is in a camera aimed in your direction, and you and the camera are not too far apart, there are not obstacles obstructing the line of sight, you are facing the camera at the time, and there is enough light, and so on; and it is only in virtue of the fact that these conditions all hold that your facial appearance causes the image on the film. [. . .]
>
> Take another example. A karate expert hits a board and splits it in two. The board splits in two *because* of the blow by the man. And if this is so it is presumably in virtue of certain noncausal conditions that hold at the time, including the board's thickness; its composition; the angle, speed, and force of the blow, etc. And it seems quite evident, moreover, that if anything noncausally a perfect twin of that board, is hit by anyone noncausally a perfect twin of that man, with a blow exactly like that blow in all noncausal respects, then that new board must also split just as did the old, because of the blow. (Sosa 1984, 273)

Sosa's argument can be filled out as follows: According to the Cartesian dualist (a dualist who is sympathetic to Descartes' account of the soul), there are many physical bodies and many souls. Consider two souls, named Stewart and Charles, and assume that each chooses at the same time *t* to go to the refrigerator for a Bud Light. Further, assume that appropriate movements occur in a body B at *t* + 1 and that the willing by Stewart caused those movements in B. What noncausal relation might connect Stewart's willing with the movements in B, where that relation is absent between Charles and B? No spatial relation can do the trick, because souls are not in space and are unable to enter into spatial relations with material objects. Thus, Stewart cannot be closer to B than Charles, or more favorably positioned with respect to B than Charles. Are there any other noncausal properties and/or relations that make it the case that movements in B are causally produced by the willing of Stewart and not of Charles? Could it be the noncausal relationship of ownership, so that Stewart and B causally intereact because Stewart owns B? But what is the sense of "owns" here? Is it legal or moral? Did Stewart inherit B, or earn it as the fruits of his labor? The obvious answer to each of these questions is "No."

At this point, says Sosa, Cartesian dualists explicate ownership in terms of direct causal interaction. We are told by them that what makes a body such as B the body of a soul such as Stewart is that the two directly causally interact. But if we then go on to ask in virtue of what noncausal relation it is that B and Stewart directly causally interact, the Cartesian dualist is unable to provide us with an answer. The answer cannot be that B and Stewart causally interact in virtue of the fact that B is owned by Stewart, because ownership is supposed to be explained in terms of causal interaction. Moreover, ownership cannot be explained in terms of a certain spatial relation, because Stewart is supposedly not located in space. In the end, it seems as if all that can be said is that B, which is supposedly the body of Stewart, causally interacts with him, period. But, according to Sosa, this will not do:

> For it is useless to be told that what makes something subject to direct causal interaction with something else is that it is indeed subject to direct causal interaction with it. And that is precisely what the answer by reference to ownership [explained in terms of causation] [...] resolves to under analysis. [...] Our picture begins to look bleak for immortal

souls. What pairs physical objects as proper mates for causal interaction is in general their places in the all-encompassing spatial framework of physical reality. It is their spatial relations that pair the piece of film with the man photographed, and distinguishes [*sic*] him as the cause from the billions of other men in existence including exact look-alikes. [. . .] One consequence for interactionism is that there can be no interaction between an immaterial soul and a material body. That of course has been the view of so many, since Gassendi to the present, that it is firmly settled as a platitude of introductory philosophy. (Sosa 1984, 274–275, 278)

What can the Cartesian dualist say in response to Sosa's argument?

On Sosa's view, the causal terms (the individual substances) of a causal relation are not able to enter into such a relation in virtue of any causal properties they possess intrinsically or *per se*, but they only acquire their causal properties by first entering into a noncausal relation which is, say, spatial in nature. Stated differently, all causal properties are possessed extrinsically or in dependence upon entrance into a noncausal spatial relation. This view is very similar to the more general ontological thesis that substantial entities, including causal agents and patients, do not possess their numerical identity (they are not the particular things that they are) intrinsically (they are not intrinsically individuated or distinct from other particular things), but rather they possess their numerical identity in virtue of their spatial relations to other subjects (they are extrinsically individuated). As a relational account of the necessary conditions of causation, Sosa's account is also similar to Locke's account of personal idenity, which we explicated in Chapter 4 and in which a person's identity over time is dependent upon (constituted by) a memory relation, instead of being dependent upon (presupposing) the persistence through time of the intrinsically individuated self that is having the memory. What Sosa presupposes, then, in his criticism of the Cartesian account of causal interaction between soul and body is that a spatial relation is the primary ontological category, and not the substantial objects and their causal properties that are the terms of the relevant relations.

We believe that Sosa's account of causation is largely mistaken. Just as a spatial relation is not the individuating principle of the substantial objects that are its terms, but those objects are intrinsically individuated, so also a spatial relation is not the individuating principle of the relevant causal properties possessed by the terms of the causal relation, but these are individuated intrinsically and possessed essentially by their bearers. Moreover, a causal relation is a productive relation that obtains or is primarily a function of the causal power and capacity of the agent and patient objects respectively. A causal relation obtains when a substance that possesses causal power exercises that power to produce the actualization of a capacity. The power of an agent and the capacity of a patient are ontologically irreducible and intrinsic causal features of those objects. They are not derivative properties. A causal agent has a power to produce an effect, and a patient has the capacity to be affected by a causal agent, *before* entering into a causal relation. In Sosa's terminology, what *pairs* the agent and the patient objects in a causal relation is the agent's exercise of its causal power upon the patient, where this exercise of causal power actualizes the respective capacity of the patient. Like the causal properties of which it is a function, the causal relation is irreducible.

In light of these comments about the nature of causal properties, consider Sosa's examples of the board and karate expert and of the physiognomy and film. How can these examples be explicated in terms of essential and fundamental causal powers and capacities? In the case of the board and the karate expert, the board has a causal capacity to break, which is a function of its thickness and composition. The board's thickness and composition can reasonably be understood as determined by the organization or arrangement of the parts of the board. Each part of the board is immediately spatially related to a contiguous part and has the causal capacity to be split apart from its immediately contiguous part. Therefore the causal capacity of the board to be split can be explained in terms of the causally attractive powers and capacities of the parts that compose it, where those parts are held in certain bonding relationships by those powers and capacities. The capacity to be separated or split apart is identical with the capacity to be moved, the capacity to be moved being possessed intrinsically by any body. The capacity to be moved is properly understood as causal in nature in that it is actualized by a causal power. Thus a capacity to be separated from a contiguous part, where contiguous parts are held together by their attractive powers, is actualized by a causal power. If the parts of the board are themselves complex, their capacities to be split apart (moved) will be further explained in the way in which the original board's capacity to be broken is explained. Therefore, contrary to Sosa, rather than the thickness and composition of the board being noncausal conditions of the board's splitting upon being hit by someone such as the karate expert, they are explicable or analyzable in terms of causal capacities and powers. Finally, with regard to the speed and force of the karate expert's blow, it is plausible to think that these are also causal, not noncausal, features of the movement of the karate expert's arm and hand. The angle of the blow is a spatial relation between the board and the hand's movement.

What about photographic imaging? Accounts of imaging typically describe how reflected light in the form of photons, which are basic packets of *energy*, move through space in waves and leave a latent image on a piece of film. In order that the film forms a latent image, it is coated with imaging layers of grains of silver-halide crystals. Chemical substances that are sensitive to the different wave lengths of red, blue, and green light are added to these grains. The chemical substances *bond* or *adhere* to the grains through powers and capacities of attraction and transfer the energy of photons to the latter, which will be released through further chemical reactions in the development of the film. As was the case with the account of the board and the karate expert, the account of photographic imaging is a causal one, whose basic categories include micro-entities held together in structural relationships that are explicable in terms of exercised and actualized powers and capacities respectively; and those relationships are altered by the introduction of exercised power, which leads to the formation of new structural relationships among those micro-entities.

Enough has been said about these specific examples introduced by Sosa. In general, a causal relation obtains when a causal power is exercised and actualizes a capacity. This is an irreducible relation, which cannot be explained in noncausal terms. But is it, nevertheless, a dependent relation in the sense that it cannot obtain unless some other noncausal relation obtains? After all, Sosa could modify his original view and accept everything that we have said about causation up to this point, yet maintain that an agent can only exercise its causal power upon a patient when the two objects are spatially related. In this case, causation would be an irreducible but dependent relation.

We believe that a causal relation is dependent in nature. When there are two objects, one with the causal power to affect the other, these two objects must stand in a noncausal pairing relation that is such that the patient is *accessible to* the agent's exercised causal power in the sense that it can be causally affected by it. Were no such noncausal pairing relation to obtain, the agent would exercise its causal power without affecting the patient. What is not evident, however, is that this noncausal pairing relation upon which the causal relation depends must be spatial in nature. We conclude this section with an explanation of why this is not obvious.

To begin with, it seems false to maintain that standing in a spatial relation is sufficient for standing in a causal relation. While being spatial in this sense imposes the condition that the agent of a causal relation stands in a spatial relation to the patient of that relation, this does not imply, as Sosa suggests, that it is because, or in virtue of, this spatial relation that the causal agent is causally paired with the affected patient. As we have already explained, they are causally paired in virtue of the agent's exercise of its causal power, which is directed upon and actualizes the patient's capacity, and the agent has the power to do this and the patient has the capacity to have this done to it ontologically, if not temporally, prior to their entering into this spatial relation. Thus, if an agent and patient are in space, they will have to be in a spatial relation with each other when they enter into a causal relation. But their being spatially related is not sufficient for their being causally related. They could exist in the spatial relation without being causally related, because the one is not exercising its causal power upon the other.

A spatial relation between two objects is not a sufficient condition of a causal relation obtaining between them. Is it a necessary condition, even for objects with the requisite causal powers and capacities? Kim thinks so:

> Causal relations must be selective and discriminating, in the sense that there can be two objects with identical intrinsic properties such that a third object causally acts on one but not the other, and, similarly, that there can be two intrinsically indiscernible objects such that one of them, but not the other, causally acts on a third object. We believe that objects with identical intrinsic properties must have the same causal powers or potentials, both active and passive (some would identify the causal powers of an object with the set of its intrinsic properties). However, objects with the same causal powers can differ in the exercise [. . .] of their powers, vis-à-vis other objects around them. This calls for a principled way of distinguishing intrinsically indiscernible objects in causal situations, and it is plausible that spatial relations provide us with the principal means of doing this. (Kim 2005, 85)

What can the Cartesian dualist say at this juncture? It looks as if the fundamental issue is whether it is possible for a nonspatial object to exist. If such an object can exist, then it is not obvious in strictly a priori or conceptual terms that it cannot interact causally with an object located in space. Moreover, if a person has good reason for believing that he is a soul which is nonspatial in nature, and if he also has good reason to believe that a certain physical body is his in virtue of his causally interacting with it, then he has good reason to believe that there must be a noncausal pairing relation in which he stands to his body, where this relation is distinct from, yet makes possible, the causal interaction between his soul (him) and his body. This is the case, even if he cannot state what this noncausal pairing relation is. This position is different from that which says that "what makes something subject to direct causal interaction with something else is that it is indeed subject to direct causal ineraction with it" (Sosa 1984, 274–275), and consonant with interpretations of Descartes which maintain that he believed soul-body causal interaction is accounted for by a more basic metaphysical relationship (see Chapter 3).

The all-important question at this point is what reason a person might have for believing that he is a nonspatial entity. As we described in Chapter 3, Descartes maintains that a body is by definition a physical object, and therefore extended in space. Given that it is extended in this way, it is divisible into substantial parts. Because a soul is simple in nature in the sense that it is not divisible into such parts, it cannot be extended in space. If a Cartesian dualist has no reason to think that his way of carving up the world is suspect and he also believes that he causally interacts with his physical body, then it seems that he has strong support for his belief in the existence of a noncausal pairing relation between his nonspatial soul and its spatial physical body, a pairing that makes their causal interaction possible, even if he cannot specify what the requisite noncausal pairing relation is.

In response, Sosa might claim that no Cartesian who (for the reasons cited in the previous paragraph) thinks he is a nonspatial entity can reasonably believe that he causally interacts with a certain physical body, without also having a knowledge of a noncausal pairing relation in which he stands to that body and which makes it causally accessible to him. It seems to us, however, that such a claim is no more obvious than the nonobvious claim that a spatial relation is a necessary condition of causal interaction between two entities. Therefore, if a person is convinced that her reasons for believing that she is a nonspatial entity and that she causally interacts with a physical body are better than any reasons she is given for believing that there can be no noncausal pairing relation between a nonspatial soul and a physical body that makes possible causal interaction between the two, then she will be justified in asserting the existence of such a relation, even though she does not know what it is.

Why Not Locate Souls in Space?

A dualist, however, has another alternative: he could hold that he is a soul that is located in the same spatial framework as his physical body, such that the necessary noncausal pairing relation is provided by the shared spatial framework. Not surprisingly, Kim (2005) believes that this non-Cartesian dualist alternative raises more problems than it solves. In this section we state four of his criticisms of the idea of a spatial soul and we respond to them.

The first problem raised by Kim concerns the location of a soul that is in space. At what point in space is it to be found?

> If my soul, as a geometric point, is in my body, it must be either in the top half of my body or its bottom half. If it's in the top half, it must be either in its left or right half, and so on, and we should be able to corner the soul into as small and specific a region of my body as we like. And why should we locate my soul in my body to begin with? Why can't we locate all the souls of this world in one tiny place, say this pencil holder on my desk, like the many thousand angels dancing on the head of a pin?
>
> It would beg the question to locate my soul where my body, or brain, is on the ground that my soul and my body are in direct causal interaction with each other; the reason is that the possibility of such interaction is what is at issue and we are considering the localizability of souls in order to make mind–body causation possible. (Kim 2005, 89)

Kim's reasoning about how a non-Cartesian dualist begs the question concerning a soul's causal interaction with its body seems to go as follows: If a non-Cartesian dualist is wondering about what makes causal interaction between a soul (Stewart) and a body B possible, then he might think (because he believes that a cause and its effect must be spatially contiguous) that what makes it possible is the fact that Stewart is located where B is located. If he then wonders about what makes it the case that Stewart is located where B is located, he might answer that it is the fact that Stewart causally interacts with B. This answer obviously begs the question, however, because it is the possibility of such interaction that is at issue.

A non-Cartesian dualist need not, however, be guilty of this question-begging reasoning. The explanation for Stewart's being located in the space where B is located is not that Stewart causally interacts with B. The explanation is simply that that is where Stewart is located. As was pointed out in the previous section in response to Sosa's argument against Cartesian dualism, the terms of a causal relationship are ontologically prior to that causal relationship. No spatial object acquires its location by being in a causal relationship. Rather, it is able to enter into a causal relationship in virtue of its location. Moreover, a non-Cartesian dualist's reason for thinking that a soul is located in the space occupied by its physical body is simply the fact that that is where it seems to be located. For example, Philip Quinn suggests that, because an individual's perceptual perspectives on the physical world are located spatially in his physical body, it is preferable to think that the soul occupies a spatial point inside the physical body, where that spatial point is most likely in its brain (Quinn 1997). Even here, however, there is another alternative. For example, Kant endorsed the view, often favored by philosophers like Augustine and Aquinas (see Chapter 2), that the soul is present in its entirety at each point in space where it is natural to locate one of its sensations—which, for all intents and purposes, means that the soul is located in every part of the space occupied by the physial body. C. D. Broad summarizes Kant's view as follows:

> Now, as far as empirical facts go, Kant thinks that it would be reasonable to say that a person's soul is present equally at every place at which it would be natural to locate any of his sensations. [. . .] In general, Kant holds that there is nothing in our experience to support the [. . .] view that the soul is located at a certain point in the region occupied by the brain. He says that he knows of nothing which would refute the Scholastic doctrine that a person's soul is present as a whole in his body as a whole in every part of it. (Broad 1953, 130, 132)

This stance was also defended by Henry More (1614–1687), who understood the soul or self to be spatially extended. This was a significant departure from Descartes, who regarded spatial extension as a sufficient condition for being physical. (The idea that nonphysical things can be spatial is widespread in modern philosophies, from Berkeley's to G. E. Moore's and H. H. Price's, which treat visual sensations or sense data as spatial but distinct from physical bodies and processes.) We will make use of this view of the soul's spatial location when we discuss Kim's next three objections to locating a soul in space.

Kim's second objection to spatializing a soul concerns the noncausal pairing relation, what he calls "the pairing problem," which is required for causal interaction between a soul and a body. "If locating souls in space is to help with the pairing problem, it must be the case that no more than one soul can occupy a single spatial point; for otherwise spatial relations would not suffice to uniquely identify each soul in relation to other souls in space" (Kim 2005, 89). At least two responses to this argument are available to the non-Cartesian dualist.

First, the non-Cartesian could simply concede the point (thus no more than one soul could be in the space of its physical body at one time) and move on. Kim then asks: "But if [. . .] the exercise of [souls'] causal powers are constrained by spatial relations, why aren't souls just material objects, albeit of a very special, and strange, kind?" (2005, 90). While the issues raised by this question go well beyond the scope of the present chapter, a brief comment is warranted. What is non-negotiable for many dualists, Cartesian and non-Cartesian alike, is the idea that the soul is a substantively simple entity, in the sense that it has no parts which are themselves substances. As we have seen in previous chapters, historically, many dualists have espoused this view, and even contemporary naturalists have labeled the natural view of the self the Simple View of the self (Nagel 1986, 43–45). Given this Simple View, what is at issue is whether locating this simple self in space is sufficient for making it a material entity. We suspect that, if a non-Cartesian dualist became convinced of the truth of this sufficiency condition, she would simply concede the point to Kim but continue to maintain that she is a soul, because what is of first importance is the soul's substantive simplicity. We also suspect that Kim would not be appeased by this concession, because he would be reluctant to concede that the soul is a substantively simple entity. At this point, the debate about the soul's substantive simplicity would have to be joined.

The second response to Kim's objection takes the same kind of line that was taken in answering the issue concerning a noncausal pairing relation as it applied to nonspatial souls: given that the non-Cartesian dualist has a good reason for thinking that souls exist and are located in the spaces occupied by their physical bodies (in the present context, this reason might be the medieval scholastic/Kantian consideration that their sensations seem to be located in the spaces occupied by their physical bodies), she is justified in holding that there is a noncausal pairing relation that makes possible causal interaction between one soul and a body—but not another soul, which is located in the same space as the first, and that body. She is justified in holding this even if she does not know what that noncausal pairing relation is.

Kim's third argument against non-Cartesian dualism concerns how it is that a spatial soul can have the requisite structure to explain its causal abilities:

> [I]f a soul, all of it, is at a geometric point, it is puzzling how it could have enough structure to account for all the marvelous causal work it is supposed to perform and how one might explain the differences between souls in regard to their causal powers. You may say: A soul's causal powers arise from its mental structure, and mental structure doesn't take up space. But what is mental structure? What are its parts and how are the parts configured in a structure? [. . .] [I]t is unclear how a wholly nonspatial mental structure could account for a soul's causal powers. (Kim 2005, 90)

In response, it is necessary to distinguish, as dualists have historically done (see our discussions of Augustine, Aquinas, and Descartes in earlier chapters), between structure or complexity at the level of thing-hood or substancehood and structure or complexity at the level of properties. A soul that is by hypothesis simple (without structure or complexity) at the level of thinghood can be complex (structured) at the level of properties. Stated differently, a lack of substantive parts is compatible with a multiplicity of properties. This is the case whether a soul is nonspatial or spatial, and, if the latter, whether it is confined to a geometric point or located in its entirety at each point in space where it experiences sensations. Furthermore, it is plausible to think, as we have already suggested earlier in this chapter and as Kim himself recognizes (2005, 85), that an entity's essential pro-perties include, at least in part, if not in whole, its intrinsic powers and capacities. Hence it does not seem the least bit implausible to say that a soul's thinking, choosing, experiencing pain, and so on are explainable in terms of its having the powers to think and choose and of exercising them, and in terms of its having the capacity to experience pain and of this capacity being actualized.

Finally, if we assume, for the sake of discussion, that a soul occupies the same space as its physical body, Kim asks how it can be that the one does not exclude the other (2005, 90). Once again, it seems to us that the non-Cartesian dualist can take the line that, if she has a good reason for believing dualism and for believing that she occu-pies the same space as that which is occupied by her physical body, she can reasonably believe that there is this kind of joint occupancy, even if she cannot explain how it is possible. She might, however, think that the possibility of joint occupancy has something to do with the way in which the two kinds of entities occupy space. If a physical object occupies a region of space in virtue of each of its substantive parts occupying distinct sub-regions of that space, and a soul occupies a region of space by being present in its entirety at each point in that space, then perhaps the possibility of joint occupancy of the same region of space is a function of the different ways in which the two occupy that space. Joint occupancy might be no odder than what we find in cases of visual sensations. While some philosophers today are direct realists and believe that we directly observe the objects around us without the mediation of sensory experience, such a position faces well-known difficulties. For one, there is the famous time lag argument. Because light travels at a finite speed, you never see a remote object as it is at precisely the time you see it. You might claim to see a remote star, and yet the star no longer exists at the time you see it. For such a reason and others (the argument from illusion, arguments from dreaming) there is some reason for claiming that our observations of objects are mediated by sensations that are located in our visual field. Our visual field is extended spatially, and double occupancy of it by a sensation and the sensed physical object is only ruptured when our visual (or other sensory) field is radically disjointed from the world, as when a subject has hallucinations and has all the sensations of being on a ship in a tempest whereas he is actually safe on solid land.

Let us explore this point a little further. Our position is akin to a view sometimes called representational realism, but it is different in an important respect. According to representational realism, we do not directly see people, buildings, and mountains but representations of them, not unlike in watching a television screen. According to representational realism, it would be true to say that you see us if your visual field matches up with (for example) our coming over to shake your hand. We adapt a view that is similar, but different. We adapt what may be called integrative realism: when you see us coming to greet you, you do not have a representation of us and then have to infer that you see us, but rather we appear to you through your sensory modalities. In veridical (reliable) experiences, there is an integration and proper functioning of organs and sensations such that, when you have the visual, auditory, and tactile sense of our greeting you by name and of our shaking your hand, these constitute the reality of what is taking place: a meeting between you and us. Under these circumstances, we are truly interacting physically and mentally.

There is, as it were, a joint occupancy of sensations, intentions, and physical movement. However, our sensory experience is also capable of disintegration. It is possible (or so we suggest) that you might have all the sensations that are indistinguishable from the authentic encounter and yet be subject to a massive, sophisticated, and sustained audio, tactile, visual hallucination. In popular idiom, it is possible that you might have a host of experiences leading you to believe your experiences are reliable, and yet you might be in the matrix. Our point here, however, is not so much about skepticism as about *occupancy*. In reliable experiences, our auditory, visual, and tactile experience of ourselves reflects and mediates our physical (and psycho-physical) interaction. We encounter problems only when our sensory experiences become altered or unhinged from the event in question. A good example of your having a sound double occupancy is when you have sensory awareness of your limbs, you feel your arms, for example, as extended in space (this is sometimes called proprioception). There is a kind of double occupancy under healthy conditions (you have a sensory awareness of your actual, extended limbs). But, as Descartes himself realized, this concord can come apart: cases arise when someone has a limb amputated and yet retains the sensory experience of having a limb. The object of this kind of experience has been called a phantom limb.

Kim believes that a careful consideration of the various questions and puzzles that arise from locating souls in space will lead us to conclude that "whatever answers might be offered to these questions [will] likely look ad hoc and fail to convince" (2005, 90). We are inclined to agree with Kim that the answers we have proposed will look ad hoc to non-dualists such as him. For example, anyone like Kim, who is persuaded that the physical world is causally closed to the causal activity of souls (see Chapter 6), will find it hard to avoid thinking anything else about these answers. But, for anyone who is either a dualist or not a convinced non-dualist, the responses that we have given to Kim will not seem ad hoc, regardless of whether or not they convince.

Property/Event Dualism or Dual Aspect Theory

It seems, then, that substance dualism (whether Cartesian or non-Cartesian) has more going for it than its critics typically admit. While the nature of the causal relationship between a soul and its physical body is mysterious, it is doubtful that this mystery rises to the level of a decisive objection against dualism. This is not only because of the reasons that support the truth of dualism, which we have discussed in this chapter and elsewhere (see Goetz 2005 and Taliaferro 1994), but also because causation of any kind, even among physical objects, is ultimately mysterious. Some philosophers argue cogently that causation among physical objects will ultimately be fundamental. That is, there may be certain causal powers (electric charge or spin) possessed by micro-particles that are foundational or intrinsic to the objects themselves, and not further accounted for by even more basic powers that underlie and explain the charge or spin. Arguably, if there is any causation at all, some causal powers will turn out to be basic, and not derived from more basic powers. If this is not a deeply vexing mystery for physical causation, it should not be one for nonphysical causation.

Nevertheless, in an effort to avoid what they believe to be the intractable problems of causal interaction in substance dualism, some philosophers have advocated a compromise between it and thorough-going physicalism or materialism (the view that denies that anything mental or psychological exists). This intermediate position affirms that any substance that exists is physical in nature, but that some physical substances have two kinds of properties and/or events, namely physical and mental or psychological. This "property/event dualism" or "dual aspect theory" is buttressed by various arguments, one of the best known of which is called "the Mary argument." What follows below is a version of it:

> Mary is a hypothetical scientist who, for whatever reason, has spent her entire life up until now locked in a room and has never experienced

pain. While locked in the room, Mary has devoted her life to learning all the physical facts that can be known about pain, such as that pain is produced by such-and-such physical objects that cause so-and-so neural happenings that lead people to utter expletives, etc. Her knowledge is exhaustive. One night, Mary is freed from the room and is invited to go bowling. As she picks up the bowling ball, she accidentally drops it on her foot and bleeps out an expletive. She asks her host what it is that she has just experienced and he informs her that she experienced pain.

Did Mary learn something new about pain? The obvious answer is "Yes." She learned for the first time what the intrinsic nature of pain is. While in the room, she only learned about extrinsic, relational features of pain. The conclusion of the Mary argument is that there are more kinds of fact (non-physical or mental/psychological facts) than physical ones, and therefore that physicalism is false. Why could not Mary learn from her studies about the intrinsic nature of pain during the time when she was in the room? Part of the answer seems to be that the ouchiness of pain (the feel, or sentient nature of pain) can only be known from the first-person perspective that Mary lacked with respect to pain. None of the features of the physical world as identified by the physical sciences (mass, size, weight, electric charge, physical structure and constitution) captures what it is to experience pain (or to think, feel, smell, taste, etc.). Another part of the answer as to why Mary learns something more when the bowling ball hits her foot seems to be that physical explanations of the intrinsic natures of things/events are typically given in terms of part–whole compositional and spatial relationships. Take the solidity of tables on which our computers presently sit. The solidity of our tables vis-à-vis the computers is explained in terms of a lattice structure of micro-parts, held together by attractive bonds that are sufficiently strong to withstand pressures to be split apart, which are exerted by the computers. Such explanations, however, will not work for an experience of pain, because it is a defining characteristic of it that it lacks a compositional event structure. It is simple in nature in the sense that it is not made up of event parts.

The Mary argument can be cast in terms of colors, smells, tastes, and so on. Its basic point is that there must be in the world two kinds of irreducible properties/events, physical and non-physical ones, which are exemplified by some substances. Nagel is an advocate of this property/event dualism (Nagel 1986, Chapter 3). What is of interest in the present context is whether property/event dualism is more successful than substance dualism at elucidating the relationship between what is mental or psychological and what is physical. Recall that the problem of causal interaction is supposedly intractable for substance dualism and provides a reason for disavowing the view. Does property/event dualism do a better job of connecting what is mental or psychological with what is physical? Consider what Nagel says on the matter:

> We have at present no conception of how a single event or thing could have both physical and phenomenological [e.g., ouchiness] aspects, or how if it did they might be related. [. . .] But if, as in the case of pain, our original concept already picks [it] out by an essential feature [ouchiness], then further discoveries about its nature have to be of things connected with this feature in a more intimate way.
>
> I am not sure of the exact character of the connection. Let us suppose, as seems unavoidable, that according to dual aspect theory both the mental and the physical properties of a mental event are essential properties of it—properties which it could not lack. [. . .] They couldn't just be *slapped together*. Both must be essential components of a more fundamental essence. As for the connection between them, it seems likely that in a rationally designed world the mental properties would be at least supervenient on the physical—a particular type of physical process being a sufficient but not inevitably a necessary condition of a particular type of mental process. (Nagel 1986, 47–48)

Nagel laments our ability to overcome the apparent contingency between the mental and physical:

We cannot directly see a necessary connection, if there is one, between phenomenological pain and a physiologically described brain state any more than we can directly see the necessary connection between increase in temperature and pressure of a gas at constant volume. In the latter case the necessity of the connection becomes clear only when we descend to the level of molecular description: till then it appears as a contingent correlation. In the psychophysical case we have no idea whether there is such a deeper level or what it could be; but even if there is, the possibility that pain might be necessarily connected with a brain state at this deeper level does not permit us to conclude that pain might be directly analyzable in physical [. . .] terms.

Even if such a deeper level existed, we might be permanently blocked from a general understanding of it. (Nagel 1986, 48–49)

Nagel says that pain might be necessarily connected with a brain state at some deeper level, but we might never know how it is so connected. Given that an experience of pain is a simple event, we know how a brain state could not be connected with it. It could not be connected through some type of part–whole analysis. What we are left with, then, on the assumption of the dual aspect theory, is that an experience of pain and a brain state are connected, though how they are connected is presently unknown to us and perhaps permanently beyond our ken. If this is the case, how is property/event dualism any superior to substance dualism, when it comes to elucidating the relationship between what is mental or psychological in nature and what is physical in nature? Is not Nagel simply reiterating Descartes' claim that the relationship is primitive? Or at least it is primitive as things presently stand? And if Descartes were concerned that Nagel might get one up on him by claiming that the nature of the relationship between an experience of pain and a brain state might one day become more perspicuous to us, he could make the same claim for the causal relationship between a soul and a body. Hence, in terms of the problem of causal interaction, there is no reason to prefer property/event dualism over substance dualism.

Why, then, does Nagel endorse the former and not the latter? His answer to this question is instructive. According to Nagel, the natural conception of the self is of an entity that is simple (without substantive parts) and indivisible (Nagel 1986, 33, 34–36, 43). However, Nagel rejects the hypothesis of the existence of the soul as an entity that is both substantively simple and indivisible, on the grounds that it is unnecessary to *postulate* its existence as the bearer of mental states, when a physical object like the brain can play this role (Nagel 1986, 29). What should be clear by now is that Nagel is misrepresenting the substance dualist position when he suggests that the soul is an entity whose existence is postulated as the bearer of mental properties. After our brief history of the soul from Plato through to Kant, it should be obvious that substance dualists are more likely to claim that the soul exists on the grounds that the self just seems to be, as Nagel concedes, a substantially simple, indivisible entity.

With this point in mind, we turn in the next chapter to the soul's existence in relationship to modern science. Some have claimed that modern science poses its own unique problems for the soul's existence. No brief history of the soul should omit a discussion of the issue; and to that discussion we now turn.

Chapter 6

The Soul and Contemporary Science

There is a resurgence of interest in the soul in light of contemporary developments in science and scientific methodology itself. The general sentiment among those in philosophy who write on the topic is that both developments in science and the methodology of science itself make belief in the soul suspect. One cannot help but wonder if this alleged challenge from science against belief in the soul's existence is much ado about nothing. In this chapter we explain why we believe that it is.

The Soul and the Brain

What might be discovered in science that poses problems for the belief in the existence of soul? According to Nancey Murphy, the main culprit is localization studies, in which regional structures or distributed systems in the brain are found to be correlated with psychological capacities like language, sight, and emotion. What the evidence from these studies supposedly suggests is that the brain itself, as opposed to the soul, is the subject of these capacities:

> A major part of current neuroscience research involves mapping regions of the brain (neuroanatomy) and studying the functions of the various regions (neurophysiology). Studies of this sort intersect,

A Brief History of the Soul, First Edition.
© 2011 Stewart Goetz and Charles Taliaferro. Published 2011 by Blackwell Publishing Ltd.

in fascinating ways, the philosophical issues [concerning the relationship of the mind to the brain]. First they provide dramatic evidence for physicalism. As neuroscientists associate more and more of the faculties once attributed to mind or soul with the functioning of specific regions or systems of the brain it becomes more and more appealing to say that it is in fact the brain that performs these functions. [. . .] With the development of CAT scans (computerized axial tomography) it has become possible to study correlations between structural abnormalities and behavior of people while they are alive. MRI scans (magnetic resonance imaging) now provide more detailed pictures, more easily revealing locations of brain damage. PET scans (positron emission tomography) allow research correlating localized brain activity with the performance of specialized cognitive tasks. (Murphy 1998, 13)

Specific examples of what Murphy has in mind are as follows: because the left of the two brain hemispheres is usually dominant for speech, "[l]eft-sided brain lesions can cause a searching for words, a limitation of vocabulary, a shortening of sentences, or a jumble of meaningless words" (Parkes 2004, 46–47). Early degeneration of neurons in the hippocampus of the brain (located in the right and left temporal lobes of the cerebral cortex) results in disturbances in working memory, whereby persons may have increasing difficulty either remembering where they placed items, recalling the names of persons to whom they were recently introduced, "or following the narratives of stories they are reading or watching on television" (Weaver 2004, 87). Multiple sclerosis can produce fronto-temporal-limbic damage in the brain, which results in an overflow of sadness, mirth, or despair (Parkes 2004, 45). In Alzheimer's disease neurons die, small holes appear throughout brain tissue, and the cerebral cortex looks shriveled in CT scans of the brain (Weaver 2004, 81). According to Malcolm Jeeves, "The nature of the [causal] interdependence increasingly uncovered by scientific research makes a substance dualism harder to maintain without tortuous and convoluted reasoning" (Jeeves 2004, 240).

Surely, however, Jeeves overstates the case against soul–body dualism. As Murphy herself points out,

[i]t is important to note that this evidence [from neuroanatomy and neurophysiology] will never amount to proof: it will always be possible for the dualist to claim that these [mental] functions belong to the mind and that mental events are merely *correlated* with events in particular regions of the brain. (Murphy 1998, 13)

After all, correlation between two things (capacities, events) is not sufficient to establish their identity. Two distinct things can be correlated and genuinely remain two distinct things. In the case of a soul and a brain, there could be soul functions and events correlated with brain functions and events. C. Stephen Evans not only agrees that correlation is not identity, but also wonders why people like Murphy (and Jeeves) are taken in by the findings of localization studies in the first place:

What, exactly, is it about these findings that are supposed to create problems for dualism? Presumably, the mere fact that the mind is causally impacted by the brain is not a problem, since most dualists have been interactionists eager to maintain that the body (and indeed the wider physical world), can in some way affect the mind. Is it a problem for dualism that this causal action takes place through the brain, rather than, say, the heart as Aristotle thought? It is hard to see why this should be a problem. Is it a problem that the causal effects should be the product of specific regions of the brain? Why should the fact that the source of the effects are localized regions of the brain, rather than the brain as a whole, be a problem for the dualist? It is hard for me to see why dualism should be thought to entail that the causal dependence of the mind on the brain should only stem from holistic states of the brain rather than more localized happenings. [. . .] We did not need neurophysiology to come to know that a person whose head is bashed in with a club quickly loses his or her ability to think or have any conscious processes. Why should we not think of neurophysiological findings as giving us detailed, precise knowledge of something that human beings have always known, or at least could have known, which is that the mind (at least in this mortal life) requires and depends on a functioning brain? We now know a lot more than we used to know about precisely *how* the mind depends on the body. However, *that* the mind depends on the body, at least prior to death, is surely not something discovered in the twentieth century. (Evans 2005, 333–334)

If Evans is correct, and we believe that he is, then what persuades people like Murphy and Jeeves that physicalism is to be preferred to dualism? At one point, she says that "science has provided a massive amount of evidence suggesting that we need not postulate the existence of an entity such as a soul or mind in order to explain life and consciousness" (Murphy 1998, 18). And Jeeves claims that "[s]ome [dualists] take a 'soul-of-the-gaps' position, much like the older 'god-of-the-gaps position,' using the concept of the 'soul' to explain those human experiences that we cannot (yet, at least) explain neurologically or biologically" (Jeeves 2004, 245).

In light of our survey, in previous chapters, of some of the major figures in the history of thought about the soul, it is hard to make a plausible case for the view that people who believe in the existence of the soul view it as a hypothetical entity whose existence is postulated in a god-of-the-gaps fashion, to account for human experiences that cannot yet be explained in physical terms. Indeed, the view seems to be thoroughly groundless. Without question, those in the Plato–Augustine–Descartes line (which includes Butler and Reid) believe in the soul's existence on the basis of what they are aware of from the first-person perspective. There is not the least bit of evidence for the idea that they arrive at their belief in the soul's existence after failing to explain various experiences in terms of what goes on in the physical world. Even in the case of Aristotle and Aquinas, who do not stress very much the first-person perspective in their thoughts about the soul, one does not find a belief in the soul that is justified in terms of the soul serving as an entity postulated in order to plug gaps in an explanatory story that cannot be completed in physical terms. On the contrary, both believe that there is positive evidence for the soul's existence. For example, each one affirms that the intellect is of such a nature that it does not make use of a bodily organ. Moreover, each one is aware of the unity of consciousness in sense experience. Thus it is reasonable to maintain that these philosophers believe in the existence of the soul, at least in part, on the basis of the nature of our psychological lives. It is true that Plato, Aristotle, Augustine, and Aquinas all believe that the soul is that entity that gives life to its body, but none of them ascribes this function to the soul on the basis of not being able to ascertain how the body could be alive on its own. Quite the opposite is the case. It was unthinkable to them that anything could have life without a soul, because the soul was by definition that which gives life. Descartes is a maverick in the history of thought when he claims that the body should be viewed as a machine that is not given life by the soul. But not even he reasons to the soul's existence on the basis of not being able to explain certain bodily motions or functions on physical mechanical principles alone. As we have already stressed, he believes in the soul's existence on the basis of first-person experience.

In light of the fact that the soul-of-the-gaps argument finds no support whatsoever from the major figures in the history of thought about the soul, one cannot help but be perplexed by Murphy's concession that, even in the face of localization studies, it will always be possible for the dualist to claim that mental functions belong to the soul and that mental events are merely correlated with events in particular regions of the brain. Why would one expect the dualist to do anything else, given that a correlation between events does not establish their identity? Any believer in the existence of the soul will wonder why he or she should not continue to believe in its existence so long as there is no good reason to give it up.

The Soul and Scientific Methodology

Instead of appealing to discovered correlations between what is mental and what goes on in the brain, some argue that the methodology of science makes belief in the soul unreasonable because it makes impossible any explanation of the movements of a human body in terms of a soul's purposeful action. For example, in an article entitled "Soul Talk," Stephen T. Asma writes: "Science seems entirely justified in its soul skepticism. [. . .] Modern medicine is a testament to the genius of methodological materialism and a mechanical [non-purposeful] approach to the human being" (Asma 2010, B6, B8). If Asma is correct, the methodology of science makes belief in the soul unreasonable because it makes impossible any appeal to the causal interaction between a soul and its physical body.

By way of giving a prolegomenon to setting forth this argument from scientific methodology, it behooves us to have a reasonably clear and concise picture of how souls are assumed by many to be causally related to their physical bodies on occasions when those souls make what we will assume are essentially undetermined choices (from here on, we will simply assume that choices are essentially undetermined). This picture is as follows: on certain occasions, we have reasons for performing incompatible actions. Because we cannot perform both actions, we must make a choice to do one or the other (or neither), and, whichever choice we make, we make that choice for a reason or purpose, where that reason provides an ultimate and irreducible teleological explanation of that choice (thus undetermined choices are not inexplicable choices). The making of a choice is a mental event that occurs in a soul, and either it or some other mental event associated with it (e.g. an intention to act) directly causally produces an effect event in that soul's physical body. In other words, there is mental-to-physical causation, and its occurrence is ultimately and irreducibly explained teleologically, by appeal to the reason that explains the making of the choice.

To put some flesh on the proverbial bones, consider the movements of our fingers right now on the keys of our keyboards as we work on different parts of this chapter. If these movements ultimately occur because of a choice, by each one of us, to type a portion of this chapter, then these physical movements are ultimately and irreducibly explained teleologically in terms of the purpose we had when we chose to write this chapter—which, we suppose, was to make clear that there are no good objections from science to the view that human beings are soul–body compounds. Hence, if the movements of our fingers are ultimately occurring because we made choices to write this chapter for a purpose, then mental events in each of our souls must be *causing* those movements to occur as we write this chapter for the purpose of making clear that there are no good objections to the view that human beings are soul–body compounds. In other words, if the view of a human being as a soul–body compound is correct, then souls cause events to occur in the physical world by making choices such as the choice to write this chapter for a purpose.

From the example of our typing this chapter, it should be clear that the claim that there is causal interaction between a soul and its physical body is *not* a "god-of-the-gaps" type of argument. As we intimated in the previous section, critics (e.g. Jeeves) often argue that theists postulate God's existence in light of an inability of science to provide a complete explanation for a physical datum (or data). This lack of a complete explanation is a gap in the scientific story. By analogy, these critics argue that a dualist postulates the existence of souls in light of an inability of science to provide a complete explanation for the movements of our fingers when we type this chapter. But this argument would be mistaken. The dualist claim is *not* that there are certain physical events (the movements of our fingers), the failure to find a complete physical causal story of which warrants appeal to the causal activity of a soul as their ultimate explanation. Rather, the claim is that an ordinary understanding of the purposeful activity of a soul–body compound entails that some physical events must occur whose ultimate causal explanation is not other physical events, but nonphysical mental events whose occurrences are explained teleologically by purposes.

What precisely is wrong with this understanding of a human being as a soul causally interacting with its body? As we have already pointed out, according to many philosophers, a serious problem for the view that souls make choices that causally produce events in physical bodies arises out of the methodology of science. Richard Taylor puts forth a lengthy argument in support of this problem, the gist of which is as follows:

> Consider some clear and simple case of what would [...] constitute the action of the mind upon the body. Suppose, for example, that I am dwelling in my thought upon high and precarious places, all the while knowing that I am really safely ensconced in my armchair. I imagine, perhaps, that I am picking my way along a precipice and visualize the destruction that awaits me far below in case I make the smallest slip. Soon, simply as the result of these thoughts and images, [...] perspiration appears on the palms of my hands. Now here is surely a case, if there is any, of something purely mental, unobservable, and wholly outside the realm of physical nature bringing about observable physical changes. [...] Here, [...] one wants to say, the mind acts upon the body, producing perspiration. (Taylor 1992, 20)

However, Taylor cautions us about such a simple supposition:

> But what actually happens, alas, is not nearly so simple as this. To say that thoughts in the mind produce sweat on the hands is to simplify the situation so grossly as hardly to approximate any truth at all of what actually happens. [...] The perspiration [...] is secreted by tiny, complex glands in the skin. They are caused to secrete this substance, not by any mind acting on them, but by the contraction of little unstriated muscles. These tiny muscles are composed of numerous minute cells, wherein occur chemical reactions of the most baffling complexity. [...] These [...] connect eventually, and in the most dreadfully complicated way, with the hypothalamus, a delicate part of the brain that is centrally involved in the emotional reactions of the organism. [...] [B]ut it is not seriously considered by those who do know something about it that mental events must be included in the description of its operations. The hypothalamus, in turn, is closely connected with the cortex and subcortical areas of the brain, so that physical and chemical changes within these areas produce

corresponding physical effects within the hypothalamus, which in turn, by a series of physical processes whose complexity has only barely been suggested, produces such remote effects as the secretion of perspiration on the surface of the hands. (Ibid., 20–21)

Taylor concludes his survey of the anatomy involved in emotional perspiration:

The important point, however, is that in describing it as best we can, there is no need, at any stage, to introduce mental or nonphysical substances or reactions. (Ibid., 21–22)

According to Taylor, while we are inclined to believe that certain physical events in our bodies are ultimately explained by mental events of nonphysical substances, as a matter of fact there is no need at any point to step outside of the physical causal story to explain the occurrences of those physical events. Kim uses the example of a neuroscientist to make the same point:

You want [or choose] to raise your arm, and your arm goes up. Presumably, nerve impulses reaching appropriate muscles in your arm made those muscles contract, and that's how the arm went up. And these nerve signals presumably originated in the activation of certain neurons in your brain. What caused those neurons to fire? We now have a quite detailed understanding of the process that leads to the firing of a neuron, in terms of complex electrochemical processes involving ions in the fluid inside and outside a neuron, differences in voltage across cell membranes, and so forth. All in all we seem to have a pretty good picture of the processes at this microlevel on the basis of the known laws of physics, chemistry, and biology. (Kim 1996, 131–132)

So, by Kim's lights, the physical story is unproblematic, but the account of raising one's arm becomes deeply puzzling when an immaterial mind is involved.

If the immaterial mind is going to cause a neuron to emit a signal (or prevent it from doing so), it must somehow intervene in these electrochemical processes. But how could that happen? At the very interface between the mental and the physical where direct and unmediated mind–body interaction takes place, the nonphysical mind must somehow influence the state of some molecules, perhaps by electrically charging them or nudging them this way or that way. Is this really conceivable? Surely the working neuroscientist does not believe that to have a complete understanding of these complex processes she needs to include in her account the workings of immaterial souls and how they influence the molecular processes involved. [. . .] Even if the idea of a soul's influencing the motion of a molecule [. . .] were coherent, the postulation of such a causal agent would seem neither necessary nor helpful in understanding why and how our limbs move. [. . .] Most physicalists [. . .] accept the causal closure of the physical not only as a fundamental metaphysical doctrine but as an indispensable methodological presupposition of the physical sciences. [. . .] If the causal closure of the physical domain is to be respected, it seems prima facie that mental causation must be ruled out. (Kim 1996, 132, 147–148)

While Kim agrees with Taylor about the lack of a need on the part of a scientist to go outside the physical explanatory story, he introduces the stronger idea that, to be successful, the physical sciences need to make the methodological assumption of the causal closure of the physical world. Is he right about this? To ensure clarity about what is at issue, consider one more example of movements of our bodies that, according to soul–body dualism, could only be adequately explained by mental causation exercised by a soul whose choice is teleologically explained by a purpose or reason. Right now, each of us is tired and feels tight in his back after typing for several minutes, so we raise our arms in order to relax. Reference to our mental activity and our purpose for acting seems not only helpful but also necessary to explain both the movements of our fingers on the typewriters while we are typing and the subsequent motions of our arms when we relax.

If we assume for the sake of discussion that we, as souls, cause our fingers and arms to move by directly causing some neural events in the motor sections of our brains, then, when we move our fingers and raise our arms for one purpose or another, we must directly cause initial neural events in our brains that ultimately lead to the movements of those extremities. In other words, in order to explain adequately (teleologically) the movements of our limbs, there must be causal openness or a causal gap in each of our brains.

In asserting the need for a teleological explanation of our finger and arm movements when we type and stretch, we are not claiming that we are always right when we provide a teleological explanation of another person's behavior. We might sometimes be wrong. But it is a huge step to conclude, from "some teleological explanations of behavior are false," that "there is ultimately no role for teleological explanations of behavior." Moreover, while we might be mistaken about whether your behavior was merely reflexive or purposeful, we are in a far better epistemic position to know whether our own behavior was purposeful or not. The following words of Alfred North Whitehead are apropos: "Scientists [and, we would add, philosophers] animated by the purpose of proving that they [and their behaviors] are purposeless constitute an interesting subject for study" (Whitehead 1958, 16).

While Kim believes that soul–body dualism implies causal openness in our brains, he also believes that it is because soul–body dualism implies the existence of this causal gap that it must be mistaken. Because the neuroscientist methodologically assumes causal closure of the physical world, what she discovers as an explanation for what occurs in our brains and limbs when we type and relax must not, and need not include reference to the mental causal activity of our souls and to the ultimate and irreducible explanatory purpose for their choice to act. Given that the principle of causal closure entails the exclusion of a soul's mental causation of a physical event and the ultimate and irreducible teleological explanation of that mental event and of its effects by a purpose, it is imperative that we examine the methodological argument from causal closure, to see if it provides a good reason to believe that the movements of our fingers and arms when we are typing and stretching must be *completely* explicable in terms of neuroscience (or any other physical science)—with the result that no reference to the causal activity of our souls and their purposes for typing and raising our arms is required.

Contrary to what Kim maintains, there is good reason to think that the argument from causal closure is unsound. To understand where it goes wrong, let us distinguish between a neuroscientist as an *ordinary human being* and a neuroscientist as a *physical scientist*. Surely a neuroscientist as an ordinary human being who is trying to understand how and why our fingers move and how our arms go up while we are typing and stretching must and would refer to us and our reasons (purposes) for acting in a complete account of why our limbs move. Must she, however, as a physical scientist, avoid making such a reference? Kim claims that she must avoid such a reference because, as a physical scientist, she must make a methodological assumption about the causal closure of the physical world. Is Kim right about this and, if he is, is such a commitment compatible with a commitment, on the part of a physical scientist as an ordinary human being, to causal openness? Or must a neuroscientist, who as a physical scientist assumes causal closure, also assume, if he is consistent, that his mention, as an ordinary human being, of choices and their teleological explanations is no more than an explanatory heuristic device that is necessary because of an epistemic gap in his knowledge concerning the physical causes of human behavior?

In order to answer these questions, it is necessary to consider what it is about physical entities that a physical scientist such as a neuroscientist is often trying to discover in his experimental work. What is the purpose of a neuroscientist's inquiry? In the case of Kim's neuroscientist, what she is trying to discover as a physical scientist is the *capacities* of particles or micro-physical entities such as neurons to be causally affected by exercised causal *powers* of other physical entities, including other neurons. For example, in his pioneering work on the brain, Wilder Penfield produced movements in the limbs of patients by stimulating their cortical motor areas with an electrode (Penfield 1975). As Penfield observed the neural impulses that resulted from stimulation by the electrode, he had to assume *during his experiments* that the areas of the brains of his patients on whom he was doing his scientific work were causally closed to other causal influences. Without this methodological assumption, he could not conclude both that it was the electrode (as opposed, say, to something "behind the scene"—such as an empirically undetectable human soul, be it that of the patient, of someone else, or of God) that causally affected the capacities of the neurons to conduct electrical impulses, and that it was the causal impulses of those neurons that causally affected the same capacities of other neurons further down the causal chain, so as to produce the movements of the limbs. There is no reason, however, to think that, because Penfield's investigation of the brain required the methodological assumption of causal closure in the areas of the brains he was studying during his experiments, he also had to be committed, as a physical scientist, to the assumption that the physical world is *universally* (in *every* context) causally closed, where universal causal closure entails that the relevant brain (neural) events can *only* be causally produced by events of other physical entities—and not, instead, by mental events of immaterial souls alone, when they indeterministically choose and intend (plan) to act for purposes. That is, there is no reason to think that, because a neuroscientist like Penfield must assume causal closure of a delimited area of the brain in the context of his experimental work in order to discover how physical entities causally interact with each other, he must also be committed, as a scientist, to the universal explanatory exclusion of mental events of souls that on certain occasions would cause the occurrence of events in the physical world. All that the neuroscientist as a physical scientist must assume is that, during his experiments, souls (either the patients themselves or others) are not causally producing the relevant events in the micro-physical entities located in the areas of the brain that he is studying. If the neuroscientist makes the universal assumption that in *any* context events in micro-physical entities can only have other physical events as causes and can never be causally explained by mental events of souls and their purposes, then he does so not as a scientist but as a *naturalist*—where a naturalist is a person who believes that the occurrence of physical events can *only* be explained in terms of the occurrence of other physical events and without any reference to ultimate and irreducible purposes of souls or mental agents.

It is relevant to note in this context that Penfield himself was not a naturalist. Rather, he was a soul–body dualist (Penfield 1975, 76, 80). One can surmise, then, that, were Penfield to have been presented with the argument from causal closure, he would have found it wanting. And for good reason. In seeking to understand how events of different physical entities affect the capacities of micro-entities such as neurons, a neuroscientist such as Penfield is seeking to learn about properties of physical entities that are essentially *conditional* or *iffy* in nature. A property that is conditional in nature is a property that is specified in terms such as: "If such-and-such is done to object O (e.g. if a cause C is exerted on O), then so-and-so will occur to O (e.g. O will move at rate R). As the Nobel physicist Richard Feynman says, scientific questions are "questions that you can put this way: 'if I do this, what will happen?' [. . .] And so the question 'If I do it what will happen?' is a typically scientific question" (Feynman 1998, 16, 45). The following description by David Chalmers of basic particles that are studied by physicists nicely captures their iffy nature:

> Basic particles [. . .] are largely characterized in terms of their propensity to interact with other particles. Their mass and charge is specified, to be sure, but all that a specification of mass ultimately comes to is a propensity to be accelerated in certain ways [moved at certain rates] by forces, and so on. [. . .] Reference to the proton is fixed as the thing that causes interactions of a certain kind that combines in certain ways with other entities, and so on. (Chalmers 1996, 153)

What Chalmers describes as a "propensity" of a particle to be accelerated is its capacity to be moved, which is such that, *if* it is actualized (triggered) by an exercised causal power of another entity (whether physical or nonphysical in nature), the particle will be necessitated to behave in a certain way. There is nothing, however, in the nature of the propensity or capacity of that particle that entails that it can only be actualized by the exercised power of a physical entity. That is, there is nothing in the nature of that propensity or capacity that entails that it cannot be actualized by persons making undetermined choices for reasons. Hence the actualization of a micro-particle's capacity to behave in a certain way, by a person, on an occasion when she makes a choice for a reason, is not excluded by anything that is discovered in a scientific study of that capacity. And it is precisely on occasions like those noted by Kim, when finger and arm movements occur seemingly for purposes, that a neuroscientist will reasonably believe that the originative micro-physical movements are traceable to the causal activity of a soul that is choosing to act for a purpose. If a neuroscientist makes the presupposition that micro-physical entities can have their capacities actualized *only* by other physical entities and never by choices made by souls for purposes, then he does so as a naturalist and not as a scientist.

Our response to the causal closure argument assumes Feynman's and Chalmers' iffy picture of micro-entities—a picture that, in addition to presenting them as iffy, is also deterministic in the sense that no effect will occur in any micro-entity unless some causal event determines or necessitates that effect to take place. Might there not, however, be random (non-deterministic) changes in the system of micro-entities as well as deterministic ones? In other words, while sometimes a neuron fires because it receives deterministic causal input from the neurons with which it is connected, at other times it fires at random (without any deterministic cause), perhaps as a result of random quantum fluctuations in a chaotic system, which are magnified at the neuronal level.

If we assume, for the sake of discussion, that neurons do some-times fire randomly, is it possible to distinguish sharply between those firings that occur randomly and those that occur as the result of being causally determined by a mental event in a soul? After all, the two kinds of firings are alike, to the extent that neither has a physically deterministic cause. We believe that it is possible to make this sharp distinction between the two kinds of firings. The way to make the distinction is in terms of contexts that are known, in the case of ourselves, through first-person experience and, in the case of others, through third-person observation. All one need do is ask how plau-sible it is to maintain that, every time a person purposefully chooses to do something such as move his fingers to type, an initial neuron just happens to fire at random (as a result of quantum fluctuations, etc.), with the result that finger movements occur that perfectly mesh with, or map onto, those that are intended by that person. Because such repeated coincidences would literally be, dare we say, miracu-lous, the only plausible view is that the neuron must not be firing randomly but because of the causal input from a soul choosing to act for a purpose.

Before proceeding, it is important to point out, in fairness to Kim, that he, too, recognizes the counterintuitive nature of the conclusion of the argument from causal closure, which is that our mental lives have no explanatory role to play in accounting for events in the physical world. Hence, in order to preserve an explanatory role for the mental, he believes that we should be committed to a reduction of the mental to the physical:

Mind-to-body causation is fundamental if our mentality is to make a difference to what goes on in the world. If I want to have the slight-est causal influence on anything outside me—to change a light bulb or start a war—I must first move my limbs or other parts of my body; somehow, my beliefs and desires must cause the muscles in my arms and legs to contract, or cause my vocal cords to vibrate. Mental cau-sation is fundamental to our conception of mentality, and to our view of ourselves as agents [...]; any theory of mind that is not able to accommodate mental causation must be considered inadequate, or at best incomplete. [...] Does this mean that we are committed willy-nilly to reductionism? The answer is no: what we have established [...] is a *conditional* thesis, "If mentality is to have any causal efficacy at all—it must be physically reducible." Those of us who believe in mental causation should hope for a successful reduction (Kim 2005, 152–153, 161).

According to Kim, then, physical reduction (reduction of the mental to the physical) enables us to preserve our belief that mentality makes a causal explanatory difference. Notice, however, the price that must be paid to embrace this "solution" to the problem of causal closure. Mentality can make such an explanatory difference, only if we give up both the idea that mental actions are ultimately and irreducibly explained by purposes and the view that we make causally indeterministic choices. While Kim is correct when he insists that none of us wants to give up on the idea of mental causation, some of us also do not want to give up on the idea that mental causation itself occurs only because mental events such as choices are indeterministic events that are ultimately and irreducibly explained by purposes. Given the high price that must be paid to endorse Kim's "solution" to the problem of causal closure, it is imperative to examine whether there is a good reason to believe in the principle of the causal closure of the physical world.

Our response to the methodological argument for causal closure is premised upon acceptance of a conception of causation that Kim also assumes, which is that causation is a *productive* or *generative* relationship between a cause and its effect (what is often called "efficient causation"). Some have argued that this conception of causation is outdated, on the grounds that the fundamental laws of physics do not mention causality (Loewer 2001). For example, laws of physics about properties such as mass, electrical charge, and motion are expressed in terms of mathematical relationships. Hence, because the fundamental concepts of physics are strictly mathematical and include neither causal productivity nor nonquantifiable powers and their exercise, we have reason to be suspicious of the relevance of the causal powers of souls and of the purposes for which they act.

Like Kim, we are not physicists, and therefore, like him, we are hesitant about engaging the present critic for fear that we might appear to be spouting off about matters beyond our intellectual purview. Nevertheless, we find Kim's own responses to this argument about the nature of causation from the perspective of contemporary physics to be persuasive (Kim 2002), and we summarize two of his points in what immediately follows.

First, Kim suggests that, if there is no productive causation anywhere, then there is no mental causation or human agency of any kind (Kim 2002, 642; Kim's response on behalf of the reality of mental causation appears puzzling until one remembers that he believes mental causation to be ontologically reducible to physical causation). This not only is unbelievable, but also seems self-refuting. After all, does not the proponent of the argument that causation is not a productive relation believe that he is trying to *produce* a belief in his listeners or readers that there is no productive causality?

Second, Kim points out that facts such as that causality is not mentioned in the fundamental laws of physics, or that the word "cause" does not appear in statements of these laws, do not show that the concept of productive causation is absent from physics. There are the mathematical laws and our *interpretation* or *understanding* of those laws:

> My impression is that disputes about the interpretation of quantum mechanics, for example, are replete with causal concepts and causal considerations; e.g., measurement (as in a measurement "having an outcome") [. . .] observation (as having a perturbational influence on the system observed [e.g. an exercise of the power of observation collapses a Schrödinger wave function]), interference, etc. [. . .] Entries on "force" in science dictionaries and encyclopedias typically begin

like this: "In dynamics, the physical agent which causes a change of momentum" . . . A force causing a body to accelerate strikes me as an instance of productive causation par excellence. (Kim 2002, 676; one might add that the concept of the mass of an object, when expressed numerically, is typically interpreted as a function of that entity's *resistance* to acceleration by a *force*).

The discussion to this point makes clear that it is thoroughly reasonable to believe that there can be *gaps* (causal openness) in the course of events in the physical world such that there is room for the explanation of some physical events in terms of a soul's causal activity, which, in turn, is ultimately explained teleologically, by recourse to a purpose. To clarify even further the relevance of what we have called the "iffy" nature of a capacity's actualization, consider the following argument for the nonexistence of explanatory gaps (causal closure) developed by Ted Honderich (1993, Chapter 3). Honderich asks us to consider a scenario in which a woman, Juliet, sees her boyfriend, Toby, and subsequently chooses to tell Toby that they should have a child. Honderich then asks how we are to view the neurological events in Juliet that correlate with what may be called the relevant teleological events (see Table 6.1):

Table 6.1   Mental–Physical Correlations in Juliet's Brain

Mental events	Juliet sees Toby	Juliet chooses to tell Toby about wanting a child	Further mental events
Neurological events	N1	N2	N3→

What, asks Honderich, is the relationships between the neurological events that we have labeled N1 and N2? In order for Juliet to have libertarian free will (and for a purpose to be explanatorily efficacious), *N2* cannot be the unavoidable (determined) effect of *N1* (or of anything else), because its unavoidability will make its correlate teleological event equally unavoidable. According to Honderich, however, it is unreasonable to think that N2 can be anything other than unavoidable in relationship to N1 and to the physical story that precedes N1. To see why it is supposedly unreasonable to think anything other than this, let N3 and subsequent neural events be the ones that lead to, and include, the movements of Juliet's lips when she tells Toby that they should have a child. Is there or is there not an unavoidable connection between N2 and what causally results from it, namely N3 and the neural and other physical events that follow N3 and yield the movements of Juliet's lips?

> If there is not a very high probability that items like [N2] will be followed by other neural events, then actions [e.g. speaking with our lips] we fully and absolutely intend will on too many occasions mysteriously not happen. So the links *after* [N2] have to be pretty tight. But then in consistency so do the neural links *before* [N2]. That is unfortunate, since the theory [of libertarian free will] needs these earlier links to be pretty loose in order for Juliet to be held really responsible for what is tied to [correlated with] [N2], her [choice] to speak [to Toby]. (Honderich 1993, 37)

Can this problem of inconsistency really be dealt with? Honderich believes that the answer to this question is "No." The correct response, however, is that there is no problem of inconsistency, and this is the case because of the iffy nature of a capacity's actualization, which in this instance is the actualization of the capacity of a neuron (N2) to fire. Honderich's own treatment of the concept of causation supports the nonexistence of the alleged inconsistency and the possible existence of explanatory gaps in the physical story. In the course of discussing the nature of causation, he asks the reader to consider the lighting of a match here and now. We quote Honderich at some length:

> When we assume that this event was the effect of the match's being struck, what are we assuming? One good reply is likely to be that it was an event that wouldn't have happened if the match hadn't been

struck. On the assumption that the striking was cause and the lighting effect, what is true is that *if the striking hadn't happened, neither
would the lighting.* [. . .] We are inclined to think [. . .] that something
else isn't true of an ordinary striking and lighting. We are reluctant
to say that *if or since the match was struck, it lit.* The explanation of
our reluctance is that even if the match was struck, had it been wet,
it wouldn't have lit. [. . .] [N]ot only the striking was required for the
lighting, but also the match's being dry. That was not all that was
required. There had to be oxygen present, and the surface on which
the match was struck had to be of a certain kind. [. . .] An event which
caused a certain effect is not necessarily such that all like events are
followed by like effects. Not all strikings are followed by lightings.
A causal circumstance for a certain effect, on the other hand, really
is such that all like circumstances *are* followed by like effects. [. . .]
[G]iven a causal circumstance, whatever else had been the case [e.g.,
the match's color had been different], the effect would still have
occurred. A necessitated event just is one for which there was a circumstance which was such that since it occurred, whatever else had
been true, the event would still have occurred. (Honderich 1993, 7–11)

It is true, as Honderich claims, that, *given* a causal circumstance, the
effect—the actualization of a capacity—had to occur; and, *since* the
circumstance occurred, the effect was necessitated to occur. But did
the circumstance—in the case of the match, the presence of oxygen,
the dryness of the match, the match's being struck, etc.—have to occur?
Was it unavoidable? There is no reason to think so, *unless one has
presupposed the truth of determinism.* Honderich says that "the causal
circumstance for an effect will typically be made up of parts which
were also effects themselves. [. . .] This fact about effects—the fact of
what you might call causal chains—is very important to determinism"
(Honderich 1993, 11). While, for the sake of the argument, it can be
conceded that causal circumstances for effects will typically be made
up of parts which were also effects themselves, this fact about causal
circumstances is not sufficient for the truth of determinism to be established. This is because what is typical is not necessarily universal. In

the case of the causal circumstance involving the match, do we think that it was unavoidable that the match be struck? Not in the least. For example, a person might strike a match in virtue of having *chosen* to have a fire in the fireplace for the purpose of staying warm. He need not, however, have *chosen* to have the fire. He might have chosen to turn up the thermostat instead for the same purpose.

What, then, about the causal circumstance that includes $N2$ and what follows from it ($N3$, subsequent neural events, and the movement of Juliet's lips)? Was that causal circumstance unavoidable? Did it have to occur? The answer to this question depends upon what one says about the relationship between $N2$ and its corresponding teleological event (Juliet's choosing to tell Toby about wanting a child). If one believes that this teleological event alone causes $N2$ (there is no physical cause of $N2$), then there is no reason to think that $N2$ had to occur, because there is no reason to think that its corresponding teleological event (cause) had to occur, unless one assumes the truth of determinism. Honderich (or Kim) might respond that it is reasonable to believe that there must be a neural event such as $N1$ that produces $N2$. Why, however, should one think that this is the case? After all, $N1$ could be the cause of Juliet's seeing Toby without also being the cause of $N2$. Moreover, one can concede that a neuroscientist such as Penfield might discover in his experimental work that actualizations of a neural capacity (neural events like $N2$) can be produced by stimulation with an electrode or by exercisings of the causal powers of certain other neurons. But why think that every actualization of a neural capacity can only be produced in these ways? Why could not an actualization of a neural capacity (e.g. $N2$) be caused by the exercising of a mental power (i.e. by a mental event) alone, and one which is made for a purpose? There is no reason to think that this cannot be the case, unless one begs the question at hand and assumes the causal closure of the physical world. Keith Campbell succinctly captures, in ontological terms, the main methodological point of this section when he states that "[a] material thing can, without ceasing to be a material thing, respond to forces other than physical ones. The brain, without ceasing to be material, can act under the influence of an immaterial mind" (Campbell 1980, 17).

Earlier in this chapter we noted that some opponents of dualism charge that belief in the soul is rightly thought of as a "soul-of-the-gaps" position, much like the older "god-of-the-gaps" position, where the concept of soul is used to explain those human experiences that we cannot (yet, at least) explain neurologically or biologically. At this juncture, it is important to make clear not only that belief in the soul is not a soul-of-the-gaps position, but also that, if the argument from causal closure is successful, it makes it impossible to explain some events in the physical world in terms of the causal activity of human souls and of their purposes for acting, and it also makes it impossible to explain other events in the physical world in terms of the causal activity of God and of God's purposes for acting. For example, Douglas Futuyma and Matthew Bagger set forth the implications of causal closure for explanations of certain events in the physical world (e.g. the resurrection of Jesus, the healings performed by Jesus) in terms of God and his causal power:

> Science is the exercise of reason, and so is limited to questions that can be approached by the use of reason, questions that can be answered by the discovery of objective knowledge and the elucidation of natural laws of causation. In dealing with questions about the natural world, scientists must act as if they can be answered without recourse to supernatural powers [. . .] of God. (Futuyma 1982, 169–170)

> [W]e can never assert that, in principle, an event resists naturalistic [physical] explanation. A perfectly substantial, anomalous event, rather than providing evidence for the supernatural, merely calls into question our understanding of particular laws. In the modern era, this position fairly accurately represents the educated response to novelty. Rather than invoke the supernatural, we can always adjust our knowledge of the natural in extreme cases. In the modern age in actual inquiry, we never reach the point where we throw up our hands and appeal to divine intervention to explain a localized event like an extraordinary experience. (Bagger 1999, 13)

Though God's powers vastly exceed those of a human soul, they are nevertheless the powers of a nonphysical, simple substance, whose actions are explained in terms of purposes. Therefore, if the argument from the causal closure of the physical world cannot be satisfactorily answered when it is directed at excluding human souls and their purposes from explaining some events in the physical world, then the failure to answer it will entail that there is no explanatory room for God and God's purposes. Christian (and other) theists would do well to think twice about conceding the soundness of the causal closure argument as it relates to human souls, while at the same time trying to preserve explanatory space for God. Any sophisticated strict naturalist will quickly point out that, if the assumption of causal closure is justified, not only does it make it impossible to explain some events in the physical world in terms of human souls and their purposes for acting but it also makes it impossible to explain other events in the physical world in terms of God's purposes for acting.

As we conclude this section, we believe that it is important to stress that our response to the causal closure argument and our defense of the possibility of soul's causal intervention in the physical world are not based on any kind of faith. Nagel discusses the possibility of a "nonphysical being [intervening] in the natural order" (Nagel 2010, 47) in the context of evaluating the contemporary intelligent design (ID) movement—which is an attempt to introduce for consideration, into the biology curricula of American public schools, the idea that some biological phenomena can only be adequately explained through the actions of an intelligent mind (as opposed to mindless evolutionary processes like random genetic mutations and natural selection). According to Nagel,

> Opponents of the scientific status of ID are moved by the fact that those who believe [that a nonphysical being's intervention in the natural order] is possible, and who therefore can regard certain empirical observations as evidence for its actuality, usually believe in the possibility as a result of faith or ecclesiastical authority, rather

than evidence. This nonscientific element, which is a necessary condition of their interpretation of the empirical evidence, is thought to undermine the scientific status of the whole position. (Ibid.)

Nagel goes on to claim that the position of the opponent of ID is no less based on an "[empirically] ungrounded assumption about how the world works, essentially a kind of naturalism" (ibid.). In other words, the position of the opponent of ID is no more reasonable than that of its proponent. However, if our argument in this section is correct, then those who believe in the possibility of a nonphysical being's intervention in the natural order do not believe what they do on faith or on ecclesiastical authority. Rather, they believe it on the basis of their own direct, introspective awareness of themselves as agents who perform mental acts for purposes that produce effects in the physical world. Given this belief, they see no problem with the idea of some other kind of nonphysical being (e.g. God) intervening in the natural order to influence the course of physical events. Similarly, opponents of ID do not hold their position on the basis of groundless nonempirical assumptions. Rather they believe, on the basis of the argument from causal closure, that causal intervention in the natural world by a nonphysical being is not possible. We have argued in this section that this argument fails.

Soul–Body Causal Interaction and the Conservation of Energy

The concern in the previous section was methodological in nature. In this section, we briefly consider an argument from a supposed principle of physics that entails that it is impossible for a soul to interact causally with its physical body. This principle is the principle of the conservation of energy.

Before stating the argument, we issue a disclaimer: we are not scientists, but philosophers. Hence we recognize our limitations in discussing a matter that falls within the scope of a specialized science.

We will leave the scientific issues to qualified scientists and we will concern ourselves with the philosophical issues that pertain to, or are raised by, the conservation-of-energy principle.

What is the principle of the conservation of energy? For purposes of simplicity, the central idea is that the total amount of energy in a closed physical system (one that is isolated from outside interference) remains constant. Hence, if a physical system is closed and the idea of a soul's causally interacting with something in that system implies the introduction of energy into it, then causal activity involving a soul is impossible. If we stick with our example from the previous section and we continue to assume, for the sake of discussion, that our souls ultimately can produce appropriate finger movements on the keyboards of our computers only by directly causing events in the motor cortices of our brains, then, under the hypothesis that the brain is a closed physical system, this causal activity of the soul would violate the principle of the conservation of energy.

As a first response to the argument against causal interactionism from the conservation-of-energy principle, it is important to point out that the argument's proponent is assuming that the concept of causation essentially involves the idea of a transfer of energy. Broad makes this point as follows:

> In the first place, it is important to notice that the [. . .] real premise [in the conservation-of-energy argument against dualism] is a tacitly assumed proposition about causation; viz., that, if a change in A has anything to do with causing a change in B, energy must leave A and flow into B. This is neither asserted nor entailed by the Conservation of Energy. What *it* says is that, *if* energy leaves A, it must appear in something else, say B; so that A and B together form a conservative system. Since the Conservation of Energy is not itself the premise for the argument against Interaction, and since it does not entail that premise, the evidence for the Conservation of Energy is not evidence against Interaction. (Broad 1960, 107)

Debates about what the nature of causation is go all the way back at least to Plato, and we are not writing a book about the history of the concept of causation. So we have to take a short cut. We will make the highly plausible assumption (to which we have already referred in discussing Kim's view of causation in the previous section) that the idea of causation is essentially that of an exercised power of a substance, a power *producing or bringing about* an effect event. This conception of causation is both highly intuitive and ancient, as Aristotle referred to it (for instance in his *Metaphysics*, I.3). As such, it does not include the idea of transference of energy. Hence a dualist would be on solid ground, were he to respond to the present objection by claiming that a soul could produce an effect in a physical system without introducing energy into that system.

In addition to this conceptual objection, some have pointed out that there seems to be empirical evidence that causation within the physical world does not always involve transference of energy. The evidence comes from quantum mechanics and from a theorem of John Bell's, appropriately called "Bell's Theorem," which shows that, if certain predicted correlations occur, then they cannot be explained through a transfer of energy from cause to effect. Robin Collins summarizes Bell's Theorem in the following:

> Quantum mechanics [. . .] does provide a good case of interaction (or at least correlation) without either energy or momentum exchange. In quantum mechanics, there are definitely correlations—and in many realist interpretations, causal interactions—without energy exchange. Consider, for example, the Einstein–Podolsky–Rosen (EPR) correlations, in which two space-like separated sequences of events—sequence A and sequence B—are correlated in law-like ways that cannot, as John Bell showed, be explained in terms of a non-instantaneous common cause. Further, since quantum mechanics predicts that EPR correlations can occur between sequences of events separated by any arbitrary distance, these correlations cannot be explained by the events in sequence A's causing the events in sequence B or vice versa, unless the causes are considered to travel faster than the speed of light. Special relativity, however, requires that any energy transfer occur at less than the speed of light (in all frames of reference), thus ruling out any causal

interaction that requires energy transfer as an explanation for these correlations. Further, quantum mechanics predicts that the correlations occur without any energy transfer. The EPR correlations have thus demonstrated that law-like correlations do not require an exchange of energy or momentum. (Collins 2008, 38–39)

Collins then summarizes two ways of responding to such correlations:

(i) the causal realist response, according to which these correlations are grounded in some instantaneous causal connection between events in A and events in B or in a non-local and thus instantaneously acting common cause; and (ii) the causal anti-realist response, according to which these correlations are not grounded in any further causal facts. If the causal realist response is adopted, the burden of proof is on the advocate of the [conservation-of-energy] objection to state why she thinks that the mind–brain interaction should require an exchange of energy when EPR interactions do not. If the causal anti-realist interpretation is adopted, then versions of dualism in which there are law-like connections between mental events and physical events without any corresponding causal interaction become much more plausible. (Collins 2008, 39)

So far we have questioned the assumption, made by those who raise the conservation-of-energy objection to dualism, that causation must involve a transfer of energy from cause to effect. However, does granting this assumption spell defeat for the dualist? It is hard to see why it should. After all, the conservation-of-energy principle applies to closed physical systems; but, if a system like the human brain is not a closed system (and we saw in the previous section that there is no methodological reason for assuming that it is), then a soul could introduce energy into it. If the introduction of this energy required an energy loss in the brain system that is equal to the amount of energy introduced by the soul, then that loss would entail a redistribution of the lost energy into some other physical system. If the conservation-of-energy principle were understood to apply to the physical universe as a whole, then the quantity of energy introduced by a soul would have to be lost at some point by the universe as a whole. Some philosophers believe that such a suggestion is ad hoc, or begs the question. Searle and Flanagan make this charge:

> All forms of substance dualism inherit Descartes' problem of how to give a coherent account of the causal relations between the soul and the body, but recent versions have an additional problem. It seems impossible to make substance dualism consistent with modern physics. Physics says that the amount of matter/energy in the universe is constant; but substance dualism seems to imply that there is another kind of energy, mental energy or spiritual energy, that is not fixed by physics. So if substance dualism is true then it seems that one of the most fundamental laws of physics, the law of conservation, must be false. Some substance dualists have attempted to cope with this problem by claiming that for each infusion of spiritual energy, there is a diminution of physical energy, thus preserving a constant amount of energy in the universe. Others have said that the mind rearranges the distribution of energy in the universe without adding to it or subtracting from it. [. . .] There is something ad hoc about these maneuvers, in the sense that the authors are convinced in advance of the truth of dualism and are trying to find some way, any way, that will make dualism consistent with physics. (Searle 2004, 29–30).

If Descartes is right that a nonphysical mind can cause the body to move, for example, when we decide to go to a concert, then physical energy must increase in and around our body, since we get up and go to the concert. In order, however, for physical energy to increase in any system, it has to have been transferred from some other physical system. But the mind, according to Descartes, is not a physical system and therefore it does not have any energy to transfer. The mind cannot account for the fact that our body ends up at the concert. [. . .] We could maintain that the principle of conservation of energy holds, but that every time a mind introduces new energy into the world—thanks to some mysterious capacity it has—an equal amount of energy departs from the physical universe—thanks to some perfectly orchestrated mysterious capacity the universe has. Unfortunately, such an assumption is totally unwarranted except as a way of saving Cartesian dualism, and, therefore, utterly begs the question. (Flanagan 1991, 21)

In light of our brief history of thought about the soul, which shows that the soul's existence is affirmed largely, if not entirely, on the basis of first-person experience and is not a theoretical postulate, it should be clear that the suggested responses to the conservation-of-energy issue are neither ad hoc nor question-begging. In other words, given that one is convinced in advance (prior to one's consideration of physics) of the truth of dualism, it is not the least bit ad hoc or question-begging to search for ways (for example, by assuming that there are equal amounts of energy entering and leaving the physical universe on the occasions when the soul moves its body) in which one might make one's belief in the soul's existence consistent with possible developments in physics.

Chapter 7

Contemporary Challenges to the Soul

As we noted in the Introduction, a great deal of philosophy today involves some form of materialism. This chapter examines six groups of objections to the soul that have been popular since the mid-twentieth century that (in general) reflect the current materialist milieu.

The Ghost in the Machine Objection

In the Introduction, we endorsed the view that the recognition of the soul and the idea that there is more to us than bodily processes and states reflects a general, commonsense approach to ourselves and the world. Gilbert Ryle radically challenges this outlook in his famous *The Concept of the Mind*, in which he likens the Cartesian view of the soul–body relationship to the belief that there is a ghost in the bodily machine. Consider the following characterization of the soul or mind as associated with Descartes. For the full effect, we cite Ryle at length:

> The official doctrine, which hails chiefly from Descartes, is something like this. With the doubtful exceptions of idiots and infants in arms every human being has both a body and a mind. Some would prefer

A Brief History of the Soul, First Edition.
© 2011 Stewart Goetz and Charles Taliaferro. Published 2011 by Blackwell Publishing Ltd.

to say that every human being is both a body and a mind. His body and his mind are ordinarily harnessed together, but after the death of the body his mind may continue to exist and function.

Human bodies are in space and are subject to the mechanical laws, which govern all other bodies in space. Bodily processes and states can be inspected by external observers. So a man's bodily life is as much a public affair as are the lives of animals and reptiles and even as the careers of trees, crystals and planets.

But minds are not in space, nor are their operations subject to mechanical laws. The workings of one mind are not witnessable by other observers; its career is private. Only I can take direct cognisance of the states and processes of my mind. A person therefore lives through two collateral histories, one consisting of what happens in and to his body, the other consisting of what happens in and to the mind. The first is public, the second private. The events in the first history are events in the physical world; those in the second are events in the mental world. (Ryle 1949, 11–12)

Ryle goes on to portray dualism as fostering a radical bifurcation:

It has been disputed whether a person does or can directly monitor all or only some of the episodes of his own private history; but, according to the official doctrine, of at least some of these episodes he has direct and unchallengeable cognisance. In consciousness, self-consciousness and introspection he is directly and authentically apprised of the present states and operations of his mind. He may have great or small uncertainties about concurrent and adjacent episodes in the physical world, but he can have none about at least part of what is momentarily occupying his mind.

It is customary to express this bifurcation of his two lives and his two worlds by saying that the things and events which belong to the physical world including his own body, are external, while the work-ings of his own mind are internal. This antithesis of outer and inner is of course meant to be construed as a metaphor, since minds, not being in space, could not be described as being spatially inside any-thing else, or as having things going on spatially inside themselves.

> But relapses from this good intention are common and theorists are found speculating how stimuli, the physical sources of which are yards or miles outside a person's skin, can generate mental responses inside his skull, or how decisions framed inside his cranium can set going movements of his extremities. (Ibid., 12)

Ryle's withering caricature of dualism was well received in many philosophical circles in the English-speaking world. According to Ryle, we are clearly a unified whole, not something "invisible, inaudible and [having] no size or weight" (ibid., 20). We actually see, hear, and touch each other, whereas the traditional view of the soul, or at least the Cartesian tradition, denies this. According to Cartesianism, "[t]he mind is its own place and in his inner life each of us lives the life of a ghostly Robinson Crusoe. People can see, hear and jolt one another's bodies, but they are irremediably blind and deaf to the workings of one another's minds and inoperative upon them" (ibid., 13). Antony Flew made a similar point when he once observed that in ordinary life we meet people, not their containers (Flew 1965). P. M. S. Hacker similarly characterized dualism as positing a little invisible person in the brain (Hacker 1987).

As part of his critique of dualism, Ryle proposed that belief in the soul/mind as a separable entity from the body is a category mistake; it involves reification, as when one treats a thing as an independent subject when it is no such thing. Here is Ryle's famous example of a category mistake:

> A foreigner visiting Oxford or Cambridge for the first time is shown a number of colleges, libraries, playing fields, museums, scientific departments and administrative offices. He then asks "But where is the University? I have seen where the members of the Colleges live, where the Registrar works, where the scientists experiment and the rest. But I have not seen the University in which reside and work the members of your University." It has then to be explained to him that the University is not another collateral institution, some ulterior counterpart to the colleges, laboratories and offices which he has

seen. The University is just the way in which all that he has already seen is organized. When they are seen and when their co-ordination is understood, the University has been seen. His mistake lay in his innocent assumption that it was correct to speak of Christ Church, the Bodleian Library, the Ashmolean Museum *and* the University, to speak, that is, as if "the University" stood for an extra member of the class of which these other units are members. He was mistakenly allocating the University to the same category as that to which the other institutions belong. (Ryle 1949, 16)

In summary, according to Ryle, Flew, and Hacker, dualism and the Platonic–Cartesian tradition of the soul do not express or reflect a general, commonsense approach to ourselves and the world. Are they right? Consider Ryle's example of the visitor to Oxford University. He is surely correct about the university not being a substance in its own right, apart from the buildings, playing fields, and other spaces of the colleges; but is there any reason to believe that Oxford University is like a person with regard to the category of being a substance? The difficulty of aligning an institution like Oxford with a person is that it appears that persons actually think and feel, whereas institutions may be described as thinking (Oxford University thinks its students should have ample opportunities to study Shakespeare) and feeling (Oxford mourned the death of its students during the Second World War) only as a metaphor. It is not literally the case that Oxford engages in reflection, though its individual members do, and they can treat their university as a distinct entity (metaphorically, in law, institutions are sometimes called legal fictions).

So persons do not seem to be akin to institutions, or somewhat muddled abstractions. What of Ryle's claim that dualism is guilty of a radical bifurcation that seems completely at odds with common sense?

We suggest that what Ryle (and Hacker and Flew) misses is that human persons are capable of radical bifurcation. A person may be so traumatized and damaged that there is a sense in which the person is *not* visible; you do not see his actual feelings and desires. Some people are psychologically so withdrawn that they are like Robinson

Crusoe or a ghost in a machine. But what Ryle and others miss is that a dualist may (and we think should) hold that, under healthy, ordinary conditions, the embodied soul functions as a unity. When you genuinely express and embody your actual thoughts and feelings, there is a singular reality, not two remote worlds being "harnessed" together. This point can be clarified by reference to a remark made by the philosopher Trenton Merricks, which is very much in the spirit of Ryle. Merricks launches the following line of reasoning: he, Merricks, kisses his wife. If dualism is true, then his wife is a soul and cannot be kissed. Dualism allows that only bodies can kiss. Hence dualism is false (personal email correspondence; but see Merricks 2007, 286, for a similar argument in print).

According to dualism, in a strict sense it is true that Merricks does not literally kiss his wife, if "his wife" is understood to refer only to his wife's soul. However, in that sense of "his wife," Merricks also neither experiences (is directly aware of) his wife's pleasures and pains nor has immediate awareness of her hopes, fears, and thoughts. All of these psychological events are accessible to him only as expressed in and through her body. And when Merricks thinks of kissing his wife, the words "my wife" normally have as their referent his wife as a soul/body unity. So, in the ordinary sense, Merricks does literally kiss his wife, just as he also experiences her pleasures and pains and is aware of the hopes, fears, and thoughts as they are manifested in the soul/body unity that is his wife.

For better or for worse, then, kissing someone requires the embodiment and cooperation of the soul. If the person you kiss is utterly affectively absent, has ill feelings for you, or is merely pretending to be affectionate, there is a sense in which you have not kissed the one you are thinking about; you are instead unwittingly being prey to a charade. We propose, then, that unfortunately human beings can fracture and (sometimes because of brain damage) wind up with their bodies in one world, and their inner identity in another; but this is not a view that dualists should accept in cases of a healthy, integrated embodiment (Taliaferro 2001c).

The Private Language Argument

Ludwig Wittgenstein was a multi-faceted powerful and yet enigmatic philosopher in the first half of the twentieth century. In his *Philosophical Investigations*, which was published posthumously, there is an argument, which has become known as the "private language argument," that is frequently interpreted as dealing a decisive blow against the dualist view of the soul or the mental. Because there are thorny questions about the interpretation of the text itself, we will simply offer a plausible version of the argument without claiming that it is in all respects Wittgenstein's.

The version of the argument to be considered here takes aim at the claim that we may know directly and immediately our own mental, subjective states. As we have seen with Augustine and Descartes, the soul tradition has indeed included some strong assertions about the infallible and incorrigible knowledge that we may claim about our own existence and about what appears to us. An important premise that is needed for the argument is that language usage must admit of correction, of ways in which language-users can determine whether they are using words correctly. Such correct use of language involves not just rules of communication (syntax and semantics), but the ability to act by the rules. Consider the following: if you do have immediate, certain access to your mental states, then it would be possible in principle for you to create a private language, a language only you know or can know. But this (or so it is argued) is impossible. Here is Anthony Kenny's representation of the argument:

> Suppose that I wish to baptize a private sensation of mine with the name "S," I fix my attention on the sensation in order to correlate the name with it. What does this achieve? When next I want to use the name "S," how will I know whether I am using it rightly? Since the sensation it is to name is supposed to be a private one, no one else can check up on my use of it. But neither can I do so for myself. Before I can check up on whether the sentence "This is S again" is

true, I need to know what the sentence means. How do I know that what I now mean by "S" was what I meant when I christened the first sensation "S"? Can I appeal to memory? No, for to do so I must call up the right memory, the memory of S; and in order to do that I must already know what "S" means. There is in the end no check on my use of "S," no way of making out a difference between correct and incorrect use of it. That means that talk of "correctness" is out of place, and shows that the private definition I have given myself is not real definition. (Kenny 1998, 340–341).

In a slightly altered version of the argument, it has been held that, if the soul exists with privileged access to its own states, there may be (unknown to us) complete inversions of meaning. This is often articulated in terms of inverted spectra thought experiments. If we both learned color words by ostension (examples), then we both would indicate the reference of "blue" by pointing to objects we thought of as blue. But what if one of us has an inverted spectrum, so that what one sees as blue the other sees as green? In such a case, arguably (and assume there are no unique neural firings involved, and hence no way to "color tag" specific neural events) we would have no way of correcting the deviant use of color terms.

Both forms of argument are designed to rule out skepticism. One obvious reply is simply to accept the possibility of skepticism. You might give a unique term to a mental state or color and simply (afterwards) not know whether you are using the term consistently. Memory is fallible. Maybe one of us does have an inverted spectrum, and this will never be known. Such skeptical hypotheses seem imaginable and, on the basis of the modal epistemic principle in Chapter 3, this fact counts against the private language argument.

This strategic reply is akin to one that can be made to a somewhat similar argument involving skepticism. If the soul is nonphysical, couldn't it be replaced regularly? Couldn't God annihilate a person's soul and then create a new one just like it, appropriately embodied? To an external observer, a person may be seen as enduring over time, and yet in actuality the observer would be (without knowing it) seeing hundreds of souls successively created and destroyed. We think there is as little harm in conceding that this is possible, as there is in conceding that the same replacement strategy could be undertaken by God vis-à-vis physical things. Perhaps you do not own one enduring book, but the one you own now will be destroyed in a few seconds and instantaneously replaced by one that is an exact look-alike.

Finally, the worry that one might be using "S" to refer to a different sensation from that referred to earlier cannot be assuaged by bringing in another speaker of the language, someone named "P," whom one trusts to confirm that one's use of "S" has remained consistent through time. After all, how does one know that P is the same person one has known for some time and now trusts? Can one appeal to one's memory? Not according to Wittgenstein (Kenny), because to do so one must call up the right memory, the memory of P, but in order to do that one must already know what "P" means. There is in the end no check on one's use of "P," no way of making out a difference between correct and incorrect uses of it. Hence, if the private language argument is sound, there is no way of making sense of *any* referring term, private or public, that we use.

Before moving to the next objection, we note that Wittgenstein himself seemed open to the possibility that our mental life is completely irreducible to the physical.

> No supposition seems to me more natural than that there is no process in the brain correlated with associating or with thinking; so that it would be impossible to read off thought-processes from brain processes. I mean this: if I talk or write there is, I assume, a system of impulses going out from my brain and correlated with my spoken or written thoughts. But why should the *system* continue further in the direction of the centre? Why should this order not proceed, so to speak, out of chaos? It is perfectly possible that certain psychological phenomena *cannot* be identified physiologically, because physiologically nothing corresponds to them. Why should there not be a psychological

regularity to which *no* physiological regularity corresponds? If this upsets our concepts of causality, then it is high time they were upset. (Wittgenstein, quoted in Kenny 1998, 344)

Ockham's Razor and Identity

Perhaps the most common objection to the traditional view of the soul involves the appeal to Ockham's razor; do not multiply entities beyond necessity. As applied to the mind–body question, this entails that, when there is no *necessity* of recognizing or affirming the existence of anything other than bodily states, you should not do so. This line of reasoning is often bolstered by the claim that, because the sciences have already established other identity relations (e.g. water is H_2O, and heat is molecular motion), we should believe, or have faith in, the scientific project of identifying mind and body. Philosophers adopting this strategy sometimes concede that the concept of being a person is quite distinct from the concept of being a body or being physical, but they then insist that this is not an insurmountable problem for an identity of human persons and bodies. In their view, the concept of being a person is neutral between a physical and a nonphysical interpretation. After all, some Christian philosophers, for example, think that God is a nonphysical person but human beings are thoroughly physical persons.

Let's begin with the idea that what satisfies the concept of being a person and our conceptions about our mental life may turn out to be the very same thing as brain states. Paul Churchland has argued that our concept of our inner mental states is quite fallible and should not be relied upon to reveal their status as physical or nonphysical. Against any argument that relies on introspection, Churchland writes:

But the argument is deeply suspect, in that it assumes that our faculty of inner observation or introspection reveals things as they really are in their innermost nature. This assumption is suspect because we already know that our other forms of observation—sight, hearing, touch, and so on—do no such thing. The red surface of an apple does not *look* like a matrix of molecules reflecting photons at certain critical wavelengths, but that is what it is. The sound of a flute does not *sound* like a sinusoidal compression wave train in the atmosphere, but that is what it is. The warmth of the summer air does not *feel* like the mean kinetic energy of millions of tiny molecules, but that is what it is. If one's pains and hopes and beliefs do not *introspectively* seem like electrochemical states in a neutral network, that may be only because our faculty of introspection, like our other senses, is not sufficiently penetrating to reveal such hidden details. (Churchland 1988, 15)

The difficulty with Churchland's reasoning is that his seemingly straightforward claim that brain states and mental states are identical begs the question against dualists or anyone else who recognizes the irreducibly nonphysical nature of mental states. Granted, seeing the redness of an apple may be caused by a matrix of molecules reflecting photons at certain critical wavelengths; but, as we saw in the last chapter, correlation is not the same as identity. And the same is true of the other examples. It is one thing to hold that a sinusoidal compression wave train in the atmosphere stimulates a subject's eardrum and brain and causes him to hear sounds (the experience of audition), but another to claim that the wave train and the hearing of the sound are identical. Similarly, the mean kinetic energy of millions of tiny molecules may cause someone to experience warm feelings, but this fact alone does not establish that warm feelings *are* mean kinetic energy.

The problem with most mind–body identity claims is that many of our mental or psychological concepts (e.g. our concepts of seeing red, of hearing sounds, and of feeling hot) are not vague; they are about *the way things seem*, and thus they are instead very distinct and precise. Identity claims seem substantive and informative when the same thing can appear in two ways. Thus it was a genuine discovery that the Morning Star, which is the planet Venus as it appears in the morning on earth, is identical with the Evening Star, which is the planet

Venus as it appears in the evening. In the case of much of the mental, however, *how something feels or appears* is the phenomenon itself, and it requires something more than mere assertion to substantiate the claim that the appearance or feeling itself (as opposed to the thing that appears or is felt) is identical with something physical.

Behaviorism (which is the view that our mental life just is our bodily behavior—e.g., being in pain just is wincing and cursing) enjoyed some popularity with B. F. Skinner in the 1960s and 1970s, and it received allegiance from Willard Quine and Daniel Dennett. But, as A. C. Ewing points out, behaviorism (as well as other forms of the identity theory) faces an enormous challenge from experience itself. Ewing suggests that first-person experience is itself an adequate refutation of the identity theory:

> In order to refute such views I shall suggest your trying an experiment. Heat a piece of iron red-hot, then put your hand on it, and note carefully how you feel. You will have no difficulty in observing that it is quite different from anything which a physiologist could observe, whether he considered your outward behavior or your brain processes. The throb of pain experienced will not be in the least like either the act of withdrawing your hand or the movement of your vocal organs to say whatever you do say, nor would it be like anything described in textbooks of physiology as happening in the nervous system or brain. I do not say that it does not happen in the brain, but it is quite distinct from anything that other people could observe if they looked into your brain. The behaviorists pride themselves on being empiricists, but in maintaining their view they are going clean contrary to experience. We know by experience what feeling pain is like and we know by experience what the physiological reactions to it are, and the two are totally unalike. (Ewing 1985, 101, 102)

Ockham's razor tells us not to multiply entities beyond necessity (to defer to simplicity) when doing so is unreasonable. However, we believe that (in the words of one of our mentors) one should not mistake simplicity for adequacy. If we seem to be subjects (souls) who have experiences of pleasure and pain, then we need to account adequately for these data. Ockham's razor can be taken too far when it is used to deny the very existence and nature of the data, as is done by Dennett. He simply wields Ockham's razor to cut reality so as to make it conform to his view that no form of dualism is acceptable. He also deems that the only worthy account of the self must be one in which the self is not retained as a simple or irreducible reality. In other words, the substantial self cannot form part of the final theory of what exists:

> You've got to leave the first person [substantial self] out of your final theory. You won't have a theory of consciousness if you still have the first person in there, because that was what it was your job to explain. All the paraphernalia that don't make any sense unless you've got a first person in there, have to be turned into something else. You've got to figure out some way to break them up and distribute their powers and opportunities into the system in some other way. (Dennett 2006, 87)

The concept of a substantial individual self and of its powers must be broken down and eliminated from doing any explanatory work of its own. Dennett reasons that, because there is no way of understanding how the brain could be a self, there is no self:

> And the trouble with brains, it seems, is that when you look in them, you discover that *there's nobody home*. No part of the brain is the thinker that does the thinking or the feeler that does the feeling, and the whole brain appears to be no better candidate for that very special role. This is a slippery topic. Do brains think? Do eyes see? Or do people see with their eyes and think with their brains? Is there a difference? Is this just a trivial point of "grammar" or does it reveal a major source of confusion? The idea that a *self* (or a person, or, for that matter, a soul) is distinct from a brain or a body is deeply rooted in our ways of speaking, and hence in our ways of thinking. (Dennett 1991, 29)

Dennett grants that ordinary language seems to support a solid affirmation of the self, but this is the result of an illusion (2006, 80–90).

We submit that this is a case of wielding Ockham's razor to the point of absurdity. Augustine's and Descartes' case for the self, based as it was upon irrefutable self-awareness, which was foreshadowed in the works of philosophers of the soul like Plato and Aristotle, contains too much truth to be dismissed by Dennett's strategy.

Argument from Neural Dependence

We have already discussed in the previous chapter the objection that the mental (conceived of as nonphysical) cannot interact with the physical, but there is another related objection that needs to be noted and addressed. Granting the possibility of mind–body interaction, why is the mental so pervasively dependent on the physical? Churchland contends that, if dualism is true, we should not expect to find the degree of dependency of the mind on the brain that we find.

> If there really is a distinct entity in which reasoning, emotion, and consciousness take place, and if that entity is dependent on the brain for nothing more than sensory experiences as input and volitional executions as output, *then one would expect reason, emotion, and consciousness to be relatively invulnerable to direct control or pathology by manipulation or damage to the brain.* (Churchland 1984, 20)

And, given this vulnerability of the mental to the physical, Searle advances the following claim: "*Mental phenomena, all mental phenomena whether conscious or unconscious, visual or auditory, pains, tickles, itches, thoughts, indeed, all of our mental life, are caused by processes going on in the brain*" (Searle 1984, 18).

We see no reason why dualism is in any way threatened by what is, in many instances, the profound dependency of mental (or psychological) processes upon bodily processes, and we believe that there are clear instances where, if we assume an intact and normally functioning brain, what goes on in our mental lives is not determined by what goes on in the brain. As we argued in Chapter 6, science is in no way incompatible with the profound dependency of the physical on the mental in cases where we choose to act freely for purposes. On such occasions, what happens in the physical world would not have occurred except for the occurrence of, and causation by, uncaused events in the mental world. Moreover, because the mental acts of choice and intention are explained teleologically, the events at which they are directed in the physical world (as when we choose to move our limbs in certain ways in order to achieve various goals, like hitting a ball and cooking a meal), are themselves purposeful in nature. Some dualists (e.g. the epiphenomenalists, who hold the view that, while the physical causally affects the mental, the mental does not causally affect the physical) go as far as to concede that the dependency of the mental on the physical is so radical that the mind or soul never exercises the kind of causal power that produces events in the physical world. However, because of the pervasive, evident experience of our mental powers to act teleologically and because of the lack of any compelling argument from science that discredits the integrity of this experience, we see no reason to embrace epiphenomenalism.

In the previous paragraph we were concerned with mental activity and its relation to the physical world, and we argued that such activity provides solid grounds for rejecting the thorough-going dependence of our mental lives on events in our body (brain). An equally important consideration for assessing the claim that what happens in our mental life is sometimes not causally produced by events in the brain comes from instances of mental passivity. More specifically, we believe that what goes on when we reason provides powerful evidence against the claim that no mental events occur that are not completely causally explained by physical events (or not completely causally explained by the physical features of physical events, if one embraces some kind of dual aspect theory discussed in Chapter 5). What we have in mind here is the passive formation of a belief, or a believing. In many (but not all) cases, believings (formations of beliefs) are causally explained by apprehending (being aware of) and believing mental *contents* such as propositions and the logical entailment relationships that obtain among them. Consider two examples.

First, take the logical entailment relationship known as *modus ponens*, whose form is as follows: If A, then B; A; therefore, B. If one apprehends (is aware) that A implies B (i.e. if one apprehends "If A, then B"), and if one also apprehends that A is the case, then one *cannot help* but come to believe that B follows from their conjunction: "If A then B; and A." In other words, upon apprehending *modus ponens*, one is *caused* to, and thereby cannot help but, believe it—where the believing is *causally explained* by that apprehension.

Second, consider *modus ponens* once again, but now assume that, in addition to believing it, one also *believes* (as well as apprehends) the antecedent of the relevant conditional, and the conditional itself. Let us say that A is "New York is north of Miami" and B is "Miami is warmer than New York in the winter." Then, given that one believes both "If New York is north of Miami, then Miami is warmer than New York in the winter" and "New York is north of Miami," then one cannot help but believe that Miami is warmer than New York in the winter. In this case, one's belief that the proposition "Miami is warmer than New York in the winter" is true is *causally explained* by one's apprehension of and belief that *modus ponens* is true *and* by one's belief that both "New York is north of Miami" and "If New York is north of Miami, then Miami is warmer than New York in the winter" are true.

If, in some cases, believings are causally explained by other mental events (apprehensions and other believings) in the way just described, then the explanation of some mental events includes other mental events, and there is *mental-to-mental causal explanation*. However, if what happens in our mental lives were, as Searle suggests, completely causally determined by brain events (or by the physical features of brain events), then the causal explanations of our believings could never include mental features such as apprehensions and other believings.

It seems to us that, with regard to believings, the thesis that what goes on in our mental lives is completely explained by processes going on in our brains is self-defeating (self-refuting); and in what immediately follows we will refer to it as "the Thesis". That is to say, it seems to us that any *argument* for the Thesis entails its falsity. Support for the view that the Thesis is self-refuting begins with the following argument for it:

1 Every mental effect event is caused only by nonmental, physical events (or caused only by non-mental, physical features of physical events; this is just a version of the Thesis).
2 Believing that the Thesis is true is a mental effect event.

   Therefore,

3 Believing that the Thesis is true is caused only by nonmental, physical events (or caused only by non-mental, physical features of physical events).

Assume, as seems thoroughly reasonable, that the advocate of the Thesis believes that the causal explanation for his believing (3) is his apprehending (1) and (2) and believing that they are true. The problem is that, if (3) is true, the apprehending and believing of (1) and (2) cannot be the causal explanation for the believing of (3), because the apprehending and believing of (1) and (2) are mental events (or mental features of physical events). Hence, if the Thesis is true, it undermines the causal explanation for believing that it is true.

An implication of the Thesis is that, if apprehensions and believings are real events, then their occurrences must be and always are epiphenomenal in the sense that whatever is mental is completely explained by what is physical. As we have already stated, we see no good reason to accept epiphenomenalism, because to have a good reason to accept it—one that is causally efficacious in producing the belief in epiphenomenalism—entails the falsity of epiphenomenalism (see Goetz and Taliaferro 2008).

Arguments from Personal Identity

What makes you the same person over time? As we recounted in Chapter 4, this issue was widely discussed in the seventeenth and eighteenth centuries in light of Locke's account of personal identity. It came into focus once again in the last three decades of the twentieth century. Bernard Williams and others argued that only continuity of bodily identity is a secure foundation of personal identity (identity of the self) through time (Williams 1973).

Here is a version of Williams' reasoning. Imagine that two human beings, A and B, are going to enter a machine in which all of the contents of their memories and other forms of consciousness (beliefs, desires, hopes, fears) are to be switched, so the person who emerges as body A will think and act as though he is person B, and person B will think and act as though he is person A. Imagine, further, that before entering the machine both persons are told that after exiting the machine one of the two will be tortured and the other will be given a great gift. Assuming that A likes gifts and does not want to be tortured, which person does he hope to be after exiting the machine? Williams uses thought experiments like this and others to erode the idea that our identity over time is principally a matter of mental continuity. Arguably, person A prior to entering the machine would want the person with body A (or who is body A) after exiting to get the gift and not be tortured, even if bodily person A after leaving the machine thinks he is B. Still other thought experiments seem to give us reason to privilege bodily rather than mental continuity. Imagine you will be tortured tomorrow, but then you will have all memory of the experience erased. One may still dread the upcoming torture even if the event will have no long-term mental effect and there will be no psychological continuity linking your experience of the torture with future experiences.

These and similar puzzles do not, in our view, raise any difficulties for the dualist concept of the soul. What they reveal instead is that both bodily and psychological continuity constitute no more than evidence for what Roderick Chisholm refers to as the strict continuity of a person over time (Chisholm 1976). As we noted in Chapters 1 and 3, switching bodies (or becoming re-embodied after the loss of one's current body) seems to be a conceivable, metaphysically possible state of affairs, which belies the idea that bodily continuity is either necessary or sufficient for personal identity over time. Similarly for psychological continuity: we can conceive of ourselves remaining the same person over time with or without any degree of psychological continuity (in the form of memories, character, etc.). Our identity is strict in so far as it does not rest on a partial or whole retention of bodily or psychological elements.

What Williams' thought experiments do bring to light is an interesting aspect of personal identity: cases may arise when there may be genuine uncertainty about personal identity from a third-person point of view. For example, a case could arise when it is not obvious whether A and B have switched bodies or merely switched mental, psychological properties. There must be a fact of the matter (which includes the possibility that neither A nor B survives the bodily and psychological changes), even though we might not know what it is. As Richard Swinburne says:

> [P]ersonal identity is something ultimate. It is unanalysable into conjunctions or disjunctions of other observable properties. Bodily continuity, continuity of memory and character, are, however, the only evidence we have of its presence; it is observable only by observing these. In general there is plenty of evidence, normally overwhelming evidence, of bodily continuity, memory and character, as to whether or not two persons are the same, which gives very clear verdicts in the overwhelming majority of cases. Yet while evidence of continuity of body, memory, and character is evidence of personal identity, personal identity is not constituted by continuity of body, memory and character. Hence the evidence may on occasion mislead, and two persons be the same, although the best evidence which we have shows that they are not and conversely. Also on occasion the evidence

of observable characteristics may give no clear verdict as to whether P_2 is the same person as P_1; but that does not mean that there is no clear answer to this question, merely that we do not know and cannot even make a reasonable guess at what it is. (Swinburne 1977, 119–120)

Argument from Evolution

In terms of evolution, some critics assume that dualists must follow Descartes in denying that some nonhuman animals are conscious, experiencing beings. Descartes believed that nonhuman animals were complex organic machines and that their behavior could (and should) be fully explained without positing a soul. Assuming that all dualists take such a position, two objections are raised. First, given the apparent continuity of features shared by human and beastly ancestral bodies, there seems to be no justification for believing that human beings have souls and beasts do not. Indeed, any demarcation between human beings as creatures with souls and ancestral beasts as creatures without seems thoroughly artificial and arbitrary. Second, evolution seems to be a thoroughly physical process. Granted that nonhuman life can be accounted for on exclusively physical grounds, why think that matters differ when it comes to human beings? Here is Churchland's version of an argument against dualism based on evolution:

> The standard evolutionary story is that the human species and all of its features are the wholly physical outcome of a purely physical process. Like all but the simplest of organisms, we have a nervous system. And for the same reason: a nervous system permits the discriminative guidance of behavior. But a nervous system is just an active matrix of cells, and a cell is just an active matrix of molecules. We are notable only in that our nervous system is more complex and powerful than those of our fellow creatures. Our inner nature differs from that of simpler creatures in degree, but not in kind. If this is the

correct account of our origins, then there seems neither need, nor room, to fit any nonphysical substances or properties into our theoretical account of ourselves. We are creatures of matter. And we should learn to live with that fact. (Churchland 1984, 21)

In reply, we do not follow Descartes with respect to nonhuman animals. We think it is reasonable to believe that many mammals have experiences, and perhaps even an awareness of themselves as distinct from others, on the basis of behavior, anatomy (possession of brain, nervous system and the like), and in some cases (dolphins, apes) language or language-like communication. We therefore (like most dualists today) do not face the objection that we arbitrarily privilege humans over nonhumans in terms of the attribution of mental states. And, in so far as it appears that nonhuman animals have mental states, there seems to be a problem with identifying such states with physical processes. We therefore do not see evolution as excluding the possession of souls by nonhuman animals.

The argument from evolution, however, does raise a broader question, which we will address in the next chapter: Is the case for and against the soul dependent on a larger debate in philosophy, about the very nature of the cosmos itself? To that question we now turn.

Chapter 8

Thoughts on the Future of the Soul

At the close of the last chapter we replied to an argument from evolution. This debate over the origin of consciousness and of the soul invites a broader form of inquiry, into one's conception of the very nature of reality and its structure. For example, if one adapts a thorough-going physicalism as one's "big picture" of the origin and nature of the cosmos, one is likely to find identity forms of physicalism (what is mental exists, but is identical with what is physical), or possibly even eliminative accounts (there is no such thing as the mental), to be more plausible than the belief that the soul exists. Matters shift if a different background is entertained. On the basis of this short history of the soul, we highlight four areas of inquiry that we believe will impact twenty-first century reflection on this topic: the first concerns the important naturalism–theism debate, which addresses ultimate background issues. The second concerns inquiry into the concept of what is physical. The third involves cross-cultural inquiry. The fourth, which may be of growing importance, involves value inquiry.

Naturalism versus Theism

At some point, an inquiry into the existence and nature of the soul must take up the deep question about the ultimate nature of the

A Brief History of the Soul, First Edition.
© 2011 Stewart Goetz and Charles Taliaferro. Published 2011 by Blackwell Publishing Ltd.

cosmos. Arguably, in the history of western philosophy, that question has most often taken shape in asking whether the cosmos is itself teleological or upheld by a teleological reality (a purposive God, as opposed to non-teleological concepts of God, as found, for example, in the works of Benedict Spinoza) or whether the cosmos is, at base, non-teleological. If one has reasons for adapting theism (the belief that there is an incorporeal, omnipotent, omniscient, all-good, omnipresent, necessarily existing Creator), then one has some reason to expect that there will be creatures who also act teleologically and have value. One also has an explanation for why there is a contingent cosmos at all, and why it persists in being.

The position that one takes in the theism–naturalism debate has important implications for one's belief about the existence and nature of the soul. As Churchland points out, a background belief that the cosmos originates in purely (and exclusively) physical processes provides a strong motivation for believing that all of life is purely and exclusively physical: "Most scientists and philosophers would cite the presumed fact that humans have their origin in 4.5 billion years of purely chemical and biological evolution as a weighty consideration of expecting mental phenomena to be nothing but a particularly exquisite articulation of the basic properties of matter and "energy" (Churchland 1995, 211). Conversely, if one has reason to believe that the origin and underlying cause the cosmos is a non-physical, purposive being, one's convictions about the nature of mental phenomena should and will differ. Part of the debate over naturalism will include reflection on the boundary between what counts as "natural" (or "nature") and what does not. Some naturalists work with the concept of the natural world as the concept of that which is described and explained by the ideal findings of the natural sciences. This conception is problematic for at least two reasons.

First, perhaps there are no (and perhaps there cannot be) ideal natural scientific findings. Second, it is conceivable that, if there is an ideal natural science, it might include God, and this would not sit well with many self-described, secular naturalists who define "naturalism" as the view that the ultimate, natural explanation of things must exclude anything purposeful or teleological in nature. For example Armstrong, whose criticisms of Plato's and Descartes' versions of dualism we examined in Chapters 1 and 3, says that naturalism is "the doctrine that reality consists of nothing but a single all-embracing spatio-temporal system" (Armstrong 1978, 261). He points out that contemporary materialism is a form of naturalism and maintains that the single, all-embracing temporal system contains nothing but the entities recognized by the most mature physics. Irreducible mental explanation (explanation that involves ineliminable reference to mental purposes and/or causes) has no place in this (or in any other) spatiotemporal system as an ultimate or basic explanatory principle. Thus Armstrong says that, "if the principles involved [in analyzing the single, all-embracing spatiotemporal system that is reality] were completely different from the current principles of physics, in particular if they involved appeal to mental entities, such as purposes, we might then count the analysis as a falsification of naturalism" (ibid., 262).

Of course, at the heart of a theistic worldview is the existence of a being that purposefully creates at least some beings (e.g. human persons) who also act for purposes. In light of this fact, it is not surprising that a naturalist philosopher like Kim makes the following remark: "The idea of an immaterial and immortal soul usually carries with it various, often conflicting, religious and theological associations that are best avoided" (Kim, 1996, 4). Perhaps they are best avoided if there is no viable theological alternative to naturalism; but, in light of the current revival of philosophical theism, we do not think it viable to avoid the theism–naturalism debate.

Given naturalism's implications for the ultimate non-reality of purposeful explanations, it is not surprising that naturalists are attracted to projects that seek to reduce what is mental to what is physical. In his important book *Secular Philosophy and the Religious Temperament*, Nagel summarizes the challenge facing the naturalistic project of reductionism:

The concepts of physical science provide a very special, and partial, description of the world that experience reveals to us. It is the world with all subjective consciousness, sensory appearances, thought, values, purpose, and will left out; what remains is the mathematically describable order of things and events in space and time.

That conceptual purification launched the extraordinary development of physics and chemistry that has taken place since the seventeenth century. But reductive physicalism turns this description into an exclusive ontology. The reductionist project usually tries to reclaim some of the originally excluded aspects of the world, by analyzing them in physical (e.g., behavioral or neurophysiological) terms, but it denies reality to what cannot be so reduced. I believe the project is doomed—that conscious experience, thought, value, and so fourth are not illusions, even though they cannot be identified with physical facts. (Nagel 2010, 25–26)

The problem facing naturalism lies in accounting for the reality of "conscious experience, thought, value, and so forth" in a cosmos that is ultimately void of purpose, thought, and value. We believe that the difficulties facing naturalism count as reasons for exploring an alternative, non-naturalist philosophy, including theism, which is more receptive to the existence of the soul.

The Physical World

In much (but not all) of the literature in the tradition of materialism, the concept of what counts as a physical event or thing is treated as unproblematic. However, idealists from George Berkeley to John Foster decidedly did *not* treat it so. These idealists wondered whether color, smells, and auditory experiences are themselves physical, and they questioned whether it is coherent to believe that material objects exist that are colored or smell or make loud noises. Ultimately, they went on to question whether even mass and shape might not be intrinsic properties of matter.

Today, some materialists are also raising questions about the nature and scope of the physical world. The difficulty in providing an uncontroversial conception of the physical is reflected in the following comments by the naturalist David Papineau about naturalism. According to Papineau, naturalism is a commitment to the completeness of physics, where physics is complete in the sense that a purely physical specification of the world, plus physical laws, will always suffice to explain what happens. Papineau is aware that the concepts of physics change over time. What categories, therefore, will qualify as "physical" in the final or ultimate physics? Papineau claims that we cannot answer this question with any certitude. At best, we can pursue a *via negativa* and specify one category that will not qualify for inclusion, namely the category of psychological attitudes such as beliefs, desires, and choices, which represent things being a certain way:

> When I say that a complete physics excludes psychology, and that psychological antecedents are therefore never needed to explain physical effects, the emphasis is on "needed." I am quite happy to allow that psychological categories *can* be used to explain physical effects, as when I tell you that my arm rose because I wanted to lift it. My claim is only that in all such cases an alternative specification of a sufficient antecedent, which does not mention psychological categories, will also be available. (Papineau 1993, 31, footnote 26)

And again:

> If you want to use the [argument that all physical effects are fully caused by purely physical prior histories], it isn't crucial that you know exactly what a complete physics would include. Much more important is to know what it won't.
>
> Suppose, to illustrate the point, that we have a well-defined notion of the *mental* realm, identified via some distinctive way of picking out properties as mental. (Thus we might identify this realm as involving intentionality, say, or intelligence, or indeed as involving consciousness— the precise characterization won't matter for the point I am about to

make.) Then one way of understanding "physical" would simply be as "non-mentally identifiable"—that is, as standing for properties which can be identified independently of this specifically mental conceptual apparatus. And then, provided we can be confident that the "physical" in this sense is complete—that is, that every non-mentally identifiable effect is fully determined by *non-mentally identifiable* antecedents—then we can conclude that all mental states must be identical with (or realized by) something non-mentally identifiable (otherwise mental states couldn't have non-mentally identifiable effects). (Papineau 2002, 41)

In short, according to Papineau we cannot say for sure what it is to be physical, but we can be sure about what it is not: it is not something that is ultimately mental in nature. Instead, it is something that is ultimately nonmentally identifiable. This conception of the physical is fully in line with Armstrong's conception of naturalism, which we highlighted in the previous section and in which any final appeal to mental entities such as purposes would count as a falsification of naturalism.

At present, philosophers are entertaining radically different concepts of the physical world. Indeed, some are inclined to believe that our own mental lives provide us with the best (and, perhaps, only) insight into the intrinsic nature of what it is to be physical. For example, Galen Strawson claims "that there is experience and that we can't be radically in error about its nature. [. . .] [F]or there to seem to be rich phenomenology or experience just is for there to be such phenomenology or experience" (Strawson 2006, 6, footnote 7). Though this sounds just like what a soul–body dualist would say, Strawson goes on to insist "that experiential phenomena 'just are' physical, so that there is a lot more to neurons than physics and neurophysiology record (or can record). No one who disagrees with this is a real physicalist, in my terms" (ibid., 7). But if experiential phenomena are physical, what does physics tell us about physical phenomena? Strawson approvingly cites Bertrand Russell's view "that 'we know nothing about the intrinsic quality of physical events except when these are mental events that we directly experience' [Russell 1956, 153]" and that, "'as regards the world in general, both physical and mental, everything that we know of its intrinsic character is derived from the mental side' [Russell 1927, 402]" (ibid., 10, footnote 20). The implication is that physics provides us with nothing more than an extrinsic characterization of the material world. Physics is mathematical, says Strawson quoting Russell, not because we know so much about the physical world (apart from our direct experience of our own mental life), but

> because we know so little; it is only its mathematical properties that we can discover. For the rest, our knowledge is negative [. . .] The physical world is only known as regards certain abstract features of its space–time structure—features which, because of their abstractness, do not suffice to show whether the physical world is, or is not, different in intrinsic character from the world of mind. (Russell 1948, 247, quoted in Strawson 2006, 10)

On this view of the physical, we have a comparatively clearer grasp of the mental than of the nonmental. Indeed, according to Strawson, "[a]ll physical stuff is energy, in one form or another, and all energy, I [believe], is an experience-involving phenomenon" (Strawson 2006, 25). What is the alternative? "[T]here is no alternative short of 'substance dualism,' a view for which [. . .] there has never been any good argument" (ibid., 25–26).

One can only wonder what Strawson's standard for a good argument is. (One might also wonder if one needs an argument at all for the existence of the soul.) If an argument is good only if it persuades everyone who hears or reads it, then there are indeed few, if any, good arguments. But if a good argument is one that starts from plausible, or at least not obviously false, premises and is logically valid, then, given our brief history of the soul, it seems that over the millenia there have been several good arguments for the existence of the soul. At least, some of those arguments do not seem any less good than good arguments that one might hear or read for physicalism. Upon reading

Strawson's work, one comes away with the impression that he does not have any argument for physicalism that is better than any argument for the soul's existence. Indeed, one comes away with the impression that Strawson has no argument for physicalism except the declaration that some view other than substance dualism must be true.

Thus, while Strawson is radically opposed to a view like Dennett's, which eliminates the self and denigrates the reality of experience (see our discussion of Dennett's view in Chapter 7), he seems to be like Dennett insofar as his key reason for physicalism is the unacceptability of dualism. After articulating his very counterintuitive denial of first-person, conscious experiences in his book *Kinds of Minds*, Dennett remarks that "[t]o some people, all this seems shocking and unlikely, I realize, but I suspect that they haven't noticed how desperate the alternatives are," the key alternative being dualism (Dennett 1996, 24).

Now neither Strawson's nor Dennett's seemingly a priori rejection of dualism should come as a surprise, especially if, as we suggested in the last section, the existence of the soul is more at home in a cosmos that is purposefully created by God—and neither Strawson nor Dennett wants to have anything to do with God. In this context, it is relevant to note some comments by Nagel who, like Strawson, affirms the irreducible nature of conscious experience (see the end of the previous section), but explicitly states that he hopes God does not exist:

> In speaking of the fear of religion [. . .] I speak from experience, being strongly subject to this fear myself: I want atheism to be true. [. . .] It isn't just that I don't believe in God and, naturally, hope that I'm right in my belief. It's that I hope there is no God! I don't want there to be a God; I don't want the universe to be like that. (Nagel 1997, 130; cf. Moreland 2008)

Debate over the soul in the future will (we predict) be shaped in part by the philosophy of the physical world. In a pejorative vein, Dennett has misleadingly referred to dualism as the view that "minds are composed of some nonphysical and utterly mysterious stuff" (Dennett 1996, 24). In view of our brief history of the soul, it should be obvious that dualists historically have treated the soul as a simple substance, which is not composed out of stuff or parts. Moreover, in light of the comments made by Strawson about our knowledge of the physical world (which we quoted above), it is more accurate to view the intrinsic nature of the mind-independent physical world as utterly mysterious. The entry "Materialism" in the prestigious *Oxford Companion to Philosophy* takes note of how it is puzzling that some materialists seem to underestimate the baffling contemporary scientific view of matter or of the physical:

> Photons and neutrons have little or no mass, and neither do fields, while particles pop out of the void, destroy each other, and pop back in again. All this, however, has had remarkably little overt effect on the various philosophical views that can be dubbed "materialism," though one might think it shows at least that materialism is not the simple no-nonsense, tough-minded alternative it might once have seemed to be.

In summary, given our present concepts of what it is to be physical, physicalism seems deeply problematic. Reflection on the soul in the future cannot afford to neglect not only the theism–naturalism debate, but also the fact that our concept of what it is to be physical is far more problematic than most physicalists acknowledge. Thus, at present, there seems to be nothing that we know about what it is to be physical that should lead us to question what we seem to know about the mental and about our belief that the soul is the substantive subject of our mental lives.

Cross-Cultured Inquiry

As western philosophy takes on board more Asian and African traditions and there is greater scope given to Muslim philosophical projects, there is bound to be renewed expansive treatments of the soul. As we write, a conference is scheduled in Iran where Muslim and Christian philosophers will meet next year to discuss the soul and possible conceptions of the afterlife. As we mentioned in Chapter 1, Hindu and Buddhist traditions also subscribe to a belief in the afterlife (in the form of reincarnation), and this invites inquiry into human nature and the self or soul. More interaction, philosophically, across continents and traditions, is likely to generate more work on the concept of the soul, and a host of alternative portraits of human nature.

Value Inquiry

Reflection on the soul has an important bearing on our conception of the good. If a radical form of materialism is true or reasonable, according to which there are no pleasures, pains, beliefs, desires, and so on, it is difficult to see how any recognizable ethic or teaching about love can survive. Consider, for example, Churchland's book, *The Engine of Reason, the Seat of the Soul,* in which he says the following to his readers:

> You came to this book assuming that the basic units of human cognition are states such as thoughts, beliefs, perceptions, desire, and preferences. That assumption is natural enough: it is built into the vocabulary of every natural language [. . .] These assumptions are central elements in our standard conception of human cognitive activity, a conception often called "folk psychology" to acknowledge it as the common property of folks generally. Their universality notwithstanding, these bedrock assumptions are probably mistaken. [. . .] Is our basic conception of human cognition and agency yet another myth, moderately useful in the past perhaps, yet false at edge or core? Will a proper theory of brain function present a significantly different or incompatible portrait of human nature? I am inclined toward positive answers to all these questions. (Churchland 1995, 8)

Fair enough. But then on page 155, he reproduces an MRI image of his wife's (Patricia Churchland's) brain and he professes his fondness for his wife. But how can there be fondness or love without thoughts, beliefs, desires, or preferences? Doesn't love involve thinking well of the beloved, desiring her well-being, preferring her company and so on? But if all these attitudes are reflections of a probably mistaken folk psychology, isn't the claim to be in love probably mistaken? Kim is well aware of the problems created by materialism for consciousness and values:

> For most of us, there is no need to belabor the centrality of consciousness to our conception of ourselves as creatures with minds. But I want to point to the ambivalent, almost paradoxical, attitude that philosophers have displayed toward consciousness. [. . .] [C]onsciousness had been virtually banished from the philosophical and scientific scene for much of the last century, and consciousness-bashing still goes on in some quarters, with some reputable philosophers arguing that phenomenal consciousness, or "qualia," is a fiction of bad philosophy. And there are philosophers [. . .] who, while they recognize phenomenal consciousness as something real do not believe that a complete science of human behavior, including cognitive psychology and neuroscience, has a place for consciousness in an explanatory/predictive theory of cognition and behavior [. . .] (Kim 2005, 10–11)

Kim then goes on to note the radical contrast between those who disparage consciousness in philosophy of mind and those philosophers who work on values, meaning, and lived experience:

> Contrast this lowly status of consciousness in science and metaphysics with its lofty standing in moral philosophy and value theory. When philosophers discuss the nature of the intrinsic good, or what is worthy of our desire and volition for its own sake, the most prominently mentioned candidates are things like pleasure, absence of pain, enjoyment, and happiness [. . .] To most of us, a fulfilling life, a life worth living, is one that is rich and full in qualitative consciousness.

We would regard life as impoverished and not fully satisfying if it never included experiences of things like the smell of the sea in a cool morning breeze, the lambent play of sunlight on brilliant autumn foliage, the fragrance of a field of lavender in bloom, and the vibrant, layered soundscape projected by a string quartet [. . .] It is an ironic fact that the felt qualities of conscious experience, perhaps the only things that ultimately matter to us, are often relegated in the rest of philosophy to the status of "secondary qualities," in the shadowy zone between the real and the unreal, or even jettisoned outright as artifacts of confused minds. (Ibid., 11–12)

Less radical forms of materialism are less threatening to our concept of what is good, but they can still wreck havoc with what we value. Searle, for example, seems to hold that, if we have genuine libertarian freedom (a person freely does x when she does x although she could have done otherwise in the exact same circumstances), we must be or contain a soul.

In order for us to have radical [libertarian] freedom, it looks as if we would have to postulate that inside each of us [our physical bodies] was a self that was capable of interfering with the causal order of nature. That is, it looks as if we would have to contain some entity that was capable of making molecules swerve from their paths. I don't know if such a view is even intelligible, but it's certainly not consistent with what we know about how the world works from physics. (Searle 1984, 92)

Goetz (2008) and Peter Unger (2006) are less skeptical about both libertarian freedom and dualism, and they have defended both.

We do not, however, wish to exaggerate the ethical implications of the traditional understanding of the soul that we have surveyed and defended in this book. In a recent, powerful book, *Body–Self Dualism in Contemporary Ethics and Politics*, Patrick Lee and Robert George argue that the traditional Platonic–Augustinian–Cartesian view of the soul has what they judge to be damaging moral implications for abortion, sexual ethics, and in other areas. We disagree.

Consider the ethics of abortion and the Patrick Lee and Robert George view of sexual ethics. Lee and George hold that the dualist tradition makes abortion more permissible than, say, their preferred more materialistic Thomistic stance, because it is unlikely that fetal life has any consciousness until eight to twelve weeks. As such, a dualist might well claim that there is no person present until at least there is consciousness, and thus a prohibition against killing persons would not rule out an early abortion. Without committing ourselves one way or the other on the permissibility of abortion, we note that dualists who believe in the impermissibility of abortion can defend their views on multiple grounds. We do not think there are compelling grounds for claiming that souls must always be conscious, or for accepting Descartes' view that consciousness is an essential property of the self. If that is the case, one may claim that the soul is present (as Lee and George hold) from conception, but not conscious. On such a view, the fate of the fetus may be the same as that of the soul. Alternatively, one may argue against abortion on the basis of a sanctity of life principle, or on the grounds that the fetus will become ensouled or an embodied person.

On sexual ethics, Lee and George argue that a traditional Platonic–Augustinian–Cartesian view of the soul will naturally lead to treating bodies in an instrumental fashion (as a means of pleasure) rather than as intrinsically valuable. In what we have sometimes called integrative dualism in this book, when we have emphasized the functional unity of the person or soul and body, there is great reason to treat the embodied person herself/himself as a good. The body is not some foreign machine that a ghost uses as a makeshift home! While we submit that views about the soul can have an important bearing on whether there can be an ethics that presupposes beliefs and desires and reasons for choosing and acting, and even about whether persons are free and thus worthy of praise or blame, we do not think that views about the soul directly impact the array of concerns raised by Lee and George.

To summarize: we believe that the future history of the soul will have implications for reflections on values, cross-cultural themes, creative reflection on the philosophy of what is physical and mental, value inquiry, and more. We hope, too, that this overview of the history of the soul and its many arguments will stimulate you not just to undertake further, deeper study of the soul's history, but to be a contributor to the soul's future.

Bibliography

Aquinas, St. Thomas. 1948. *Summa theologica*, Vols. I–III. Translated by Fathers of the English Dominican Province. Allen, Texas: Christian Classics.

Aquinas, St. Thomas. 1949. *On Spiritual Creatures*. Translated by M. C. Fitzpatrick. Milwaukee: Marquette University Press.

Aquinas, St. Thomas. 1957. *Summa contra Gentiles, Book Four: Salvation.* Translated by Charles J. O'Neil. New York: Image Books.

Aquinas, St. Thomas. 1964. *Summa theologiae*, Vol. XIII: Ia.90–102. Translated by E. Hill. New York: McGraw-Hill.

Aquinas, St. Thomas. 1965. *Summa theologiae*, Vol. VI: Ia.27–32. Translated by C. Velecky. New York: McGraw-Hill.

Aquinas, St. Thomas. 1968a. *On Being and Essence*, 2nd rev. ed. Translated by A. Maurer, C. S. B. Toronto: The Pontifical Institute of Mediaeval Studies.

Aquinas, St. Thomas. 1968b. *Summa theologiae*, Vol. XII: Ia.84–89. Translated by P. T. Durbin. New York: McGraw-Hill.

Aquinas, St. Thomas. 1970. *Summa theologiae*, Vol. 11: Ia.75–83. Translated by T. Sutter. New York: McGraw-Hill.

Aquinas, St. Thomas. 1975. *Summa contra Gentiles, Book Two: Creation.* Translated by J. F. Anderson. Notre Dame: University of Notre Dame Press.

Aquinas, St. Thomas. n.d. *Commentary on the First Epistle to the Corinthians.* Translated by Fabian Larcher. Available at www.aquinas.avemaria.edu/Aquinas-Corinthians-Sec2.pdf

Aquinas, St. Thomas. 1984. *Questions on the Soul*. Translated by James H. Robb. Milwaukee: Marquette University Press.

A Brief History of the Soul, First Edition.
© 2011 Stewart Goetz and Charles Taliaferro. Published 2011 by Blackwell Publishing Ltd.

Aristotle. 1962. *Nicomachean Ethics*. Translated by Martin Oswald. Indianapolis: Bobbs-Merrill.

Aristotle. 1973. *Nicomachean Ethics*. Translated by W. D. Ross. In *An Introduction to Aristotle*, 2nd ed., edited by Richard McKeon. Chicago: University of Chicago Press.

Aristotle. 1984a. *De anima*. Translated by J. A. Smith. In *The Complete Works of Aristotle*, Vol. I, edited by Jonathan Barnes. Princeton: Princeton University Press.

Aristotle. 1984b. *Generation of Animals*. Translated by A. Platt. In *The Complete Works of Aristotle*, Vol. I, edited by Jonathan Barnes. Princeton: Princeton University Press.

Aristotle. 1986. *De anima*. Translated by Hugh Lawson-Tancred. New York: Penguin Books.

Armstrong, D. 1978. "Naturalism, Materialism, and First Philosophy." *Philosophia* 8: 261–276.

Armstrong, D. 1999. *The Mind–Body Problem: An Opinionated Introduction*. Boulder, CO: Westview Press.

Asma, S. T. 2010. "Soul Talk." *The Chronicle of Higher Education: The Chronicle Review*. May 7, pp. B6–B8.

Augustine, St. 1947. *The Immortality of the Soul*. Translated by Ludwig Schopp. New York: CIMA Publishing Company.

Augustine, St. 1950a. *Against the Academics*. Translated by John J. O'Meara. Westminster, MD: The Newman Press.

Augustine, St. 1950b. *The Greatness of the Soul*. Translated by Joseph M. Colleran. In *The Greatness of the Soul and The Teacher*. Edited by Johannes Quasten and Joseph Plumpe. New York: The Newman Press.

Augustine, St. 1961. *Confessions*. Translated by R. S. Pine-Coffin. New York: Penguin Books.

Augustine, St. 1964. *On Free Choice of the Will*. Translated by A. S. Benjamin and L. H. Hackstaff. Indianapolis: Bobbs-Merrill Company, Inc.

Augustine, St. 1991. *The Trinity*. Translated by E. Hill. New York: New City Press.

Augustine, St. 1993. *The City of God*. Translated by M. Dods. New York: The Modern Library.

Augustine, St. 2002. *On Genesis*. Translated by E. Hill. New York: New City Press.

Augustine, St. 2003. *Letters 100–155*. Translated by R. Teske. New York: New City Press.

Augustine, St. 2004. *Letters 156–210*. Translated by R. Teske. New York: New City Press.

Bagger, M. 1999. *Religious Experience, Justification, and History*. Cambridge: Cambridge University Press.

Baker, L. R. 2000. *Persons and Bodies: A Constitution View*. Cambridge: Cambridge University Press

Blakeslee, S. 1995. "How the Brain Might Work." *New York Times*, March 21, Section C, page 1.

Blanke, O. 2009. "Out-of-Body Experience." In T. Bayne, A. Cleeremans, and P. Wilren (eds.), *The Oxford Companion to Consciousness*. Oxford: Oxford University Press, pp. 492–494.

Broad, C. D. 1953. *Religion, Philosophy, and Psychical Research*. New York: Harcourt, Braceand Co.

Broad, C. D. 1960. *The Mind and Its Place in Nature*. Paterson, NJ: Littlefield, Adams, & CO.

Butler, J. 1897. *The Analogy of Religion: To Which Are Added Two Brief Dissertations: I. Of Personal Identity; II. Of The Nature of Virtue and Correspondence with Dr. Samuel Clarke*. Edited by W. E. Gladstone. Oxford: Clarendon Press.

Campbell, K. 1980. *Body and Mind*. Notre Dame, IN: University of Notre Dame Press.

Carey, B. 2008. "Standing in Someone Else's Shoes, Almost for Real." Available at www.nytimes.com/2008/12/02/health/02mind.html

Chalmers, D. 1996. *The Conscious Mind: In Search of a Fundamental Theory*. New York: Oxford University Press.

Chisholm, R. M. 1976. *Person and Object: A Metaphysical Study*. La Salle, IL: Open Court.

Chisholm, R. M. 1994. "On the Observability of the Self." In Q. Cassam (ed.), *Self-Knowledge*. Oxford: Oxford University Press, pp. 94–108.

Churchland, P. M. 1984. *Matter and Consciousness*. Revised edition. Cambridge, MA: MIT Press.

Churchland, P. M. 1995. *The Engine of Reason, the Seat of the Soul*. Cambridge, MA: MIT Press.

Collins, R. 2008. "Modern Physics and the Energy Conservation Objection to Mind–Body Dualism." *The American Philosophical Quarterly*, 45: 31–42.

Cooper, J. W. 1989. *Body, Soul, and Life Everlasting*. Grand Rapids, MI: Wm. B. Eerdmans Publishing Company.

Dennett, D. 1991. *Consciousness Explained.* Boston: Little, Brown and Company.

Dennett, D. 1996. *Kinds of Minds: Toward and Understanding of Consciousness.* New York: Basic Books.

Dennett, D. 2006. "You Have to Give Up Your Intuitions about Consciousness." In S. Blackmore (ed.), *Conversations about Consciousness.* Oxford: Oxford University Press, pp. 79–91.

Descartes, R. 1958. *Descartes' Philosophical Writings.* Translated by Norman Kemp Smith. New York: The Modern Library.

Descartes, R. 1967. *The Philosophical Work of Descartes.* Translated by E. S. Haldane and G. R. T. Ross, Vols. I–II. Cambridge: Cambridge University Press.

Descartes, R. 1970. *Descartes: Philosophical Letters.* Edited and translated by A. Kenny. Oxford: Clarendon Press.

Descartes, R. 1984. *The Philosophical Writings of Descartes*, Vol. II. Translated by J. Cottingham, R. Stoothoff, and D. Murdoch. Cambridge: Cambridge University Press.

Descartes, R. 1985. *The Philosophical Writings of Descartes*, Vols. I–II. Translated by J. Cottingham, R. Stoothoff, and D. Murdoch. Cambridge: Cambridge University Press.

Evans, C. S. 2005. "Separable Souls: Dualism, Selfhood, and the Possibility of Life After Death." *Christian Scholar's Review*, 34: 327–340.

Ewing, A. C. 1985. *The Fundamental Questions of Philosophy.* London: Routledge.

Feynman, R. 1998. *The Meaning of It All.* Reading, MA: Perseus Books.

Flanagan, O. 1991. *The Science of the Mind*, 2nd ed. Cambridge, MA: MIT Press.

Flanagan, O. 2002. *The Problem of the Soul.* New York: Basic Books.

Flew, A. 1965. "A Rational Animal." In J. R. Smythies (ed.), *Brain and Mind.* New York: Humanities Press, pp. 111–127.

Foster, J. 1993. "The Succinct Case for Idealism." In H. Robinson (ed.), *Objections to Physicalism.* Oxford: Clarendon Press, pp. 293–313.

Futuyma, D. 1982. *Science on Trial: The Case for Evolution.* New York: Pantheon Books.

Gilson, E. 1960. *The Christian Philosophy of Saint Augustine.* Translated by L. E. M. Lynch. New York: Random House.

Goetz, S. 2005. "Substance Dualism." In J. B. Green and S. L. Palmer (eds.), *In Search of the Soul.* Downers Grove, IL: Inter Varsity Press, pp. 33–60.

Goetz, S. 2008. *Freedom, Teleology, and Evil.* London: Continuum.

Goetz, S., and C. Taliaferro. 2007. "Theistic Argument from Consciousness." In P. Draper (ed.), *Naturalism and Theism: Philosophers' Debate The Evidence.* Available at: http:infidels. org.

Goetz, S., and C. Taliaferro. 2008. *Naturalism.* Grand Rapids, MI: Eerdmans.

Gombay, A. 2007. *Descartes.* Oxford: Blackwell.

Hacker, P. M. S. 1987. *Appearance and Reality.* Oxford: Blackwell.

Hasker, W. 1999. *The Emergent Self.* Ithaca: Cornell University Press.

Hoffman, P. 1986. "The Unity of Descartes' Man." *Philosophical Review,* 95: 339–370.

Honderich, T. 1993. *How Free Are You? The Determinism Problem.* New York: Oxford University Press.

Hume, D. 1978. *A Treatise of Human Nature,* 2nd ed. Edited by L. A. Selby-Bigge and revised by P. H. Nidditch. Oxford: Clarendon Press.

Jeeves, M. 2004. "Toward a Composite Portrait of Human Nature." In M. Jeeves (ed.), *From Cells to Souls—and Beyond: Changing Portraits of Human Nature.* Grand Rapids, MI: Eerdmans Publishing Company, pp. 233–249.

Kant, I. 1965. *Critique of Pure Reason.* Translated by Norman Kemp Smith. New York: St. Martin's Press.

Kenny, A. 1998. *A Brief History of Western Philosophy.* Oxford: Blackwell.

Kim, J. 1996. *Philosophy of Mind.* Boulder, CO: Westview Press.

Kim, J. 1998. *Mind in a Physical World.* Cambridge, MA: MIT Press.

Kim, J. 2002. "Book Symposia: *Mind in a Physical World.*" *Philosophy and Phenomenological Research,* 65: 674–677.

Kim, J. 2005. *Physicalism, or Something Near Enough.* Princeton: Princeton University Press.

Kim, J. 2006. *Philosophy of Mind,* 2nd ed. Boulder, CO: Westview Press.

Krauss, L. M. 2009. "God and Science Don't Mix." *The Wall Street Journal,* June 26.

Lee, P., and R. P. George. 2008. *Body–Self Dualism in Contemporary Ethics and Politics.* Cambridge: Cambridge University Press.

Leibniz, G. 1973. *Leibniz: Discourse on Metaphysics/Correspondence with Arnauld/Monadology.* Translated by G. R. Montgomery. La Salle, IL: Open Court.

Lewis, C. S. 2007. *The Collected Letters of C. S. Lewis: Narnia, Cambridge, and Joy 1950–1963.* Edited by W. Hooper. New York: Harper San Francisco.

Locke, J. 1975. *An Essay concerning Human Understanding.* Edited by P. H. Nidditch. Oxford: Clarendon Press.

Loewer, B. 2001. "Review of Mind in a Physical World: An Essay in the Mind–Body Problem and Mental Causation, by Jaegwon Kim." *Journal of Philosophy*, 98: 315–324.

Lycan, W. 2009. "Giving Dualism Its Due." *Australasian Journal of Philosophy*, 87: 551–563.

Lyons, W. 2001. *Matters of the Mind*. New York: Routledge.

McGinn, C. 1991. *The Problem of Consciousness*. Oxford: Basil Blackwell.

Malebranche, N. 1980. *Nicolas Malebranche: The Search after Truth*. Translated by T. M. Lennon and P. J. Olscamp. Columbus, OH: Ohio State University Press.

Martin, R., and J. Barresi. 2000. *Naturalization of the Soul: Self and Personal Identity in the Eighteenth Century*. New York: Routledge.

Martin, R., and J. Barresi. 2006. *The Rise and Fall of Soul and Self: An Intellectual History of Personal Identity*. New York: Columbia University Press.

Matthews, G. B. 1992. *Thought's Ego in Augustine and Descartes*. Ithaca: Cornell University Press.

Matthews, G. B. 2000. "Internalist Reasoning in Augustine for Mind–Body Dualism." In J. P. Wright and P. Potter (eds.), *Psyche and Soma: Physicians and Metaphysicians on the Mind–Body Problem from Antiquity to Enlightenment*. Oxford: Oxford University Press, pp. 133–145.

Matthews, G. B. 2005. *Augustine*. Oxford: Blackwell.

Merricks, T. 2007. "The Word Made Flesh: Dualism, Physicalism, and the Incarnation." In P. Van Inwagen and D. Zimmerman (eds.), *Persons; Human and Divine*. Oxford: Oxford University Press, pp. 281–300.

Moreland, J. P. 2008. *Consciousness and the Existence of God: A Theistic Argument*. New York: Routledge.

Murphy, Nancey. 1998. "Human Nature: Historical, Scientific, and Religious Issues." In W. S. Brown, N. Murphy, and H. Newton Malony (eds.), *Whatever Happened to the Soul? Scientific and Theological Portraits of Human Nature*. Minneapolis: Fortress Press, pp. 1–29.

Nagel, T. 1979. "What Is It Like to Be a Bat?" In T. Nagel, *Mortal Questions*. Cambridge: Cambridge University Press, pp. 165–180.

Nagel, T. 1986. *The View from Nowhere*. Oxford: Oxford University Press.

Nagel, T. 1997. *The Last Word*. Oxford: Oxford University Press.

Nagel, T. 1998. "Conceiving the Impossible and the Mind–Body Problem." *Philosophy*, 73: 337–352.

Nagel, T. 2010. *Secular Philosophy and the Religious Temperament*. Oxford: Oxford University Press.

Neuhaus, R. J. 2002. *As I Lay Dying: Meditations upon Returning.* New York: Basic Books.

The New English Bible: The New Testament. 1970. 2nd ed. Oxford: Oxford University Press

The New English Bible: The Old Testament. 1970. Oxford: Oxford University Press.

O'Daly, G. 1987. *Augustine's Philosophy of Mind.* Berkeley: University of California Press.

Papineau, D. 1993. *Philosophical Naturalism.* Oxford: Blackwell.

Papineau, D. 2002. *Thinking about Consciousness.* Oxford: Oxford University Press.

Parkes, D. 2004. "The Vulnerability of Persons: Religion and Neurology." In Malcolm Jeeves (ed.), *From Cells to Souls—and beyond: Changing Portraits of Human Nature.* Grand Rapids, MI: Eerdmans Publishing Company, pp. 34–57.

Penfield, W. 1975. *The Mystery of the Mind.* Princeton: Princeton University Press.

Perry, J. 1975. *Personal Identity.* Berkeley: University of California Press.

Plantinga, A. 2007. "Materialism and Christian Belief." In P. Van Inwagen and D. Zimmerman (eds.), *Persons: Human and Divine.* Oxford: Clarendon Press, pp. 99–141.

Plato. 1961. *The Collected Dialogues of Plato.* Edited by E. Hamilton and H. Cairns. *Meno,* translated by W. K. C. Guthrie. *Phaedo,* translated by H. Tredennick. *Phaedrus,* translated by R. Hackforth. *Theaetetus,* translated by F. M. Cornford. *Timaeus,* translated by B. Jowett. Princeton: Princeton University Press.

Plato. 1998. *Phaedo.* Translated by E. Brann, P. Kalkavage, and E. Salem. Newburyport, MA: Focus Publishing.

Popper, K., and J. C. Eccles. 1977. *The Self and Its Brain.* New York: Routledge.

Quinn, P. L. 1997. "Tiny Selves: Chisholm on the Simplicity of the Soul." In L. E. Hahn (ed.), *The Philosophy of Roderick M. Chisholm.* Chicago: Open Court, pp. 55–67.

Quinton, A. 1975. "The Soul." In J. Perry (ed.), *Personal Identity.* Berkeley: University of California Press, pp. 53–72.

Reid, T. 1872. *The Works of Thomas Reid,* Vols. I–II, 7th ed. Edited by W. Hamilton. Edinburgh: Maclachlan & Stewart.

Russell, B. 1927. *The Analysis of Matter*. London: Routledge.

Russell, B. 1948. *Human Knowledge: Its Scope and Its Limits*. London: Routledge.

Russell, B. 1956. "Mind and Matter." In B. Russell, *Portraits from Memory*. Nottingham: Spokeman.

Ryle, G. 1949. *The Concept of Mind*. New York: Barnes and Noble.

Searle, J. 1984. *Minds, Brains, and Science*. Cambridge, MA: Harvard University Press.

Searle, J. 1992. *The Rediscovery of the Mind*. Cambridge, MA: MIT Press.

Searle, J. 1997. *The Mystery of Consciousness*. New York: New York Review, Inc.

Searle, J. 2004. *Mind: A Brief Introduction*. Oxford: Oxford University Press.

Sosa, E. 1984. "Mind–Body Interaction and Supervenient Causation." In P. A. French, T. E. Uehling, Jr., and H. K. Wettstein (eds.), *Midwest Studies in Philosophy*, Vol. 9. Minneapolis: University of Minnesota Press, pp. 271–281.

Strawson, G. 2006. *Consciousness and Its Place in Nature: Does Physicalism Entail Panpsychism?* Exeter, UK: Imprint Academic.

Strawson, G. 2009. *Selves*. Oxford: Clarendon Press.

Stump, E. 1995. "Non-Cartesian Substance Dualism and Materialism without Reductionism." *Faith and Philosophy*, 12: 505–531.

Stump, E. 2003. *Aquinas*. New York: Routledge.

Swinburne, R. 1977. *The Coherence of Theism*. Oxford: Oxford University Press.

Swinburne, R. 1997. *The Evolution of the Soul*. Revised edition. Oxford: Clarendon Press.

Taliaferro, C. 1994. *Consciousness and the Mind of God*. Cambridge: Cambridge University Press.

Taliaferro, C. 1997. "Possibilities in the Philosophy of Mind." *Philosophy and Phenomenological Research*, 57: 127–137.

Taliaferro, C. 2001a. "Emergentism and Consciousness: Going Beyond Property Dualism." In K. Corcoran (ed.), *Soul, Body, and Survival*. Ithaca: Cornell University Press, pp. 59–72.

Taliaferro, C. 2001b. "Sensibility and Possibilia: A Defense of Thought Experiments." *Philosophia Christi*, 3: 403–420.

Taliaferro, C. 2001c. "The Virtues of Embodiment." *Philosophy*, 76: 111–125.

Taliaferro, C. 2005. *Evidence and Faith: Philosophy and Religion since the Seventeenth Century*. Cambridge: Cambridge University Press.

Taliaferro, C. 2009. "The Virtues of Dualist Modal Thought Experiments." In A. Battyany and A. Elitzur (eds.), *Irreducibly Conscious*. Universitatsverlag WINTER: Heidelberg, pp. 113–133.

Taliaferro, C. 2011. "All Souls." In M. Baker and S. Goetz (eds.), *The Soul Hypothesis*. London: Continuum, pp. 26–40.

Taliaferro, C., and J. Evans. 2010. *The Image in Mind*. London: Continuum.

Taylor, A. E. 1955. *Aristotle*. New York: Dover Publications.

Taylor, R. 1992. *Metaphysics*, 4th ed. Englewood Cliffs, NJ: Prentice Hall.

Teske, R. 2001. "Augustine's Theory of Soul." In E. Stump and N. Kretzman (eds.), *The Cambridge Companion to Augustine*. Cambridge: Cambridge University Press, pp. 116–123.

Unger, P. 2006. *All the Power in the World*. Oxford: Oxford University Press.

Van Dyke, C. 2007. "Human Identity, Immanent Causal Relations, and the Principle of Non-Repeatability: Thomas Aquinas on the Bodily Resurrection." *Religious Studies*, 43: 373–94.

Van Dyke, C. 2009. "Not Properly a Person: The Rational Soul and 'Thomistic Substance Dualism.'" *Faith and Philosophy*, 26: 186–204.

Van Inwagen, P. 2002. *Metaphysics*, 2nd ed. Boulder, CO: Westview.

Van Inwagen, P., and D. Zimmerman. 2007. *Persons: Human and Divine*. Oxford: Clarendon Press.

Weaver, G. 2004. "Embodied Spirituality: Experiences of Identity and Spiritual Suffering among Persons with Alzheimer's Dementia." In Malcolm Jeeves (ed.), *From Cells to Souls—and Beyond: Changing Portraits of Human Nature*. Grand Rapids, MI: Eerdmans Publishing Company, pp. 77–101.

Whitehead, A. N. 1958. *The Function of Reason*. Boston: Beacon Press.

Williams, B. 1973. *Problems of the Self*. Cambridge: Cambridge University Press.

Wright, N. T. 1992. *The New Testament and the People of God*. Minneapolis: Fortress.

Wright, N. T. 2003. *The Resurrection of the Son of God*. Minneapolis: Fortress

Zimmerman, D. 1991. "Two Cartesian Arguments for the Simplicity of the Soul." *American Philosophical Quarterly*, 28: 217–226.

Index

A Brief History of the Soul, First Edition.
© 2011 Stewart Goetz and Charles Taliaferro. Published 2011 by Blackwell Publishing Ltd.